INTERNATIONAL DEVELOPMENT IN FOCUS

# Overweight and Obesity in Saudi Arabia

## Consequences and Solutions

MOHAMMED ALLUHIDAN, REEM F. ALSUKAIT,
TAGHRED ALGHAITH, MEERA SHEKAR,
NAHAR ALAZEMI, AND CHRISTOPHER H. HERBST, EDITORS

 WORLD BANK GROUP

# Contents

## Boxes

## Figures

## Photos

## Tables

# Foreword

Overweight and obesity are both a disease and a biological risk factor linked to noncommunicable diseases. More than half of the adult population in Saudi Arabia is overweight, and one out of five is considered obese. These rates echo what is seen in other Gulf Cooperation Countries, representing an alarming regional challenge. Overweight and obesity have a large impact on the economy—through reduced productivity, increased disability, increased health-care costs, and reduced life expectancy. As Saudi Arabia undergoes massive economic transformation through Vision 2030, addressing this issue will contribute significantly to building its human capital, ensuring higher economic growth, and sustaining a workforce that is healthy and prepared for a productive future. While the causes of overweight and obesity are complex and numerous, several innovative and multisectoral evidence-based interventions are emerging globally as promising. Saudi Arabia has already embarked on the design and implementation of several such interventions and is committed to further expanding and scaling up such efforts in order to meet national goals and achieve results.

This book, produced under the leadership of the Saudi Health Council, builds on this work and is an output of the close collaboration between the Saudi Health Council and World Bank staff, as well as renowned researchers and experts, who came together to sound the alarm on the remaining challenges while highlighting the opportunities that lie ahead. We highly appreciate the opportunity to contribute toward this book and look forward to continuing our collaboration to help reverse the trend of overweight and obesity in Saudi Arabia. We hope that the lessons learned in Saudi Arabia will also be useful globally.

**Issam Abousleiman**
Regional Director
Gulf Cooperation Council Countries
The World Bank

**Keiko Miwa**
Director for Human Development
Middle East and North Africa Region
The World Bank

# Acknowledgments

This report was produced by the Health Policy and Economics unit of the Saudi Health Council (SHC) with technical support from the World Bank. It is an output of the 2021 Reimbursable Advisory Services (RAS) program between the World Bank and Saudi Arabia.

Taghred Alghaith (SHC), Reem F. Alsukait (World Bank), and Christopher H. Herbst (World Bank) led the production of the document. The book is edited jointly by individuals from the SHC and the World Bank: Taghred Alghaith (SHC), Reem F. Alsukait (World Bank), Mohammed Alluhidan (SHC), Meera Shekar (World Bank), Nahar Alazemi (SHC), and Christopher H. Herbst (World Bank).

The chapters were written by a combination of SHC and World Bank staff, as well as select stakeholders from Saudi Arabia. Contributing authors from the SHC included Adwa Alamri, Nahar Alazemi, Taghred Alghaith, and Mohammed Alluhidan. Contributing authors from the World Bank include Reem F. Alsukait, Tim Bruckner, Erik Finlekstein, Mariam M. Hamza, Christopher H. Herbst, Eileen Lee, Barry Popkins, Severin Rakic, Shu Wen Ng, and Meera Shekar. The team is very grateful for the administrative support provided by Fatima Mansouri (team assistant, World Bank) and Hope Steele (editor consultant, World Bank)

Throughout this work, the SHC and the World Bank team benefited from the overall guidance and support from Nahar Alazemi (Secretary-General of SHC), Issam Abousleiman (Regional Director, Gulf Cooperation Council [GCC] Countries, World Bank), and Rekha Menon (Practice Manager, Middle East and North Africa Health, Nutrition, and Population Global Practice, World Bank). Sameh El-Saharty (former Program Leader, Human Development in GCC, World Bank) and Larisa Marquez (Operations Officer, World Bank) provided additional guidance to the team.

# About the Editors

**Nahar Alazemi** is the Secretary General of the Saudi Health Council, whose mission is to facilitate and establish regulations that ensure coordination and integration among health stakeholders to improve and enhance health care in Saudi Arabia. Alazemi has more than 25 years of management experience in the health sector, including as Assistant Deputy Minister for Hospital Affairs at the Saudi Ministry of Health as well as Executive Director of Medical Affairs and Executive Director of Academic Training Affairs at the King Fahd Medical City. He is board certified in family medicine and is a member of the Board of the College of Medicine at the Medical School in King Fahd Medical City. As a practicing physician, he was head of the home care unit and head of the emergency department at the Armed Forces Hospital in Tabuk (Saudi Arabia). Alazemi is an Adjunct Assistant Professor in family medicine at King Saud bin Abdulaziz University for Health Sciences; he has contributed and participated in many local and international conferences, seminars, and scientific events. He holds a bachelor's degree in medicine and surgery from the College of Medicine at King Saud University in Riyadh, a child health diploma from the Royal College of Physicians and Surgeons in Edinburgh, and an executive master's degree in health administration from Washington University in St. Louis, Missouri.

**Taghred Alghaith** is the General Director of the National Health Economics and Policies General Directorate in the Saudi Health Council. She oversees the generation of evidence for policy making, as well as the design, review, and implementation of transformational health care strategies for Saudi Arabia. In line with the ongoing health sector reform efforts there, her focus is on programs and interventions to reduce cost, achieve greater responsiveness, and increase efficiency in health care services provision. Alghaith holds a PhD in management science from Lancaster University (United Kingdom) and a master's degree in health and hospital administration from King Saud University (Saudi Arabia).

**Mohammed Alluhidan** is the Head of the Health Economics Unit (HEU) of the Saudi Health Council. He oversees the work program of the HEU, including capacity building in health economics and the generation and dissemination of evidence to help inform policy in the health sector. His research interests include economic evaluation in health care, health policy research and analytics, and health system efficiency. He holds a bachelor's degree in health science from Simon Fraser University (Canada) and a master's degree in medicine from the University of Sydney (Australia), and he is pursing further education in health economics and policy at Lancaster University (United Kingdom).

**Reem F. Alsukait** is a Health Specialist in the World Bank's Health, Nutrition, and Population Global Practice and an Assistant Professor in the Community Health Department at King Saud University. Her work lies at the intersection of public health, nutrition, and policy. She is based in Saudi Arabia, where she is supporting the World Bank's engagement in the health sector, specifically in the areas of nutrition-related diseases, such as obesity and noncommunicable diseases, along with other areas such as using behavioral economics and COVID-19-related responses. Alsukait holds a bachelor's degree from King AbdulAziz University (KAU), a master's degree in public health from Tufts University's School of Medicine, and a PhD in food and nutrition policy and programs from Tufts University's Friedman School of Nutrition Science and Policy, where she received the 2020 Joan M. Bergstrom Award for Excellence in Global Nutrition.

**Christopher H. Herbst** is the World Bank's Program Leader for Human Development in the Gulf Region. He coordinates the Bank's engagement in health, education and social protection in Bahrain, Kuwait, Oman, Qatar, Saudi Arabia, and United Arab Emirates. Previously he was a Senior Health Specialist in the World Bank's Health, Nutrition, and Population Global Practice, leading the Bank's engagement in the health sector in Saudi Arabia. Prior to that, Herbst worked in more than 25 low-, middle-, and high-income countries in Africa, Asia, and the Middle East. His research and publications focus on health systems strengthening, noncommunicable diseases, health financing, service delivery, and health workforce issues. His academic background is in public health, political science, and economics. Herbst holds a bachelor's degee from King's College London, a master's degree from the London School of Economics, and a PhD from Lancaster University, United Kingdom.

**Meera Shekar** is Global Lead for nutrition with the World Bank's Health, Nutrition and Population Global Practice, managing key partnerships and firmly positioning nutrition within the World Bank's new initiative on human capital. She steered the repositioning of the nutrition agenda that led to the new global Scaling-up Nutrition (SUN) movement and was a founding member of the Catalytic Financing Facility for Nutrition that evolved into the Power of Nutrition. She is Chair of the SUN executive committee and has been one of the principals for the aid-architecture for nutrition within the G8 and G20 agenda-setting process. She led the development of the first global Investment Framework for Nutrition and co-leads (with the Bill and Melinda Gates Foundation) the Nutrition Financing working group for the Nutrition for Growth (N4G) summit hosted by Japan in 2020. She has a PhD in international nutrition, epidemiology, and population studies from Cornell University; has consulted and published extensively; and is on various advisory boards and panels, including the Essential Living Standards index (forthcoming), Legatum Institute (United Kingdom), and the advisory group at Gates Ventures.

# Abbreviations

| | |
|---|---|
| ACE2 | angiotensin-converting enzyme 2 |
| ALI | acute lung injury |
| ANSA | National Agreement for Healthy Nutrition (Mexico) |
| AOR | adjusted odds ratio |
| ARDS | acute respiratory distress syndrome |
| BMI | body mass index |
| BMI z-score | body mass index standard deviation score |
| CI | confidence interval |
| COVID-19 | coronavirus disease 2019 |
| DALY | disability-adjusted life year |
| EPIC | Environmental Policy Integrated Climate model |
| FBDG | food-based dietary guidelines |
| FCNL | fruits, vegetables, nuts, and legumes |
| FOP | front of package |
| FOPL | front-of-package labeling |
| FVNL | fruit, vegetables, nuts, and legumes |
| g | grams |
| GBD | Global Burden of Disease |
| GCC | Gulf Cooperation Council |
| GDP | gross domestic product |
| HALE | healthy life expectancy |
| HFSS | high in fat, sugar, and salt |
| ICU | intensive care unit |
| IMV | invasive mechanical ventilation |
| kcal | kilocalorie |
| $kg/m^2$ | kilogram per square meter |
| LCMV | lymphocytic choriomeningitis virus |
| mL | milliliters |
| MTL | multiple traffic light |
| NCD | noncommunicable disease |
| NIP | nutrition information panel |
| NPM | nutrient profiling model |
| NSS | nonsugar sweeteners |
| OECD | Organisation for Economic Co-operation and Development |

| | |
|---|---|
| OR | odds ratio |
| PAF | population attributable risk fraction |
| PPP | purchasing power parity |
| PPPs | public-private partnerships |
| RCT | randomized controlled trials |
| SDIL | Soft Drink Industry Levy (the United Kingdom) |
| SFDA | Saudi Food and Drug Administration |
| SHIS | Saudi Health Interview Survey |
| SPHeP | Strategic Public Health Planning model |
| SSB | sugar-sweetened beverage |
| TFA | trans fatty acid |
| UPP | ultraprocessed product |
| VSL | value of a statistical life |
| WHO EMRO | World Health Organization Eastern Mediterranean Regional Office |
| WHO | World Health Organization |
| YLD | years of life disabled |
| YLL | years of life lost |

# 1 Overview

*CHALLENGES AND OPPORTUNITIES FOR OBESITY PREVENTION IN SAUDI ARABIA*

MOHAMMED ALLUHIDAN, REEM F. ALSUKAIT,
TAGHRED ALGHAITH, MEERA SHEKAR, NAHAR ALAZEMI,
AND CHRISTOPHER H. HERBST

## INTRODUCTION

Overweight and obesity—categories of abnormal or excessive fat accumulation that result in a body mass index (BMI) of more than 25 and 30, respectively—are a major global epidemic that has grown substantially. Worldwide, obesity has nearly tripled since 1975. In 2016, 39 percent of adults ages 18 years and above were overweight, and 13 percent were obese. Most of the world's population lives in countries where overweight and obesity kill more people than does underweight. This has made overweight and obesity one of the key public health challenges of today.

Overweight and obesity are particularly alarming in Saudi Arabia. More than half of the adult population in Saudi Arabia is overweight, and one out of five is obese. Overweight and obesity together constitute both a disease and a biological risk factor linked to numerous noncommunicable diseases (NCDs). The prevalence of all NCDs—such as diabetes, cardiovascular diseases, and cancers—has increased substantially in recent decades, and today they are the leading cause of disability and death in Saudi Arabia. Diabetes prevalence alone has increased by 99 percent over a recent decade in Saudi Arabia, from 1.4 million cases in 2009 to 2.7 million in 2019.

In addition to the health burden, obesity comes with a large economic toll on society, including through its impact on human capital—the knowledge, skills, and health needed for people to realize their full potential as productive members of society and contribute toward economic growth ambitions. Under Vision 2030, Saudi Arabia's strategic framework to reduce its dependence on oil, diversify its economy, and develop public service sectors such as health and education, the country is aiming for a 3 percent reduction in obesity and a 10 percent decrease in diabetes prevalence by 2030. Achieving this will require the development and implementation of interventions that draw on the latest data and evidence, an emphasis on prioritizing prevention over treatment, and a commitment to work across sectors, within and outside of the health sector.

While the causes of overweight and obesity are complex and numerous, several innovative and multisectoral evidence-based interventions are emerging globally as promising: these aim to address the main behavioral risk factors of obesity, such as unhealthy diets and inadequate physical activity. Saudi Arabia has already embarked on the design and implementation of several such interventions and is committed to further expanding and scaling up such efforts in order to meet national goals and achieve results. This report builds on this work by laying out the remaining challenges while highlighting the opportunities lying ahead.

## OBJECTIVE AND SCOPE OF THIS REPORT

The aim of this report is to provide new evidence and analysis on obesity in Saudi Arabia in order to support its planning efforts on obesity prevention. The objectives are to examine the current prevalence of obesity and its risk factors, to estimate the country's health and economic burden associated with obesity, to explore the relationship between obesity and COVID-19, and to identify existing obesity prevention efforts implemented in Saudi Arabia and ways to enhance their impact based on the latest evidence. Furthermore, the report explores the use of a food system approach to connect human health and the environment, including through the production of a Saudi Arabia–specific nutrient profiling model to help guide nutrition- and obesity-related policies.

The chapters in the report focus primarily on unhealthy diets and physical inactivity as the two main modifiable risk factors for obesity. Modifying these risk factors will result in added health benefits beyond reducing obesity. Specifically, these risk factors—such as high salt consumption that results in increased hypertension risk—contribute directly to NCDs and also have a mediated effect on NCDs as determinants of obesity. The report does not focus on treatment for obesity in individuals, such as bariatric surgeries in health care settings, focusing instead on the most effective and cost-effective population-wide prevention approaches to curb obesity.

## ORGANIZATION OF THE REPORT

Chapter 2 provides a detailed and comprehensive situational analysis of overweight and obesity's prevalence rates, trends, and consequences in Saudi Arabia. The prevalence of overweight and obesity is high in the country across all age and sex groups. The rates have been consistently increasing during the past three decades, especially—and most alarmingly—among children. This is especially concerning when one considers that the majority of Saudis are young and the prevalence rates will likely increase as the population ages if no action is taken. Furthermore, the chapter shows that having a high BMI is one of the main drivers of morbidity and mortality in Saudi Arabia, making it a key priority for government action.

Chapter 3 reviews the latest research on obesity determinants and risk factors in Saudi Arabia. It focuses on understanding the main obesity determinants in the country and confirms that only a small percentage of the Saudi population meets dietary recommendations and very few engage in regular physical activity at a sufficient level. Not surprisingly, adolescents and children appear to follow similar unhealthy lifestyles. Addressing these risk factors will require multisectoral and population-wide approaches beyond an individual-level focus.

Chapter 4 provides a forecasting analysis of the health burden of obesity in Saudi Arabia. It presents a picture of the forthcoming developments in the country, particularly the important impact that childhood obesity will have on the NCD disease burden. The forecasting study puts a special focus on six major causes of disability and death associated with high BMI: ischemic heart disease, stroke, type 2 diabetes, breast cancer, colon cancer, and leukemia. The links between lack of physical activity and unhealthy diet on overweight and obesity are well documented. Reductions in overweight and obesity from 2020 to 2050 have the potential to substantially improve overall health and reduce the NCD burden. The chapter shows how obesity's health burden will increase in the next three decades if nothing is done and calculates how modest changes in diet and physical activity can reduce the disability-adjusted life year burden from obesity by 4–8 percent.

Chapter 5 models the economic burden of obesity in Saudi Arabia. Explaining the different methodologies used to capture direct and indirect costs of obesity, it calculates the estimated direct costs of obesity to be 7 percent of current health expenditure. Absenteeism caused by obesity may reduce gross domestic product by 1.42 percent annually. Such costs can be prevented and minimized through high-impact, multicomponent interventions that reduce the risk factors of obesity.

Chapter 6 reviews the global literature on the link between obesity and COVID-19 and emphasizes the need for investment and intervention. The chapter demonstrates that, while physical distancing and stay-at-home policies may have exacerbated adverse weight and health situations, the overweight and obese populations face a greater risk of severe consequences from COVID-19 than those with a healthy weight, including hospitalization, intensive clinical care requirements, and death. Moreover, obesity is likely to reduce the effectiveness of both treatment for those with severe infection and vaccines through mechanisms similar to those responsible for the greater primary infection risk. The chapter shows that there is an opportunity to step up research and collect more high-quality data on the relationship between BMI and COVID-19 in areas with a relatively young population such as Saudi Arabia.

Chapter 7 provides an in-depth review of current nutrition- and obesity-related policies in Saudi Arabia and considers the evidence to date on additional policies implemented elsewhere. The chapter notes the multiple stakeholder groups and current strategies and policies in place to address obesity (for example, the Saudi Center of Disease Control Obesity Strategy 2020–30). While many measures have already been implemented in Saudi Arabia, the chapter highlights the need for monitoring and evaluation of existing interventions and provides a review of evidence on additional policies for potential consideration in the country.

The document ends with chapter 8, which uses a food systems approach to nutrition- and obesity-related policies in Saudi Arabia and culminates with designing a Saudi Arbia–specific nutrient profiling model. The chapter reviews lessons learned from other countries with integrated and systems-based strategies (Chile, Mexico, and the United Kingdom). A nutrient profiling model to cohesively guide policy implementation is needed. The chapter provides an in-depth discussion of different considerations for designing such a model and culminates with the way forward for a Saudi Arbia–specific nutrient profiling model.

## CONCLUSIONS

This document provides a comprehensive assessment of obesity in Saudi Arabia, considering both the health and economic burdens posed to the country. It represents and further builds on a strong commitment by the Saudi government to address the rising problem of obesity in the country—particularly among youth. While obesity is complex, evidence-based interventions do exist and can focus on an integrated, systems-based approach to maximize impact. Additionally, effective implementation and monitoring of interventions to increase healthy diet, boost physical activity, and encourage a healthier lifestyle overall are critical for reducing obesity's health and economic burdens and thus the overall obesity and NCD burden in Saudi Arabia.

# 2 Prevalence, Trends, and Consequences of Overweight and Obesity in Saudi Arabia

SEVERIN RAKIC, MOHAMMED ALLUHIDAN, REEM F. ALSUKAIT, ADWA ALAMRI, CHRISTOPHER H. HERBST, ASSIM ALFADDA, SAMEH EL-SAHARTY, TAGHRED ALGHAITH, AND KHALED ALABDULKAREEM

## KEY MESSAGES

- Between 1975 and 2016, levels of overweight and obesity in Saudi Arabia increased significantly, with rates higher among women than men.
- Three out of five adults in Saudi Arabia had overweight or obesity in 2019.
- Childhood overweight and obesity rates have more than tripled in Saudi Arabia in the past four decades and will likely increase as the population ages.
- One-third of all children and adolescents 5–19 years of age in Saudi Arabia had overweight or obesity in 2016, which is twice the global average of 18 percent.
- The sex gap reversed around 1999–2002; boys are now showing higher rates of overweight and obesity than girls.

## BACKGROUND

Obesity is currently a major public health issue in Saudi Arabia. Over the past several decades, the country has witnessed economic growth accompanied by technological transformations and changes in the population's standards of living, leading to major negative changes in lifestyle. Physical inactivity, sedentary behaviors, and the consumption of calorie-dense food and sugar-sweetened beverages have significantly increased, contributing to the country's increase of overweight and obesity. Subsequently, overweight and obesity have led to an increase in lifestyle-related noncommunicable diseases (NCDs), such as diabetes mellitus, cardiovascular diseases, chronic respiratory diseases, and cancers.

*Overweight* and *obesity* are defined as abnormal or excessive accumulation of fat, which presents a risk to health. Body mass index (BMI) is the most frequently used measure of an individual's weight in relation to height. Adults over age 18 with a BMI of 25 or more but less than 30 kilograms per square meter ($kg/m^2$) are considered to be overweight, and those with a BMI of greater than or equal to 30 kg/m² are considered obese. Children with a BMI greater than 1 standard deviation above the median, according to the World Health Organization's references for school-age children and adolescents, are considered to be overweight; those with a BMI greater than 2 standard deviations above the median are considered obese (WHO 2020). The prevalence of overweight and obesity is calculated as a percentage of a defined population with a BMI higher than 25 kg/m².

Accumulation of abdominal fat (central adiposity) has been strongly associated with an increased risk of cardiovascular diseases. BMI provides no indication of body fat distribution, and abdominal fat mass can vary considerably within a narrow range of total body fat and BMI. Therefore, other indicators need to complement the measurement of BMI to identify individuals at increased risk of obesity-related morbidity due to an accumulation of abdominal fat. Waist circumference and waist-to-hip ratio (the waist circumference divided by the hip circumference) have been suggested as an additional measures of body fat distribution (WHO 2011). The waist-to-hip ratio is an additional proxy for central adipose tissue, which has recently received attention as a marker of "early health risk" (Ashwell and Gibson 2016).

The objective of this chapter is to establish a clear and comprehensive picture of the prevalence, trends, and consequences of overweight and obesity in Saudi Arabia. The chapter starts with a description of the methodology and data sources used. It continues with a review of trends and current prevalence of overweight and obesity in Saudi Arabia in the next section. Morbidity and mortality attributable to high BMI in Saudi Arabia are discussed in the subsequent section, and then the chapter concludes.

## METHODS

Analysis in this chapter was based on secondary data from international databases, recent nationally representative surveys in Saudi Arabia—the World Health Survey 2019 (MOH 2020) and the Saudi Health Interview Survey 2013 (MOH and IHME n.d.)—and recent peer-reviewed publications. Annually published Saudi Arabia health statistics were of limited use in assessing obesity-related mortality and morbidity, as they did not cover NCD cases and deaths in sufficient detail. Two international databases were used instead (box 2.1):

- The World Health Organization's Global Health Observatory data repository (WHO 2020) was used as a source of data on trends and prevalence and of overweight and obesity among adults, adolescents, and children in Saudi Arabia.
- The Institute for Health Metrics and Evaluation's Global Burden of Disease Compare/Viz Hub tool (IHME 2020) was used as a source of data on morbidity and mortality attributable to high BMI in Saudi Arabia.

The analysis relied on the descriptive report of the 2019 World Health Survey (MOH 2020), which included anthropometric measurements, blood pressure measurements, and biochemical measurements. However, lack of access to the survey database prevented the development of multivariate logistic regression models based on the most recent data on overweight and obesity in the Saudi Arabian population.

**BOX 2.1**

## Data sources: methodologies and limitations

The World Health Organization's Global Health Observatory's section with body mass index (BMI) data was built on the population-based studies that had measured height and weight in people ages 5 years and older to estimate trends from 1975 to 2016. Data sources included data collected on samples of a national, subnational, or community population. A Bayesian hierarchical model was used to estimate trends for mean BMI and for prevalence of high BMI in children, adolescents, and adults. For Saudi Arabia, the data sources included 15 surveys conducted between 1985 and 2013. Four national data collections were conducted between 2006 and 2013 in Saudi Arabia: 2005 survey based on the World Health Organization's STEPwise approach to NCD surveillance and conducted among 15–64 year olds, 2007 World Health Survey among the population 18 years and older, 2011–12 Time for an Adolescent Health Surveillance System among 10–19 year olds, and 2013 Saudi Health Interview Survey among those 15 years old and older. An important limitation of the Global Health Observatory repository is unavailability of estimates for 2017 and subsequent years.

The Institute for Health Metrics and Evaluation coordinated the Global Burden of Disease Study 2017, which estimated the burden of diseases, injuries, and risk factors for 195 countries and territories and enabled access to detailed results for its Global Burden of Disease Compare/Viz Hub tool. The study produced estimates by pulling in diverse data sources, including censuses, vital registrations, disease registries, surveys (both local and international), and

scientific literature. Some of the data sources used are publicly available. Other sources are shared by partners or through the network of collaborators.

The 2019 Saudi Arabia World Health Survey was designed to provide up-to-date and reliable estimates of the priority health-related indicators, at the national level, by urban and rural residence and for each administrative area. The survey sample frame was based on the 2010 Saudi Arabia Population and Housing Census. As part of the sampling process, the country was divided into regions and subregions, with each subregion divided into quarters and quarters divided into census enumeration areas that were treated as primary sampling units. A nationally representative sample of 10,000 households was selected from the 13 administrative regions. The survey followed a stratified, three-stage sample design (primary sampling units, households, and adults of age 15 or more years) with a probability proportional to population size. A total of 9,336 households was successfully interviewed, with a response rate of 96.8 percent.

The 2013 Saudi Health Interview Survey was a national multistage survey of the Saudi population age 15 years or older. Households were randomly selected from a national sampling frame maintained by the Saudi Arabia Census Bureau. The country was divided into 13 regions, and each region was divided into subregions and blocks. Households were randomly selected from each block. An adult was randomly selected from the household. A total of 12,000 households were contacted, and 10,735 participants completed the survey (response rate of 89.4 percent).

*Sources:* GBD 2017 Mortality Collaborators 2018; IHME 2020; Memish et al. 2014; MOH 2020; MOH and IHME n.d.; NCD-RISC 2017.

## TRENDS AND PREVALENCE OF OVERWEIGHT AND OBESITY

### Adults

Comparisons of prevalence in adult populations over long time periods are usually based on age-standardized rates. While the crude prevalence shows what proportion of the population is affected by overweight or obesity at a specific time, it is not appropriate to use it for comparing a population over a longer time because the age and sex structure of the adult population changes. For example, patterns of BMI increase in the adult Saudi population in the 1980s are likely to be very different from those in 2010s, because the median age of the Saudi population increased. As age is the most important characteristic that affects prevalence of overweight and obesity, age-standardized prevalence is one indicator included in the NCD Global Monitoring Framework (WHO 2014).

The prevalence of overweight and obesity among adults in Saudi Arabia has been increasing for four decades. The data available in its Global Health Observatory database for 1975–2016 show a continuous rise of both overweight and obesity (hereafter, overweight/obesity when considered together) as well as obesity prevalence among adults in Saudi Arabia (figure 2.1). The four-decades-long increase resulted in an age-standardized prevalence of overweight/obesity of 69.7 percent in 2016, with an age-standardized prevalence of overweight at 34.3 percent and of obesity at 35.4 percent. The prevalence of obesity was one of the highest worldwide. Mean BMI increased by 5.2 percent among adults (from 27.1 kg/m$^2$ to 28.5 kg/m$^2$) between 2000 and 2016. Both overweight and obesity are currently more prevalent among women than among men in Saudi Arabia. However, the increasing overweight/obesity prevalence among men brought it close to the overweight/obesity prevalence among women. While prevalence of overweight/obesity among men doubled over the past four decades, the prevalence of obesity increased fivefold.

Findings from the nationally representative data in Saudi Arabia show consistent prevalence and trends of overweight and obesity. The 2019 World Health Survey (MOH 2020) found the overall prevalence of overweight/obesity to be 58.4 percent and confirmed that overweight and obesity were still higher among women than men in Saudi Arabia. Obesity prevalence was found to increase with age. Additionally, measures of central adiposity showed increased waist circumference in 30.1 percent of respondents, while 91.3 percent of respondents had a waist-to-hip ratio above normal. The survey highlighted the differences in prevalence of overweight and obesity between regions (figure 2.2), with Jawf, Bahah, and Najran having the highest prevalence of overweight and obesity. These findings were consistent with the 2013 Saudi Health Interview Survey (MOH and IHME n.d.) for Saudi nationals.

FIGURE 2.1

**Age-standardized prevalence of overweight and obesity among the 18 years and older population of Saudi Arabia, by sex, 1975–2016**

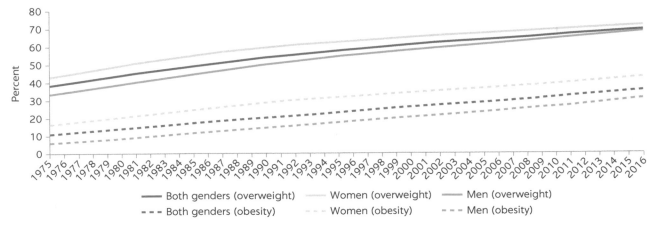

*Source:* WHO 2020.

FIGURE 2.2

**Percent distribution of overweight by region in Saudi Arabia**

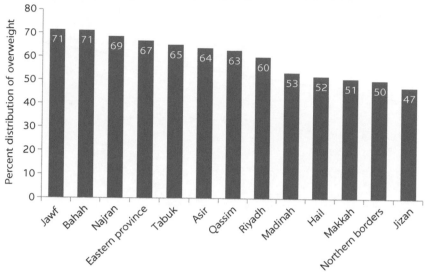

*Source:* MOH 2020.

## Children and adolescents

Children who have overweight or obesity often carry the extra weight into adolescence and adulthood, leading to lifelong health problems. They are at higher risk of early onset obesity-related health problems, including type 2 diabetes, high blood pressure, and sleep disorders (WHO 2014). It might also impact their psychological well-being by generating low self-esteem, depression, and social isolation.

BMI standard deviation scores (BMI z-scores) are measures of relative weight adjusted for child age and sex. The BMI z-scores are calculated relative to an external reference, either national or international (such as the World Health Organization's child growth standards). Children with a BMI greater than 1 standard deviation above the median, according to the World Health Organization's child growth standards, are considered to have overweight, and those with a BMI greater than 2 standard deviations above the median to have obesity (WHO 2020).

The prevalence of overweight and obesity is significantly increasing among children ages 5–9 years. The crude prevalence of overweight/obesity among those children in Saudi Arabia reached 36.5 percent and the prevalence of obesity was 18.5 percent in 2016 (WHO 2020). Mean BMI increased by 8.3 percent among children between 2000 and 2016. Both overweight and obesity rates were higher and increased faster among boys than among girls (figure 2.3). The historical data illustrate that the sex gap in overweight prevalence reversed in the late 1990s. The reversal subsequently contributed to a reversal of the sex gap among overweight adolescents, where prevalence is now higher among males than females. Unlike data from the 2019 World Health Survey (MOH 2020) and the Saudi Health Interview Survey 2013 (MOH and IHME n.d.), recent nationally representative data on childhood obesity do not exist. However, subpopulations cross-sectional studies show that the crude prevalence of obesity was 21.3 percent among boys and

FIGURE 2.3

**Crude prevalence of overweight and obesity among Saudi Arabian children ages 5–9 years, by sex, 1975–2016**

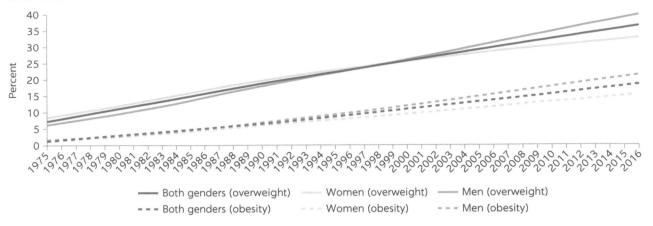

Source: WHO 2020.
Note: Crude prevalence is calculated as the percentage of a defined population with a BMI greater than 1 (overweight) or 2 (obesity) standard deviations above the median according to the World Health Organization's child growth standards. The prevalence of overweight is sum of the prevalence of obesity and the prevalence of overweight.

15.4 percent among girls 5–9 years of age in 2016 and confirmed that boys in Saudi Arabia have a significantly higher BMI than girls (Al-Agha and Mahjoub 2018; Al-Hazzaa et al. 2020).

The prevalence of both overweight and obesity is rising among children and adolescents ages 10–19 years. The crude prevalence of overweight among children and adolescents ages 10–19 years was 35.1 percent, while obesity was 16.7 percent in 2016 (figure 2.4). Mean BMI increased by 5.7 percent among children between 2000 and 2016. Overweight and obesity rates were higher and increased faster among male than female children and adolescents ages 10–19 years. The historical data illustrate that the sex gap in overweight prevalence reversed early in the 2000s; the prevalence is now higher among males than females. The crude prevalence of obesity reached 19.0 percent in male and 13.6 percent in female children and adolescents in 2016. Recent cross-sectional studies found an even higher prevalence of obesity of 17.6–20.2 percent among schoolchildren (Al-Hussaini et al. 2019) and 27.0 percent among male adolescents (Alazzeh et al. 2018), confirming that male adolescents have significantly higher BMI than female adolescents in Saudi Arabia (Al-Hazzaa and Albawardi 2019). The proportion of adolescents having a waist-to-height ratio above 0.50 was 33.1 percent, with significant differences between male (36.0 percent) and female adolescents (30.3 percent) (Al-Hazzaa and Albawardi 2019).

## Obesity in overweight population

Among all age groups, the prevalence of obesity is continuously increasing in the overweight population of Saudi Arabia. There are more and more people with obesity in the overweight population of Saudi Arabia (figure 2.5). The prevalence of adults with obesity has surpassed half of the population of adults with a BMI of 25 kg/m² or higher. The same applies for the population of children

FIGURE 2.4

**Crude prevalence of overweight and obesity among Saudi Arabian children and adolescents ages 10–19 years, by sex, 1975–2016**

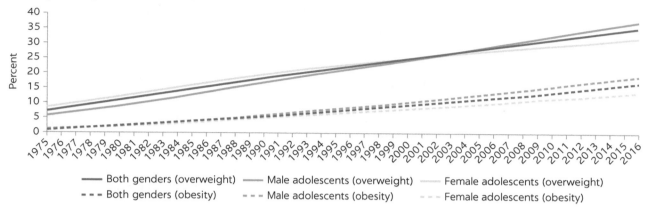

*Source:* WHO 2020.
*Note:* Crude prevalence is calculated as the percentage of a defined population with a BMI greater than 1 (overweight) or 2 (obesity) standard deviations above the median according to the World Health Organization's child growth standards. The prevalence of overweight is the sum of the prevalence of obesity and the prevalence of overweight.

FIGURE 2.5

**Prevalence of obesity in overweight population of Saudi Arabia, 1975–2016**

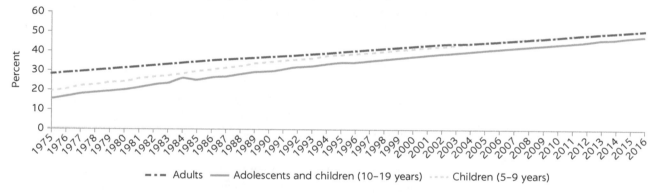

*Source:* WHO 2020.
*Note:* Based on the crude prevalence of overweight and obesity among children and adolescents (5–19 years) and the age-standardized prevalence of overweight and obesity among adults.

ages 5–9 years with overweight: the prevalence of obesity in this group increased to 50.7 percent. The prevalence of adolescents and children with obesity tripled in the overweight population ages 10–19 years over the past four decades, reaching 47.6 percent in 2016.

## CONSEQUENCES OF OVERWEIGHT AND OBESITY: BOTH A DISEASE AND A RISK FACTOR

Overweight and obesity are both a disease and a contributing risk factor to the high prevalence of NCDs in Saudi Arabia. Diabetes prevalence in Saudi Arabia increased from 13.4 percent to 16.7 percent between 2013 and 2019. Additionally,

10.6 percent of the population had impaired glucose tolerance (MOH 2020). The number of people with diabetes and those with impaired glucose tolerance are expected to increase to 6.1 million and 4.7 million, respectively, by 2030. The overall 10-year high/intermediate cardiovascular disease risk tends to increase in Saudi Arabia with increasing age in both men and women, being higher in men than women (33.1 percent versus 17.1 percent). The prevalence of high blood pressure was 13.5 percent of the Saudi Arabian population ages 15 and older (MOH 2020). Previous estimates from the 2013 Saudi Health Interview Survey (MOH and IHME n.d.) showed that almost half of individuals with high blood pressure were unaware they had hypertension (47 percent). The prevalence of these NCDs will likely rapidly increase as the population ages in Saudi Arabia.

Overweight and obesity are significantly associated with diabetes and prediabetes in Saudi Arabia. Obesity has been considered the most important factor related to insulin resistance in the country (Alneami and Coleman 2016). Multiple studies conducted in Saudi Arabia have reported that high BMI had a significant association with both diabetes and impaired glucose tolerance (Aldossari et al. 2018; Alhazmi et al. 2017; Al Mansour 2019). Women with impaired glucose tolerance were found to be 2.3 times more likely to have obesity and women with diabetes were 6.6 times more likely to have obesity than women without diabetes (Al-Zahrani et al. 2019).

Central adiposity particularly increases risk of cardiovascular diseases in the Saudi Arabian population. A multivariable logistic regression model found that low physical activity, prolonged sitting time, and high central adiposity were associated with high/intermediate risk for cardiovascular disease in Saudi Arabia: for men, adjusted odds ratio (AOR) = 2.38) with 95 percent confidence interval (CI) of 1.67–3.41; for women, AOR = 3.35 with 95 percent CI of 1.92–5.87 (AlQuaiz et al. 2019). The risk for cardiovascular disease was found to be higher in the children who have abdominal adiposity (Al-Agha and Mahjoub 2018). The severity of overall and abdominal obesity in Saudi children ages 5–15 years has been associated with a greater prevalence of cardiovascular risk factors (Alissa et al. 2020).

Obesity was found to be a significant risk factor for hypertension in Saudi Arabia. The prevalence of hypertension and prehypertension linearly and proportionally increases with the level of obesity (Aldiab et al. 2018). The risk of hypertension was found to be increasing in the Saudi Arabian population with age, obesity (AOR = 2.24 with 95 percent CI of 1.89–2.65), diabetes, and hypercholesterolemia (El Bcheraoui et al. 2014). Additionally, the risk of hypertension was 3.5 times higher among individuals with obesity than among those with normal body weight (AOR = 3.49 with 95 percent CI of 1.42–8.63) (Al-Hamdan et al. 2010).

Hypertension among adolescents is an emerging public health problem in Saudi Arabia for which obesity was found to be a significant risk factor (Hothan et al. 2016). A school-based cross-sectional study of males ages 15–17 years found 9.0 percent of adolescents to have prehypertension and 17.2 percent to have hypertension (Bandy et al. 2019). Overweight and obesity (AOR = 10.43 with 95 percent CI of 4.63–23.46), insufficient physical activity, positive family history of hypertension, and smoking showed a significant relationship with systolic hypertension in the adolescents. A correlation between high BMI and elevated blood pressure was also confirmed among female adolescents in Saudi Arabia (Al-Agha and Mahjoub 2018).

## Morbidity attributable to overweight and obesity

Morbidity attributable to high BMI and related NCDs is significantly contributing to the disease burden in Saudi Arabia. A disability-adjusted life year (DALY) metric quantifies a population's morbidity and mortality burden. One DALY can be thought of as 1 year of healthy life that is lost. DALYs provide a summary measure for national and international health statistics systems and can be used by governments to prioritize allocation of health resources. Using DALYs as a measure of the burden of disease also allows one to estimate the impact that changing risk factors would have on reducing the burden of disease. The Institute for Health Metrics and Evaluation (IHMA 2020) estimated that high BMI contributed to 11 percent of total DALYs in Saudi Arabia in 2017. DALYs associated with NCDs contributed to 65.17 percent of the overall burden of disease in Saudi Arabia, while 15.7 percent of the overall burden of NCDs was attributable to high BMI (figure 2.6). Overweight and obesity contributed most significantly to the burden of diabetes, kidney diseases, cardiovascular diseases, and chronic respiratory diseases (figure 2.7). The majority of NCD cases affect the working-age population (30–65 years old). There are no available data disaggregated by income.

## Mortality attributable to overweight and obesity

Because of limitations in Saudi Arabian data, the Institute for Health Metrics and Evaluation's hub was used to assess mortality attributable to high BMI. Existing health statistics do not routinely provide information needed to monitor and evaluate the progress made in implementing obesity- and/or overweight-related policies and programs. The Ministry of Health's annual *Statistical Yearbook* includes the number of deaths reported to the ministry's hospitals (MOH 2019). No data are collated and published on deaths determined by other types of facilities. The quality of the most recent set of mortality data is questionable, as

FIGURE 2.6

**Causes of disability-adjusted life years in Saudi Arabia in 2017**

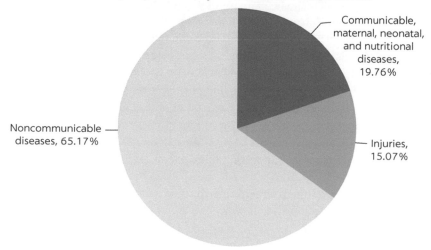

*Source:* IHME 2020.

**FIGURE 2.7**

**Morbidity attributable to high BMI in Saudi Arabia, both sexes, all ages, 2017**

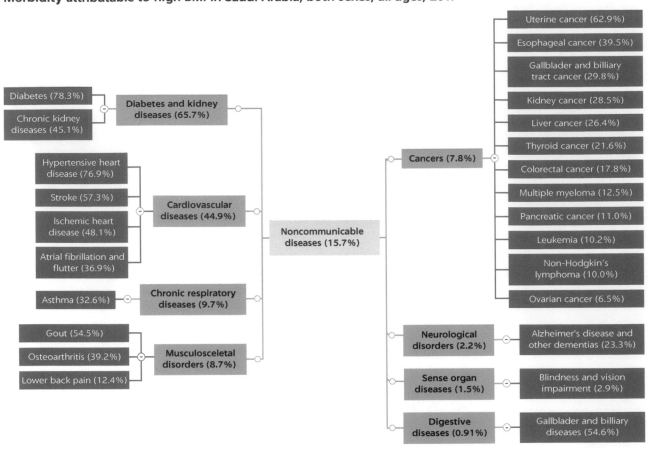

*Source:* IHME 2020.

more than a third of the hospital deaths were reported as symptoms, signs, or abnormal findings. A portion of the unclassified deaths might be caused by NCDs. All the limitations made the Saudi Arabian data unusable for assessing how much overweight and obesity contribute to mortality in Saudi Arabia. The Institute for Health Metrics and Evaluation's Global Burden of Disease Compare/Viz Hub (IHME 2020) data were used instead in this section.

High BMI was ranked as the second among all the risk factors contributing to mortality in Saudi Arabia, contributing to 18 percent of total deaths in 2017. The ranking rose from the fifth to the second position over the last three decades (figure 2.8). The number of deaths attributable to high BMI increased by 208 percent during the same period (from 5,600 to 17,400 deaths). The share of total deaths attributable to high BMI more than doubled between 1990 and 2017—from 6.9 percent to 18.4 percent of all deaths (figure 2.9). The mortality rate attributable to high BMI increased by 46.7 percent (from 34.5 to 50.5 per 100,000 population). High BMI ranked as the first among all risk factors contributing to the mortality of women (with one-fifth of all deaths among women attributable to high BMI) and population ages 15–49 years (with 12.6 percent of all deaths attributable to high BMI) in 2017. If the current trend continues, high

FIGURE 2.8

**Ranking of risk factors contributing to mortality in Saudi Arabia, both sexes, all age groups, all causes of death, 1990 and 2017**

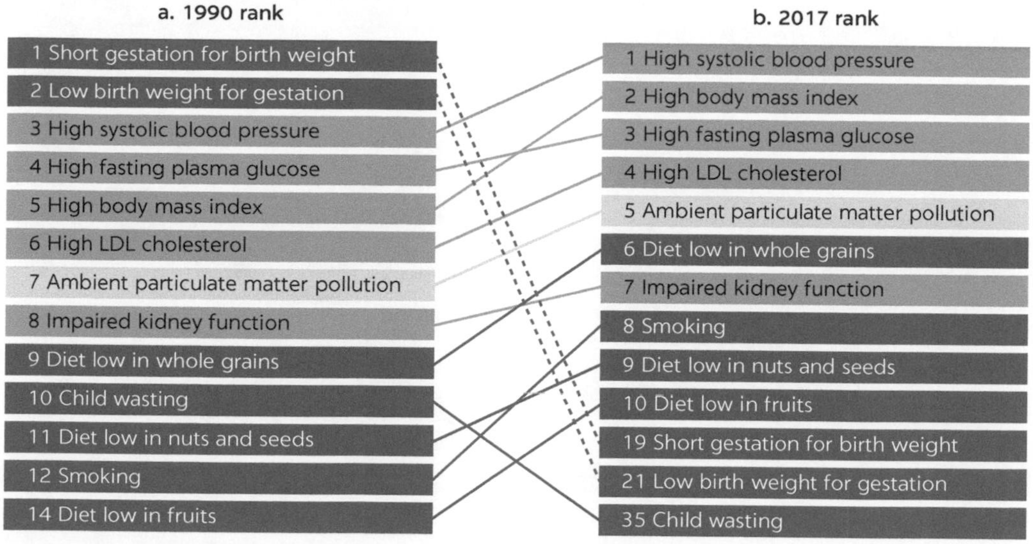

a. 1990 rank
1 Short gestation for birth weight
2 Low birth weight for gestation
3 High systolic blood pressure
4 High fasting plasma glucose
5 High body mass index
6 High LDL cholesterol
7 Ambient particulate matter pollution
8 Impaired kidney function
9 Diet low in whole grains
10 Child wasting
11 Diet low in nuts and seeds
12 Smoking
14 Diet low in fruits
b. 2017 rank
1 High systolic blood pressure
2 High body mass index
3 High fasting plasma glucose
4 High LDL cholesterol
5 Ambient particulate matter pollution
6 Diet low in whole grains
7 Impaired kidney function
8 Smoking
9 Diet low in nuts and seeds
10 Diet low in fruits
19 Short gestation for birth weight
21 Low birth weight for gestation
35 Child wasting

*Source:* IHME 2020.
*Note:* Green = environmental/occupational risks; dark blue = behavioral risks; light blue = metabolic risks. LDL = low-density lipoprotein.

FIGURE 2.9

**Percentage of total deaths in Saudi Arabia attributable to high body mass index, both sexes, all age groups, all causes of death, 1990–2017**

Percentage of total deaths
24
20
16
12
8
4
0
1990 1991 1992 1993 1994 1995 1996 1997 1998 1999 2000 2001 2002 2003 2004 2005 2006 2007 2008 2009 2010 2011 2012 2013 2014 2015 2016 2017
Both genders
Women
Men

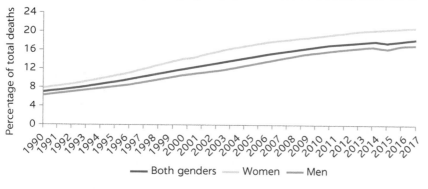

*Source:* IHME 2020.

BMI might rank as the number one risk factor contributing to mortality in all other population groups in Saudi Arabia.

More than a quarter of deaths caused by NCDs were attributable to high BMI in 2017. About two-thirds of all deaths in Saudi Arabia (65.2 percent) were caused by NCDs in 2017. The majority of the NCD deaths were attributable to metabolic risks, and 27.4 percent of the NCD deaths were attributable to high BMI. Half of the deaths attributable to high BMI were caused by ischemic heart disease (49.5 percent), followed by stroke (18.5 percent), chronic kidney disease (10.7 percent), diabetes (7.8 percent), and cancers (6.0 percent) (figure 2.10). Most of the deaths attributable to high BMI occurred in the population 40–79 years of age.

FIGURE 2.10

**Number of deaths in Saudi Arabia attributable to high body mass index, both sexes, all age groups, 2017**

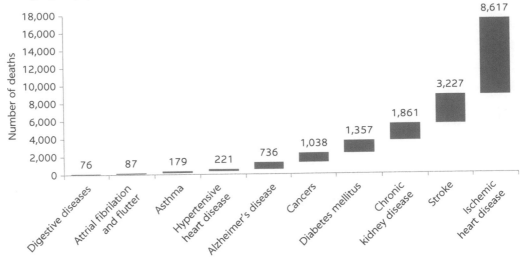

*Source:* IHME 2020.

## CONCLUSIONS

The already high prevalence of overweight and obesity among adults, adolescents, and children continues to rise in Saudi Arabia. The prevalence of overweight and obesity has been increasing for four decades, and the prevalence of obesity in Saudi Arabia has now reached one of the highest levels in the world. The prevalence of obesity in the overweight population of Saudi Arabia has also been increasing, reaching one-half in almost all population groups. Overweight among adults is higher in women, but the trend might reverse in the future, following the reversal of trends among children and adolescents.

High BMI is one of the main drivers of morbidity and mortality from NCDs in Saudi Arabia. NCDs are currently the leading cause of death and contribute significantly to the burden of disease in the country. High BMI was ranked in 2017 as the second among all the risk factors contributing to mortality in Saudi Arabia: more than a quarter of deaths caused by NCDs were attributable to high BMI in 2017. Obesity predisposes the Saudi Arabian population to diabetes, hypertension, and dyslipidemia, thus contributing to the development of NCDs. Overweight and obesity contribute significantly to the burden of diabetes, chronic kidney disease, cardiovascular diseases, and chronic respiratory diseases.

Population growth and longer life expectancy are expected to increase the proportion of older individuals in Saudi Arabia in the future. Since NCDs disproportionately affect older age groups, the burden of obesity and NCDs can be expected to continue rising. Existing health statistics do not routinely provide information needed to monitor and evaluate the progress made in implementing obesity- and overweight-related policies and programs. Improvement of the NCD surveillance system is of critical importance to ensuring the regular provision of the information needed to develop obesity-related policies and legislation.

## REFERENCES

Al-Agha, A. E., and A. O. Mahjoub. 2018. "Impact of Body Mass Index on High Blood Pressure among Obese Children in the Western Region of Saudi Arabia." *Saudi Medical Journal* 39 (1): 45–51. doi:10.15537/smj.2018.1.20942.

Alazzeh, A. Y., E. M. AlShammari, M. M. Smadi, F. S. Azzeh, B. T. AlShammari, S. Epuru, S. Banu, R. Bano, S. Sulaiman, J. C. Alcantara, S. A. Ashraf, and S. Qiblawi. 2018. "Some Socioeconomic Factors and Lifestyle Habits Influencing the Prevalence of Obesity among Adolescent Male Students in the Hail Region of Saudi Arabia." *Children* 5: 39. doi:10.3390/children5030039.

Aldiab, A., M. M. Shubair, J. M. Al-Zahrani, K. K. Aldossari, S. Al-Ghamdi, M. Househ, H. A. Razzak, A. El-Metwally, and H. Jradi. 2018. "Prevalence of Hypertension and Prehypertension and Its Associated Cardioembolic Risk Factors; A Population Based Cross-Sectional Study in Alkharj, Saudi Arabia." *BMC Public Health* 18: 1327. doi:10.1186/s12889-018-6216-9.

Aldossari, K. K., A. Aldiab, J. M. Al-Zahrani, S. H. Al-Ghamdi, M. Abdelrazik, M. A. Batais, S. Javad, S. Nooruddin, H. A. Razak, and A. El-Metwally. 2018. "Prevalence of Prediabetes, Diabetes, and Its Associated Risk Factors among Males in Saudi Arabia: A Population-Based Survey." *Journal of Diabetes Research* 2018: 2194604. doi:10.1155/2018/2194604.

Al-Hamdan, N., A. Saeed, A. Kutbi, A. J. Choudhry, and R. Nooh. 2010. "Characteristics, Risk Factors, and Treatment Practices of Known Adult Hypertensive Patients in Saudi Arabia." *International Journal of Hypertension* 2010: 168739. doi:10.4061/2010/168739.

Alhazmi, R. S., A. A. B. Ahmed, M. H. Alshalan, Z. D. Alfuhigi, S. F. Alhazm, A. N. Aldughmi, N. N. Alshammari, A. E. Alruwaili, G. S. Alenezi, T. S. Alanazi, and S. A. Almadani. 2017. "Prevalence of Diabetes Mellitus and Its Relation with Obesity in Turaif (Saudi Arabia) in 2017." *Electronic Physician* 9 (10): 5531–35. doi:10.19082/5531.

Al-Hazzaa, H. M., and N. M. Albawardi. 2019. "Activity Energy Expenditure, Screen Time and Dietary Habits Relative to Sex among Saudi Youth: Interactions of Sex with Obesity Status and Selected Lifestyle Behaviours." *Asia Pacific Journal of Clinical Nutrition* 28 (2): 389–400. doi:10.6133/apjcn.201906_28(2).0022.

Al-Hazzaa, H. M., A. M. Alhowikan, M. H. Alhussain, and O. A. Obeid. 2020. "Breakfast Consumption among Saudi Primary-School Children Relative to Sex and Socio-Demographic Factors." *BMC Public Health* 20: 448. doi:10.1186/s12889-020-8418-1.

Al-Hussaini, A., M. S. Bashir, M. Khormi, M. AlTuraiki, W. Alkhamis, M. Alrajhi, and T. Halal. 2019. "Overweight and Obesity among Saudi Children and Adolescents: Where Do We Stand Today?" *Saudi Journal of Gastroenterology* 25 (4): 229–35. doi:10.4103/sjg.SJG_617_18.

Alissa, E. M., R. H. Sutaih, H. Z. Kamfar, A. E. Alagha, and Z. M. Marzouki. 2020. "Relationship between Pediatric Adiposity and Cardiovascular Risk Factors in Saudi Children and Adolescents." *Archives de Pediatrie* 27 (3): 135–9. doi:10.1016/j.arcped.2019.12.007.

Al Mansour, M. A. 2019. "The Prevalence and Risk Factors of Type 2 Diabetes Mellitus (DMT2) in a Semi-Urban Saudi Population." *International Journal of Environmental Research and Public Health* 17: 7. doi:10.3390/ijerph17010007.

Alneami, Y. M., and C. L. Coleman. 2016. "Risk Factors for and Barriers to Control Type-2 Diabetes among Saudi Population." *Global Journal of Health Science* 8 (9): 10–19. doi:10.5539/gjhs.v8n9p10.

AlQuaiz, A. M., A. R. Siddiqui, A. Kazi, M. A. Batais, and A. M. Al-Hamzi. 2019. "Sedentary Lifestyle and Framingham Risk Scores: A Population-Based Study in Riyadh City, Saudi Arabia." *BMC Cardiovascular Disorders* 19: 88. doi:10.1186/s12872-019-1048-9.

Al-Zahrani, J. M., A. Aldiab, K. K. Aldossari, A. Al-Ghamdi, M. A. Batais, S. Javad, S. Nooruddin, N. Zahid, H. A. Razzak, and A. El-Metwally. 2019. "Prevalence of Prediabetes, Diabetes and Its Predictors among Females in Alkharj, Saudi Arabia: A Cross-Sectional Study." *Annals of Global Health* 85 (1): 109. doi:10.5334/aogh.246.

Ashwell, M., and S. Gibson. 2016. "Waist-to-Height Ratio as an Indicator of 'Early Health Risk': Simpler and More Predictive than Using a 'Matrix' Based on BMI and Waist Circumference." *BMJ Open* 6: e010159. doi:10.1136/bmjopen-2015-010159.

Bandy, A., M. M. Qarmush, A. R. Alrwilly, A. A. Albadi, A. T. Alshammari, and M. M. Aldawasri. 2019. "Hypertension and Its Risk Factors among Male Adolescents in Intermediate and

Secondary Schools in Sakaka City, Aljouf Region of Saudi Arabia." *Nigerian Journal of Clinical Practice* 22: 1140–46. doi:10.4103/njcp.njcp_507_18.

El Bcheraoui, C., Z. A. Memish, M. Tuffaha, F. Daoud, M. Robinson, S. Jaber, S. Mikhitarian, M. Al Saeedi, M. A. AlMazroa, A. H. Mokdad, and A. A. Al Rabeeah. 2014. "Hypertension and Its Associated Risk Factors in the Kingdom of Saudi Arabia, 2013: A National Survey." *International Journal of Hypertension* 2014: 564679.

GBD 2017 Mortality Collaborators. 2018. "Global, Regional, and National Age-sex-specific Mortality and Life Expectancy, 1950-2017: A Systematic Analysis for the Global Burden of Disease Study 2017." *Lancet* 392 (10159): 1684–735. doi:10.1016/S0140-6736(18)31891-9. Erratum in: *Lancet* 393 (10190): e44.

Hothan, K. A., B. A. Alasmari, O. K. Alkhelaiwi, K. M. Althagafi, A. A. Alkhaldi, A. K. Alfityani, M. M. Aladawi, S. N. Sharief, S. El Desoky, and J. A. Kari. 2016. "Prevalence of Hypertension, Obesity, Hematuria and Proteinuria amongst Healthy Adolescents Living in Western Saudi Arabia." *Saudi Medical Journal* 37 (10): 1120–26. doi:10.15537/smj.2016.10.14784.

IHME (Institute for Health Metrics and Evaluation). 2020. GBD Compare/Viz Hub, database, University of Washington, Seattle. https://vizhub.healthdata.org/gbd-compare.

Memish, Z. A., C. El Bcheraoui, M. Tuffaha, M. Robinson, F. Daoud, S. Jaber, S. Mikhitarian, M. Al Saeedi, M. A. AlMazroa, A. H. Mokdad, and A. A. Al Rabeeah. 2014. "Obesity and Associated Factors: Kingdom of Saudi Arabia, 2013." *Preventing Chronic Disease* 11: E174. doi:10.5888/pcd11.140236.

MOH (Ministry of Health). 2019. *Statistical Yearbook 2018*. Riyadh: Ministry of Health. https://www.moh.gov.sa/en/Ministry/Statistics/book/Documents/book-Statistics.pdf.

MOH (Ministry of Health). 2020. "World Health Survey Saudi Arabia (KSAWHS) 2019 Final Report." Ministry of Health Riyadh.

MOH and IHME (Ministry of Health and Institute for Health Metrics and Evaluation). n.d. *Saudi Health Interview Survey Results*. Washington, DC: University of Washington. http://www.healthdata.org/sites/default/files/files/Projects/KSA/Saudi-Health-Interview-Survey-Results.pdf.

NCD-RISC (Noncommunicable Diseases Risk Factor Collaboration). 2017. "Worldwide Trends in Body-Mass Index, Underweight, Overweight, and Obesity from 1975 to 2016: A Pooled Analysis of 2416 Population-Based Measurement Studies in 128·9 Million Children, Adolescents, and Adults." *Lancet* 390: 2627–42. doi:10.1016/S0140-6736(17)32129-3.

WHO (World Health Organization). 2011. *Waist Circumference and Waist-Hip Ratio: Report of a WHO Expert Consultation, Geneva, 8–11 December 2008*. Geneva: World Health Organization.

WHO (World Health Organization). 2014. *Noncommunicable Diseases Global Monitoring Framework: Indicator Definitions and Specifications*. Geneva: World Health Organization.

WHO (World Health Organization). 2020. *The Global Health Observatory*. Geneva: World Health Organization. https://www.who.int/data/gho.

# 3 Determinants of Overweight and Obesity in Saudi Arabia

REEM F. ALSUKAIT, SEVERIN RAKIC, MOHAMMED ALLUHIDAN,
ADWA ALAMRI, RANA SABER, ALI ALSHEHRI, KHALED ALABDULKAREEM,
AND SHAKER ALOMARY

## KEY MESSAGES

- Overweight and obesity have increased in Saudi Arabia alongside a major shift in lifestyles affecting all levels of Saudi Arabian society, from children and adolescents to adults.
- Only a small percentage of the Saudi population meets dietary recommendations.
- Increased obesity among children and adolescents in Saudi Arabia has been commensurate with increased consumption of ultraprocessed foods and beverages, such as fast foods.
- Excessive energy intake and low consumption of fruits, vegetables, and whole grains is related to the increase in body mass index.
- Very few Saudis regularly engage in a sufficient level of physical activity. Sedentary lifestyles—including long commutes, sedentary office jobs, and prolonged television watching—contribute to the physical inactivity of adults in Saudi Arabia.
- Individual risk factors—lack of physical activity and unhealthy diet—need to be addressed along with population-oriented policies to encourage healthier lifestyles.
- Successful policy interventions must tackle societal trends and systems that support excess energy intake and are not conducive to increasing energy expenditure (see chapters 7 and 8).

## INTRODUCTION

Overweight and obesity increased in Saudi Arabia alongside a major shift in lifestyles. Over the past several decades, Saudi Arabia has witnessed economic growth, accompanied by technological transformations and changes in the population's standards of living. Currently, 83 percent of the Saudi population live in urban settings, which has changed the choice and availability of food, in turn promoting higher energy intake and less energy expenditure. Energy intake positively predicts body weight, while total energy expenditure per kilogram of body weight negatively predicts it.

Dietary habits are determined by individual preferences and broader sociocultural factors. These include household lifestyle patterns, family and community pressures, and social norms. In addition, broader economic forces (for example, globalization and changes to the food system and to agricultural practices) and commercial forces (for example, marketing of unhealthy foods and reduced availability of healthy foods) play an oversized role in influencing consumer food habits. This chapter reviews the most recent evidence on these risk factors in Saudi Arabia and synthesizes it with the objective of identifying modifiable risk factors, high at-risk groups, and remaining knowledge gaps.

## METHODS

A social ecological model lens (figure 3.1) was used to investigate the determinants of obesity in Saudi Arabia. Social ecological models emphasize multiple levels of influence—such as sociocultural, community, and governmental levels—and how they interact to enable healthy lifestyles. This review focuses mainly on the inner circle of behavioral risk factors (diet, individual behaviors, and physical activity) while acknowledging their interaction with other layers such as socioeconomic and cultural influences and the food and built environments.

FIGURE 3.1

**Determinants of Obesity**

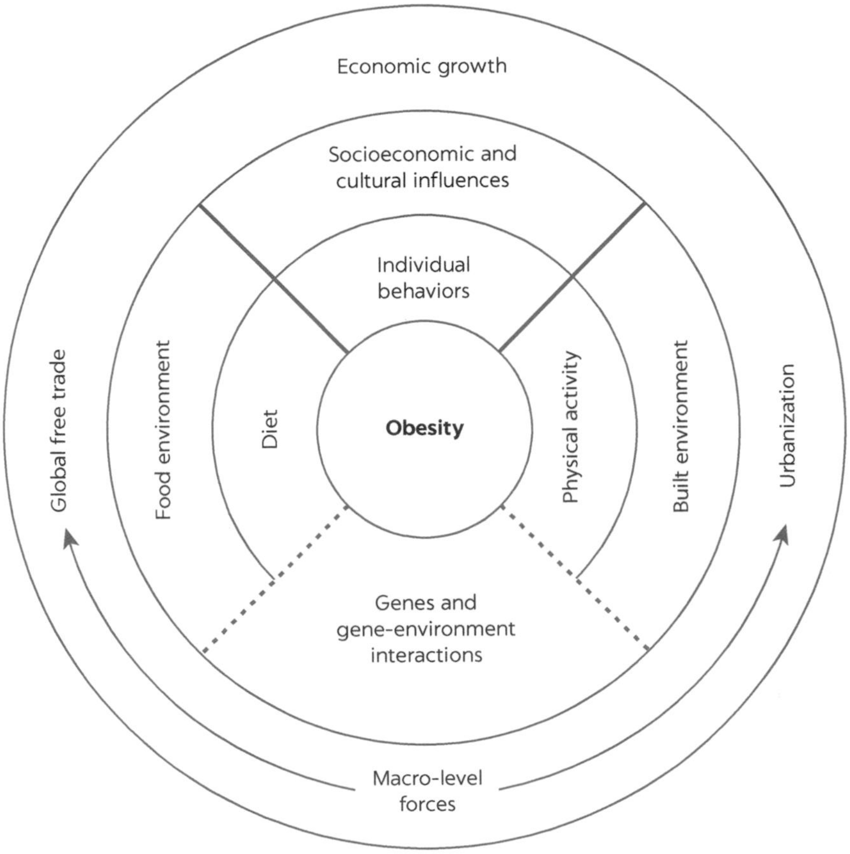

*Source:* Malik and Hu 2017.

Risk factors associated with increased body mass index (BMI) are well researched in Saudi Arabia. However, the majority of the evidence is cross-sectional, and there is a need for longitudinal and randomized controlled trial studies to increase the strength of the evidence and establish causality between risk factors and disease outcomes (AlAbdulKader, Tuwairqi, and Rao 2020). This review draws on peer-reviewed publications and recently collected national surveys. Findings from the peer-reviewed publications, identified through the PubMed (using "obesity" and "Saudi" in combination with search terms, such as "diet," "fruit," "fast food," and "inactivity"), supported the analysis of the contribution of dietary behaviors and physical inactivity to the development of overweight and obesity in the Saudi population. Whenever possible, recent publications—not older than five years—were used in the analysis.

The following national surveys were used:

- The 2019 World Health Survey (MOH 2020) was used as a source of data on the intake of fruits and vegetables as well as on the physical activity level among the adult Saudi population.
- The 2017 and 2018 Household Sports Practice Surveys (GASTAT 2017, 2018) were used as a source of recent data on the physical activity of the Saudi Arabia population.
- The 2013 Saudi Health Interview Survey (MOH and IHME n.d.) was used as a source of data on dietary habits and the level of physical activity among the adult Saudi population.

## DIETARY BEHAVIORS CONTRIBUTING TO OVERWEIGHT AND OBESITY

Excessive energy intake contributes to an increase in overweight and obesity prevalence. The energy intake positively predicts body weight, while total energy expenditure per kilogram of body weight negatively predicts it. Based on the Food and Agriculture Organization's food balance sheets, the availability of kilocalories per capita in Saudi Arabia increased from 1,717 in 1961 to 3,194 in 2017 (FAO 2020). National cross-sectional surveys in Saudi Arabia found that the excess of food energy supply was 1,448 kilojoules per day in 1996 and that the excess increased by 519 kilojoules per day in 2004 (Vandevijvere et al. 2015). A recent study confirmed a significant difference in the mean daily energy intake between girls ages 8–11 years with obesity (intake of 2,677 plus or minus 804 kilocalories per day) and normal weight (intake of 1,806 plus or minus 403 kilocalories per day) (Al-Kutbe et al. 2017). The number of calories consumed per day was found to differ significantly between Saudi children ages 9–12 years who have obesity and those who have normal weight, with daily energy intake being higher by about 300 kilocalories among children with obesity (Alturki, Brookes, and Davies 2018b).

### Dietary behaviors of the adult population

A comprehensive diet history questionnaire was last used in 2013 in a nationally representative survey. The 2013 Saudi Health Interview Survey used a 42-item questionnaire to ask respondents about their typical weekly consumption of specified food and beverage items, the type of oil or fat most often used for meal preparation, and the usual type of dairy products and bread in the household

(MOH and IHME n.d.). The data were used for an indirect estimation of energy intake and for energy-adjusted daily food and beverage consumption estimates (Moradi-Lakeh et al. 2016).

The majority of the adult Saudi population was not complying with the dietary guidelines. The 2013 Saudi Health Interview Survey found that the recommendations of the MOH dietary guidelines were met by 5.2 percent of respondents for fruit, 7.5 percent for vegetables, 31.4 percent for nuts, and 44.7 percent for fish (Moradi-Lakeh et al. 2016). There was considerably higher consumption of processed meat and sugar-sweetened beverages than recommended, particularly among younger groups of respondents. More than 81.0 percent of Saudis consumed fewer than three servings of fruit and vegetables per day. Vegetable oils were the most common type of oil or fat used to prepare food (84.5 percent), while the use of olive oil was reported by 5.3 percent of respondents. The likelihood of meeting the dietary recommendations increased with age; it was higher among women, among those who consumed at least two servings of meat or chicken per day, among those who visited a health care facility for a routine medical exam within the previous three years, and among those who have been diagnosed with hypertension (El Bcheraoui et al. 2015).

The intake of whole grains and their products is less than optimum among adults in Saudi Arabia. The 2013 Saudi Health Interview Survey found that white bread was the most commonly used type of bread (79.1 percent). Those who reported usually consuming brown bread constituted 20.1 percent and those who usually consumed Saudi-specific traditional breads constituted 0.8 percent of the survey respondents (Moradi-Lakeh et al. 2016). A small sample study of Saudi adults in Riyadh found that 57.3 percent of the participants did not, on a daily basis, consume any kind of whole grains or their products (Al Tamimi 2016). The Institute for Health Metrics and Evaluation (IHME 2020) estimated that low intake of whole grains was the most significant dietary risk contributing to the development of noncommunicable diseases (NCDs) in Saudi Arabia in 2017.

The prevalence of an insufficient intake of fruits and vegetables among adults increased between 2013 and 2019. Because of the climate, Saudi Arabia traditionally has no major production of fruits and vegetables and Saudis did not consume many fruits and vegetables, except for dates (El Bcheraoui et al. 2015). The 2019 World Health Survey (MOH 2020) showed that only 6.9 percent of the population ages 15 years and older had five or more servings of fruits or vegetables per typical day in 2019 (6.7 percent of men and 7.1 percent of women). All age groups and both sexes had low consumption of fruit and vegetables. Insufficient intake of fruit and vegetables in 2019 was not related to residence, marital status, wealth, or education. Saudi respondents consumed fruit and vegetables marginally less than non-Saudis. The 2019 World Health Survey found that consumption of fruits and vegetables was lowest among the populations of Hail (2.0 percent), Najran (3.0 percent), and Alqaseem (3.7 percent). In 2019, the consumption of fruit and vegetables decreased even further than the already-low consumption found in the 2013 Saudi Health Interview Survey: 7.6 percent of the Saudi population had a sufficient intake of fruit and vegetables in 2013.

## Dietary behaviors of children and adolescents

Children and adolescents in Saudi Arabia also have a low daily intake of fruits and vegetables. A majority of children ages 7–12 years do not consume fruits

(69.0 percent) or vegetables (71.4 percent) on a daily basis on weekdays (Alsubaie 2018). Daily consumption of fruit was positively associated with daily consumption of vegetables. Daily consumption of vegetables inversely correlated with daily consumption of sweets: odds ratio (OR) = 0.6 with 95 percent confidence interval (CI) of 0.4–0.9. More than 70 percent of adolescents ages 15–19 years do not consume vegetables daily, and more than 80 percent of adolescents do not consume fruit daily (Al-Hazzaa and Albawardi 2019). Overweight and obesity was found to be significantly and inversely associated with weekly vegetable intake (OR = 1.29 with 95 percent CI of 1.03–1.59) among Saudi adolescents ages 14–19 years (Al-Hazzaa et al. 2012). Consumption of fruits and vegetable is lower among the physically inactive than among active adolescents.

Increased obesity among children and adolescents in Saudi Arabia has been commensurate with the increased consumption of fast foods. Obesity among children ages 6–15 years in Riyadh was significantly associated with fast-food intake, with 72.5 percent of the children with overweight or obesity consuming fast food at least four times per week (Almuhanna et al. 2014). Children who frequently eat at fast-food restaurants have higher intakes of fatty foods, unwanted energy, sugar-sweetened beverages, sweet and savory snacks, and highly salted foods; they also have reduced intakes of dietary fibers, milk, water, fruits, and vegetables. A study conducted in Riyadh found that intake of fast food per week was higher among children with obesity ages 9–11 years compared with normal-weight children, regardless of whether the fast food was consumed outside or inside the home (Alturki, Brookes, and Davies 2018a). The same study noted that larger portion sizes were preferred by children with obesity, and that the taste of fast foods, a child-friendly menu, and meal cost were the main reasons for parents taking their children to fast-food restaurants. Parents who regularly ate fast-food meals with their children, controlled the type and/or portion size for their children, and ordered from the "healthy meals menu" for their children were less likely to have children with obesity. Adolescent Saudi girls (ages 13–18 years) and young adult Saudi women (ages 19–29 years) eat fast food primarily because they enjoy the taste and convenience, preferring international (70.9 percent) over local restaurants (29.1 percent) when buying fast food (AlFaris et al. 2015). A high snack frequency of more than twice per day was observed in 33 percent of Saudi children and adolescents, of whom 72.2 percent preferred unhealthy crisps, sweets, and carbonated beverages (Al-Agha et al. 2020).

Consumption of sugar-sweetened beverages contributes to energy intake among Saudi children and adolescents. Overweight and obesity were found to be significantly associated with the consumption of sugar-sweetened beverages (OR = 1.32 with 95 percent CI at 1.08–1.62) among Saudi adolescents ages 14–19 years (Al-Hazzaa et al. 2012). Waist circumference and BMI were positively correlated with sugar-sweetened carbonated beverage intake in Saudi boys and adolescents ages 10–19 years (Collison et al. 2010). High intake of sugar-sweetened carbonated beverages correlated strongly with total energy intake and was positively associated with poor dietary choices. Fast-food meal intake, savory snacks, iced desserts, and added sugar consumption correlated with sugar-sweetened carbonated beverages intake in both boys and girls. Consumption of sugar-sweetened carbonated beverages was higher in older adolescents (Collison et al. 2010).

Other dietary behaviors also contribute to the increase in overweight and obesity in Saudi Arabia. More than 79 percent of the children enrolled in primary schools in Riyadh skip daily breakfast, with children in private schools consuming breakfast more frequently than those attending public schools (Al-Hazzaa et al. 2020). Overweight and obesity were found to be significantly and inversely associated with frequency of breakfast (OR = 1.44 with 95 percent CI at 1.20–1.71) among Saudi adolescents ages 14–19 years (Al-Hazzaa et al. 2012). A study of Saudi female students showed that greater energy intake in the morning and mid-morning was correlated with a lower risk of overweight and obesity, while greater energy intake in the evening was associated with a higher risk of overweight and obesity (Alamri 2019).

## PHYSICAL INACTIVITY AS A RISK FACTOR IN THE DEVELOPMENT OF OVERWEIGHT AND OBESITY

Regular physical activity helps in the prevention of hypertension, overweight, and obesity; it can also improve mental health, quality of life, and well-being. Additionally, it helps to prevent and treat NCDs such as heart disease, stroke, diabetes, and breast and colon cancer (WHO 2018). All forms of physical activity can provide health benefits if undertaken regularly and with sufficient duration and intensity. In 2013, the World Health Assembly endorsed the Global Action Plan on the Prevention and Control of NCDs and agreed on a set of nine global voluntary targets, which include a 10 percent relative reduction in the prevalence of insufficient physical activity by 2025 (WHO 2013).

One of the Vision 2030 goals is to increase the percentage of individuals who practice sports at least once a week from 13 percent to 40 percent. To track progress toward that goal, data on physical activity levels in Saudi Arabia have been collected by the General Authority for Statistics through the Household Sport Practice Surveys (GASTAT 2017, 2018). The most recent data on time spent on physical activity during a typical week, and the intensity of the activity, come from the 2019 World Health Survey (MOH 2020). Additional data on sedentary habits (time spent on watching television and time spent sitting daily) are available from the 2013 Saudi Health Interview Survey (MOH and IHME n.d.). All the surveys used the same threshold of 150 metabolic equivalent minutes per week to classify physical activity level as sufficient or insufficient.

### Physical activity among adults

More than 80 percent of the Saudi Arabian population ages 15 years and older do not engage regularly in sufficient physical activity. Findings from recent surveys indicate that the prevalence of insufficient physical activity among adults declined from 85.1 percent (GASTAT 2017) to 80.3 percent (MOH 2020) between 2017 and 2019. The 2019 World Health Survey found that 19.7 percent of Saudi Arabia's population (18.4 percent of women and 20.8 percent of men) had sufficient levels of physical activity per week. The level of physical activity was highest among the 15–29 age group (21.1 percent) and was decreasing with age. Populations living in urban areas reported slightly higher levels of physical activities than those from rural areas. Men in Saudi Arabia are more physically active than women (figure 3.2).

More than a half of those engaged in a sufficient level of physical activity practice walking. Additionally, the 2018 Household Sport Practice Survey found that one-quarter of the population ages 15 years and older played football, while others who were physically active practiced other types of sport activities, including weight training, running, and swimming. Most of the respondents practiced a physical activity at public facilities (59.0 percent), at sport centers (15.1 percent), or at home (14.8 percent) three or four times per week (GASTAT 2017). About a fifth of physically active respondents used modern electronic fitness tracking applications to monitor heart rate and calories burned, for example, while practicing. The most important reasons for Saudi adults to be physically active were to maintain health and lose weight (Al-Hazzaa 2018). The weather, culture, lack of time, and lack of exercising facilities are among factors that might make it difficult for Saudis to be physically active (El Bcheraoui et al. 2016).

Sedentary lifestyles—including long commutes, sedentary office jobs, and significant screen time—contribute to the physical inactivity of adults in Saudi Arabia. The 2013 Saudi Health Interview Survey showed that more than half of Saudis spend four or more hours or more per day sitting (figure 3.3). Working-age men and women are considered to be a vulnerable

FIGURE 3.2

**Engagement of men and women in sufficient physical activity in Saudi Arabia, 2017–19**

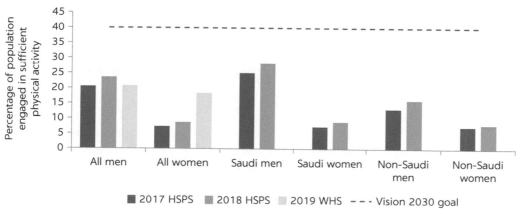

*Sources:* GASTAT 2017, 2018; MOH 2020.
*Note:* HSPS = Household Sports Practice Survey; WHS = World Health Survey.

FIGURE 3.3

**Time spent sitting per day, by sex and age group, 2013**

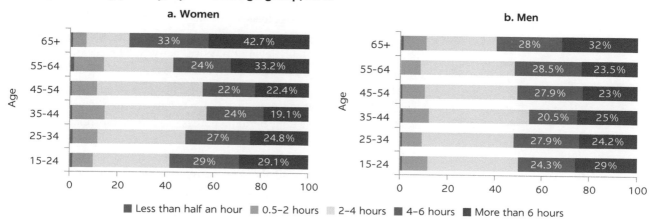

*Source:* MOH and IHME n.d..
*Note:* Based on the responses to the question on sedentary behavior: "How much time do you usually spend sitting or reclining on a typical day?"

group because of the nature of their primarily office-based work (Albawardi et al. 2017; Almuzaini and Jradi 2019). Desk-based employees, including office workers, spend more than two-thirds of their working day in a seated position. Lengthy sitting time in the workplace often exceeds the time spent sitting during leisure time. Playing computer, mobile, and/or internet games, using social media on various devices, watching television, and/or multitasking (for example, watching television while using a mobile device) all contribute to daily screen time. A recent study in Saudi Arabia found that about 76 percent of adults with obesity were spending more than 9 hours per day on various screens (Mattoo et al. 2020).

About a third of adults in Saudi Arabia spend four or more hours per day watching television. Prolonged television watching is associated with an increase in sitting time, the intake of energy-dense foods, and the consumption of foods commonly advertised on television, which all result in higher BMI levels. On average, adults in Saudi Arabia spent about 25 hours per week watching television; prolonged television watching was found to be associated with both very low BMI values and very high BMI values (Al-Hanawi et al. 2020). Prolonged television watching is likely to increase the BMI values of individuals with obesity faster than it is to increase the levels of those with moderate BMI values, thus additionally increasing their risk of suffering from NCDs.

## Physical activity among children and adolescents

Children of physically inactive parents are more likely to be physically inactive. The progression or regression of obesity from childhood to adulthood depends on the habits developed in childhood within the family milieu. Parents can encourage physical activity and limit screen time and can influence other activities that affect their children's health. Unlike habits that can be enforced verbally, physical activity needs to be practiced by the parents within the family to establish a desirable role model for the child. Physically active parents in Saudi Arabia were found to be inspiring their children to be more physically active in adulthood (Mattoo et al. 2020). A lack of space in the home environment to perform physical activity was identified as a significant risk factor for development of obesity among children in Saudi Arabia (Alturki, Brookes, and Davies 2018b).

A systematic review of physical activity in Saudi Arabia showed that the majority of children and youth in Saudi Arabia were not active enough to meet the recommended weekly level of physical activity. The review found that physical inactivity is highly prevalent among Saudi children at an early age (Al-Hazzaa 2018). The physical activity level in Saudi preschool children declines by 23.4 percent from age 4 to age 6, while screen time increases by 22.5 percent during the same period. There is a significant correlation between Saudi children's activity levels during physical education lessons and their activity levels outside of school time. Boys who were active during physical education classes were likely to be active outside school, and vice versa. Inactive Saudi boys ages 8–12 years are 17 percent more overweight than their active peers.

Screen time contributes to the physical inactivity of children and adolescents in Saudi Arabia. Sedentary behaviors are highly prevalent among Saudia Arabian adolescents, with 84.0 percent of males and 91.2 percent of females daily spending more than two hours on a screen (Al-Hazzaa 2018). A study of Saudi children ages 6–13 years showed the mean of screen viewing time to be 3.23 (plus or minus 1.7) hours per day, with boys showing significantly higher screen viewing time than girls. This study suggested that excessive screen time increased the chances of children going late to bed, reduced their total night's sleep, and impacted negatively on breakfast intake (Al-Hazzaa et al. 2019). Close to 75 percent of Saudi adolescents reported screen time of at least two hours a day, and 23.9 percent reported viewing screens 6 hours or more per day (Saquib et al. 2017).

The finding that Saudi women are much less active than Saudi men applies to adolescents also. The systematic review by Al-Hazzaa (2018) further found the average prevalence of physical activity to be somewhat moderate (55.5 percent) among adolescent males and very low among adolescent females (21.9 percent). It also showed that physical activity correlated with healthy dietary habits (breakfast, fruit, vegetables, and milk intakes), while sedentary behaviors were associated with greater consumption of sugar-sweetened drinks, fast foods, cake and doughnuts, and energy drinks among Saudi adolescents. The most important reasons for engaging in physical activity among adolescents are health, losing or maintaining weight, recreation, and socializing. The most important barrier to practicing physical activity is the lack of time, followed by the lack of an appropriate place (especially for female adolescents) and the lack of facility and resources. Female adolescents exercise mostly at home, while males exercise mostly in public areas, commonly with their friends.

## SOCIOECONOMIC AND CULTURAL INFLUENCES

Lower education, but not income, was associated with higher BMI among adults (figure 3.4). This indicates that lack of knowledge about nutrition, lack of access to information, and the inability to have a balanced and nutritious diet had a large influence on increased BMI. However, unlike other high-income countries, in Saudi Arabia the highest rates of overweight and obesity were found in the

FIGURE 3.4

**Percent distribution of overweight and obesity by education level in Saudi Arabia, 2019**

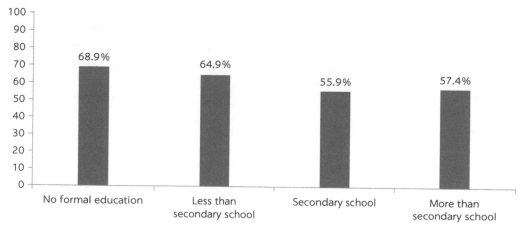

*Source:* MOH 2020.

fourth quintile of wealth (63.5 percent prevalence) compared with only 55 percent in the lowest wealth quintile (MOH 2020).

Similarly, the risk of children becoming affected by overweight and obesity is found to be linked with higher socioeconomic levels, especially family income, and associated with lifestyle changes such as sedentary life and unhealthy dietary habits (Al-Hussaini et al. 2019). The majority of children and adolescents were found to be leading a sedentary lifestyle, following an unhealthy diet (low in nutritional value yet high in caloric content), as well as exhibiting unhealthy dietary habits (Al-Agha et al. 2020).

Determinants of obesity differ between men and women in Saudi Arabia. The risk of obesity among women increases with age and being married or previously married (Memish et al. 2014). Women who had more education than high school were less likely to have obesity than those who had a primary school education or less. Multiple pregnancies were considered to be a specific risk factor for increased food intake, coupled with cultural beliefs that women should not practice any form of physical activity until 40 days after delivery, thus leading to weight gain and evidently increasing BMI in women as compared with men (Al-Qahtani 2019). Men who were previously married or who consumed three or more servings of meat per day were more likely to have obesity (Memish et al. 2014). The risk of obesity was lower among men who reported high levels of physical activity than among inactive men. Income level and employment status, as well as soda consumption and the consumption of red meat, were found to be significant in explaining gender differences in BMI (Al-Hanawi, Chirwa, and Kamninga 2020).

Eating time and occasion are also associated with overweight and obesity in Saudi Arabia. Emotional eating (excessive consumption of food in response to stressful periods such as anxiety and depression) is an additional harmful dietary habit significantly associated with a higher BMI (Al-Agha et al. 2020). Eating a lot was found to be a stress-coping strategy for 15.0 percent of girls ages 15–19 years attending secondary schools in Riyadh (Raheel 2014).

Parenting style and knowledge affects overweight and obesity among children in Saudi Arabia. A high proportion of parents of children ages 6–10 years with overweight (64.3 percent) or obesity (90.0 percent) did not know their children had excess body weight and misclassified their child's weight status in a study conducted in Alqaseem (Al-Mohaimeed 2016). This finding indicates that parents in Saudi Arabia are unaware of the signs and/or cut-off values for childhood obesity and that certain cultural perceptions exacerbate the misperception of children's weight. Additionally, a study of Saudi mothers of preschool children found that Saudi mothers may be more prone to follow indulgent feeding practices that have been previously associated with child obesity (Mosli et al. 2019).

Culturally, Arab parents tend to prioritize spiritual and educational goals for their children. This could be at the expense of sports or physical activities (Sharara et al. 2018). Inactive social gatherings focused on food or sitting games are the predominant leisure activity (Ali, Baynouna, and Bernsen 2010). In addition to the hot weather, the built environment in Saudi Arabia encourages the use of cars and hinders opportunities for outdoor exercise (Donnelly et al. 2018). Together, these factors discourage physical activity and promote a sedentary lifestyle, ultimately leading to more weight gain and higher obesity rates.

## FOOD ENVIRONMENT

The pervasive marketing of junk food is a significant risk factor for childhood obesity. In a 2018 online survey in Gulf Cooperation Council countries, half of respondents mentioned being exposed to food advertisements every day and three-quarters of respondents said they were concerned about children's exposure to fast food advertising, with 23 percent indicating their child asks for fast food after watching these ads (McLaren 2018). Smart phones constitute the largest platform for logging into social networks, with 260 minutes (4.3 hours) a day as an estimated average of logging per person using smart phones (MCIT 2019). Saudi Arabia ranked first among Arab countries and second worldwide in the use of Snapchat. WhatsApp and Facebook had the top rates of social networking platforms use, with 22 percent for WhatsApp and 21 percent for Facebook (MCIT 2019).

## CONCLUSIONS

Only a small percentage of the Saudi population meets the country's dietary recommendations. Excessive energy intake and low consumption of fruits, vegetables, and whole grains is related to the increase in BMI. The consumption of sugar-sweetened beverages contributes to energy intake among Saudi children and adolescents. The increased obesity among children and adolescents in Saudi Arabia has been commensurate with the increased consumption of fast foods.

Very few Saudis regularly engage in a sufficient level of physical activity. Sedentary lifestyles—including long commutes, sedentary office jobs, and prolonged television watching—contribute to the physical inactivity of adults in Saudi Arabia. The chance of children in Saudi Arabia being physically inactive increases with a high level of physical inactivity of their parents. The finding that Saudi women are much less active than Saudi men extends to adolescents in Saudi Arabia. All the factors contributed to increases in the prevalence of overweight and obesity among children, adolescents, and adults in Saudi Arabia.

The majority of Saudi Arabian adolescents and children were found to be leading a sedentary lifestyle and following an unhealthy diet (one low in nutritional value yet high in caloric content). Overweight and obesity are higher and have been increasing faster among male than female adolescents and children. Overall, mean BMI increases most rapidly among children ages 5–9 years, further highlighting the magnitude and urgency of addressing the childhood obesity challenge in Saudi Arabia. If no changes to risk factors take place, high BMI and the overall NCD burden in Saudi Arabia will increase over time.

Together, these results point out many critical roles, beyond the level of individual control, that different sectors can play to help prevent overweight and obesity in Saudi Arabia. Individual risk factors—lack of physical activity and unhealthy diet—need to be addressed along with population-oriented policies to encourage healthier eating and physical activity. Successful policy interventions must tackle societal trends and systems that encourage excess energy intake and are not conducive to increasing energy expenditure (see chapters 7 and 8).

## REFERENCES

AlAbdulKader, A. M., K. Tuwairqi, and G. Rao. 2020. "Obesity and Cardiovascular Risk in the Arab Gulf States." *Current Cardiovascular Risk Reports* 14 (7). doi:10.1007/s12170-020 -00642-8.

Al-Agha, A. E., Y. M. Mabkhoot, A. S. Bahwirith, A. N. Mohammed, R. Ragbi, E. Allhabi, B. K. Dumyati, and A. Milyani. 2020. "Various Causative Factors and Associated Complications of Childhood Obesity in Jeddah, Western Region, Saudi Arabia." *Annals of African Medicine* 19 (1): 15–19. doi:10.4103/aam.aam_8_19.

Alamri, E. S. 2019. "The Association between the Timing of Energy Intake and the Risk of Overweight and Obesity among Saudi Female University Students." *Saudi Medical Journal* 40 (12): 1272–77. doi:10.15537/smj.2019.12.24686.

Albawardi, N. M., H. Jradi, A. A. Almalki, and H. M. Al-Hazzaa. 2017. "Level of Sedentary Behaviour and Its Associated Factors among Saudi Women Working in Office-Based Jobs in Saudi Arabia." *International Journal of Environmental Research and Public Health* 14: 659. doi:10.3390/ijerph14060659.

AlFaris, N. A., J. Z. Al-Tamimi, M. O. Al-Jobair, and N. M. Al-Schwaiyat. 2015. "Trends of Fast Food Consumption among Adolescent and Young Adult Saudi Girls Living in Riyadh." *Food and Nutrition Research* 59: 26488. doi:10.3402/fnr.v59.26488.

Al-Hanawi, M. K., G. C. Chirwa, and T. M. Kamninga. 2020. "Decomposition of Gender Differences in Body Mass Index in Saudi Arabia Using Unconditional Quantile Regression: Analysis of National-Level Survey Data." *International Journal of Environmental Research and Public Health* 17: 2330. doi:10.3390/ijerph17072330.

Al-Hanawi, M. K., G. C. Chirwa, L. A. Pemba, and A. M. N. Qattan. 2020. "Does Prolonged Television Viewing Affect Body Mass Index? A Case of the Kingdom of Saudi Arabia." *PLoS One* 15 (1): e0228321. doi:10.1371/journal.pone.0228321.

Al-Hazzaa, H. M. 2018. "Physical Inactivity in Saudi Arabia Revisited: A Systematic Review of Inactivity Prevalence and Perceived Barriers to Active Living." *International Journal of Health Sciences* 12 (6): 50–64.

Al-Hazzaa, H. M., N. A. Abahussain, H. I. Al-Sobayel, D. M. Qahwaji, and A. O. Musaiger. 2012. "Lifestyle Factors Associated with Overweight and Obesity among Saudi Adolescents." *BMC Public Health* 12: 354. doi:10.1186/1471-2458-12-354.

Al-Hazzaa, H. M., and N. M. Albawardi. 2019. "Activity Energy Expenditure, Screen Time and Dietary Habits Relative to Gender among Saudi Youth: Interactions of Gender with Obesity Status and Selected Lifestyle Behaviours." *Asia Pacific Journal of Clinical Nutrition* 28 (2): 389–400. doi:10.6133/apjcn.201906_28(2).0022.

Al-Hazzaa, H. M., A. M. Alhowikan, M. H. Alhussain, and O. A. Obeid. 2020. "Breakfast Consumption among Saudi Primary-School Children Relative to Sex and Socio-Demographic Factors." *BMC Public Health* 20: 448. doi:10.1186/s12889-020-8418-1.

Al-Hazzaa, H. M., M. H. Alhussain, A. M. Alhowikan, and O. A. Obeid. 2019. "Insufficient Sleep Duration and Its Association with Breakfast Intake, Overweight/Obesity, Socio-Demographics and Selected Lifestyle Behaviors among Saudi School Children." *Nature and Science of Sleep* 11: 253–63. doi:10.2147/NSS.S225883.

Al-Hussaini, A., M. S. Bashir, M. Khormi, M. AlTuraiki, W. Alkhamis, M. Alrajhi, and T. Halal. 2019. "Overweight and Obesity among Saudi Children and Adolescents: Where Do We Stand Today?" *Saudi Journal of Gastroenterology* 25 (4): 229–35. doi:10.4103/sjg.SJG_617_18.

Ali, H. I., L. M. Baynouna, and R. M. Bernsen. 2010. "Barriers and Facilitators of Weight Management: Perspectives of Arab Women at Risk for Type 2 Diabetes." *Health and Social Care in the Community* 18 (2): 219–28. doi:10.1111/j.1365-2524.2009.00896.x.

Al-Kutbe, R., A. Payne, A. de Looy, and G. A. Rees. 2017. "A Comparison of Nutritional Intake and Daily Physical Activity of Girls Aged 8–11 Years Old in Makkah, Saudi Arabia, According to Weight Status." *BMC Public Health* 17: 592. doi:10.1186/s12889-017-4506-2.

Al-Mohaimeed, A. A. 2016. "Parents' Perception of Children's Obesity, in Al-Qassim, Saudi Arabia." *Journal of Family and Community Medicine* 23: 179–83. doi:10.4103/2230-8229.189134.

Almuhanna, M. A., M. Alsaif, M. Alsaadi, and A. Almajwal. 2014. "Fast Food Intake and Prevalence of Obesity in School Children in Riyadh City." *Sudanese Journal of Paediatrics* 14 (1): 71–80.

Almuzaini, Y., and H. Jradi. 2019. "Correlates and Level of Physical Activity and Body Mass Index among Saudi Men Working in Office-Based Jobs." *Journal of Community Health* 44 (4): 815–21. doi:10.1007/s10900-019-00639-4.

Al-Qahtani, A. M. 2019. "Prevalence and Predictors of Obesity and Overweight among Adults Visiting Primary Care Settings in the Southwestern Region, Saudi Arabia." *BioMed Research International* 2019: 8073057. doi:10.1155/2019/8073057.

Alsubaie, A. S. R. 2018. "Intake of Fruit, Vegetables and Milk Products and Correlates among School Boys in Saudi Arabia." *International Journal of Adolescent Medicine and Health* 2018: 2018005.

Al Tamimi, J. Z. 2016. "Consumption of Whole Grains by a Sample of Saudi Adults." *International Journal of Nutrition and Food Sciences* 5 (2): 117–23. doi:10.11648/j.ijnfs.20160502.14.

Alturki, H. A., D. S. K. Brookes, and P. S. W. Davies. 2018a. "Comparative Evidence of the Consumption from Fast Food Restaurants between Normal-Weight and Obese Saudi Schoolchildren." *Public Health Nutrition* 21 (12): 2280–90. doi:10.1017/S1368980018000757.

Alturki, H. A., D. S. K. Brookes, and P. S. W. Davies. 2018b. "Obesity Prevention Interventions in Saudi Arabian Children—Building the Evidence Base: An In-Depth Analysis of Sociodemographic Characteristics and Dietary Habits of Obese and Normal Weight Schoolchildren." *Global Epidemic Obesity* 6 (1). doi:10.7243/2052-5966-6-1.

Collison, K. S., M. Z. Zaidi, S. N. Subhani, K. Al-Rubeaan, M. Shoukri, and F. A. Al-Mohanna. 2010. "Sugar-Sweetened Carbonated Beverage Consumption Correlates with BMI, Waist Circumference, and Poor Dietary Choices in School Children." *BMC Public Health* 10: 234. doi:10.1186/1471-2458-10-234.

Donnelly, T. T., A.-A.b. M. Al-Thani, K. Benjamin, Al-H. Al-Khater, T. S. Fung, M. Ahmedna, and A. Welsh. 2018. "Arab Female and Male Perceptions of Factors Facilitating and Inhibiting Their Physical Activity: Findings from a Qualitative Study in the Middle East." *PLoS One* 13 (7): e0199336. doi:10.1371/journal.pone.0199336.

El Bcheraoui, C., M. Basulaiman, M. A. Al Mazroa, M. Tuffaha, F. Daoud, S. Wilson, M. Y. Al Saeedi, F. M. Alazani, M. E. Ibrahim, E. A. Ahmed, S. A. Hussain, R. M. Salloum, O. Abid, M. F. Al-Dossary, Z. A. Memish, A. A. Al Rabeeah, and A. H. Mokdad. 2015. "Fruit and Vegetable Consumption among Adults in Saudi Arabia, 2013." *Nutrition and Dietary Supplements* 7: 41–9.

El Bcheraoui, C., M. Tuffaha, F. Daoud, H. Kravitz, M. A. Al Mazroa, M. Al Saeedi, Z. A. Memish, M. Basulaiman, A. A. Al Rabeeah, and A. H. Mokdad. 2016. "On Your Mark, Get Set, Go: Levels of Physical Activity in the Kingdom of Saudi Arabia, 2013." *Journal of Physical Activity and Health* 13 (2): 231–8.

FAO (Food and Agriculture Organization of the United Nations). 2020. FAOSTAT, database. Rome: Food and Agriculture Organization of the United Nations. http://www.fao.org/faostat/en/#home.

GASTAT (General Authority for Statistics). 2017. *Bulletin of Household Sports Practice Survey.* Riyadh: General Authority for Statistics. https://www.stats.gov.sa/sites/default/files/bulletin_of_household_sports_practice_survey_2017_en.pdf.

GASTAT (General Authority for Statistics). 2018. *Bulletin of Household Sport Practice Survey.* Riyadh: General Authority for Statistics. https://www.stats.gov.sa/sites/default/files/household_sport_practice_survey_2018_en.pdf.

IHME (Institute for Health Metrics and Evaluation). 2020. GBD Compare/Viz Hub, database. Seattle: University of Washington. https://vizhub.healthdata.org/gbd-compare.

Malik, V. S., and F. B. Hu. 2017. "Obesity Prevention." In *Disease Control Priorities, Third Edition,* vol. 5, *Cardiovascular, Respiratory, and Related Disorders,* edited by D. Prabhakaran, S. Anand, T. A. Gaziano. J.-C. Mbanya, Y. Wu, and R. Nugent, 117–34. Washington, DC: World Bank.

Mattoo, K., M. Shubayr, M. Al Moaleem, and E. Halboub. 2020. "Influence of Parental Physical Activity and Screen Time on the BMI of Adult Offspring in a Saudi Population." *Healthcare* 8: 110. doi:10.3390/healthcare8020110.

MCIT (Ministry of Communications and Information Technology). 2019. "Over 18 Million Users of Social Media Programs and Applications in Saudi Arabia." MCIT Media Center News. https://www.mcit.gov.sa/en/media-center/news/89698.

McLaren, Kerry. 2018. "Fast Food Advertising Influences GCC Residents to Make Unhealthy Choices." YouGov Media Center. https://mena.yougov.com/en/news/2018/10/01/fast-food-advertising-influences-gcc-residents-mak/.

Memish, Z. A., C. El Bcheraoui, M. Tuffaha, M. Robinson, F. Daoud, S. Jaber, S. Mikhitarian, M. Al Saeedi, M. A. AlMazroa, A. H. Mokdad, and A. A. Al Rabeeah. 2014. "Obesity and Associated Factors—Kingdom of Saudi Arabia, 2013." *Preventing Chronic Disease* 11: E174.

MOH (Ministry of Health). 2020. "World Health Survey Saudi Arabia (KSAWHS) 2019 Final Report." Ministry of Health, Riyadh.

MOH and IHME (Ministry of Health and Institute for Health Metrics and Evaluation). n.d. *Saudi Health Interview Survey Results*. Seattle: University of Washington. http://www.healthdata.org/sites/default/files/files/Projects/KSA/Saudi-Health-Interview-Survey-Results.pdf.

Moradi-Lakeh, M., A. El Bcheraoui, F. Afshin, F. Daoud, M. A. AlMazroa, M. Al Saeedi, M. Basulaiman, Z. A. Memish, A. A. Al Rabeeah, and A. H. Mokdad. 2016. "Diet in Saudi Arabia: Findings from a Nationally Representative Survey." *Public Health Nutrition* 20 (6): 1075–81. doi:10.1017/S1368980016003141.

Mosli, R. H., J. A. Bakhsh, M. A. Madami. A. F. Sindi, A. F. Barasheed, H. A. Kutbi, and H. K. Al-Wassia. 2019. "Indulgence and Stress around Feeding: Initial Evidence from a Qualitative Study of Saudi Mothers." *Appetite* 138: 242–51. doi:10.1016/j.appet.2019.03.036.

Raheel, H. 2014. "Coping Strategies for Stress Used by Adolescent Girls." *Pakistan Journal of Medical Sciences* 30 (5): 958–62. doi:10.12669/pjms.305.5014.

Saquib, N., J. Saquib, A. Wahid, A. A. Ahmed, H. E. Dhuhayr, M. S. Zaghloul, M. Ewid, and A. Al-Mazrou. 2017. "Video Game Addiction and Psychological Distress among Expatriate Adolescents in Saudi Arabia." *Addictive Behaviors Reports* 6: 112–17. doi:10.1016/j.abrep.2017.09.003.

Sharara, E., C. Akik, H. Ghattas, and C. Obermeyer. 2018. "Physical Inactivity, Gender and Culture in Arab Countries: A Systematic Assessment of the Literature." *BMC Public Health* 18: 639. doi:10.1186/s12889-018-5472-z.

Vandevijvere, S., C. C. Chow, K. D. Hall, E. Umali, and B. A. Swinburn. 2015. "Increased Food Energy Supply as a Major Driver of the Obesity Epidemic: A Global Analysis." *Bulletin of the World Health Organization* 93: 446–56. doi:10.2471/BLT.14.150565.

WHO (World Health Organization). 2013. *Global Action Plan for the Prevention and Control of Noncommunicable Diseases 2013–2020*. Geneva: World Health Organization.

WHO (World Health Organization). 2018. *Global Action Plan on Physical Activity 2018–2030: More Active People for a Healthier World*. Geneva: World Health Organization.

# 4 Forecasting the Health Burden of Overweight and Obesity on Noncommunicable Diseases in Saudi Arabia

EILEEN LEE, TIM BRUCKNER, MOHAMMED ALLUHIDAN, REEM F. ALSUKAIT, TAGHRED ALGHAITH, CHRISTOPHER H. HERBST, ABDULAZIZ ALTOWAIJRI, AND SALEH ALQAHTANI

## KEY MESSAGES

- The burden of noncommunicable diseases (NCDs) is expected to increase from 2020 to 2050.
- An elevated body mass index (BMI) is the top risk factor for NCD-related death and disability.
- The six major causes of disability and death associated with elevated BMI are ischemic heart disease, stroke, type 2 diabetes, breast cancer, colon cancer, and leukemia.
- Reductions in overweight and obesity have the potential to substantially improve overall health and reduce the NCD burden.
- This chapter presents 10 models of potential scenarios; these include no change, moderate modifications, and ambitious modifications to population risk factors.
- In the ambitious scenario, a reduction of 20 percent in overweight and obesity is expected to avert 59,279 and 110,712 deaths for females and males, respectively, by 2050.

## BACKGROUND

The disability and life years lost due to noncommunicable diseases (NCDs) in Saudi Arabia are substantial. In 2020, disability-adjusted life years (DALYs) in Saudi Arabia due to NCDs are estimated at a loss of 5,964,386. (DALY numbers are losses.) This value represents 65.17 percent of overall DALYs (all-cause DALYs are 9,151,937) in the Saudi population.[1]

The overall burden of NCDs in Saudi Arabia is expected to increase because of changes in population distribution (that is, population aging), increasing life expectancy, and decreasing fertility rates, as discussed in chapters 2 and 3. In 2020, cardiovascular diseases, diabetes, and cancers accounted for approximately one-third of the overall NCD burden. The proportion of the population over 50 years of age is projected to increase more than twofold, from 15.09 percent (of the total population) in 2020 to 36.64 percent in 2050.

Elevated body mass index (BMI) is a major risk factor for NCD-related death and disability. High BMI is expected to contribute to 15.73 percent of the total NCD DALY burden in Saudi Arabia (IHME 2018b). A BMI greater than 25 is a major risk factor for heart disease, stroke, and diabetes burden. (BMI is measured is measured as kilograms per square meter, or kg/m². ). Approximately 71 percent of the population over 45 years in Saudi Arabia is overweight or obese (measured as having a BMI greater than 25.0 and 30.0, respectively) (MOH 2020). The high prevalence of these (hereafter overweight/obesity, when considered together) in Saudi Arabia makes BMI reduction a top priority for reducing the burden of NCDs.

The six major causes of disability and death associated with raised BMI are ischemic heart disease, stroke, type 2 diabetes, breast cancer,[2] colon cancer, and leukemia. In 2020, these six conditions are estimated to contribute 23.62 percent of all NCD DALYs. This proportion is expected to increase to 33.94 percent by 2050 as the population ages. Of these conditions, ischemic heart disease and stroke are the top two contributors to NCD DALYs (17.01 percent). These conditions affect both men and women and, more recently in Saudi Arabia, even those as early as in their 40s.

The links between lack of physical activity and low intake of fruits and vegetables on overweight/obesity are well documented. The NCD burden caused by overweight/obesity can be reduced by modifying diet and exercise (Catenacci and Wyatt 2007; Samdal et al. 2017) (figure 4.1). Peer-reviewed literature on policy interventions to modify BMI via exercise shows the interventions to have short-term effects (Millar et al. 2011). Any single policy intervention in itself appears to be insufficient to significantly reduce the prevalence of overweight/obesity. Therefore, it is likely that a combination of these efforts will be needed to reduce the NCD burden. This chapter offers 10 health scenarios for Saudi Arabia's future, with the assumption of no change to population risk factors and

**FIGURE 4.1**

**Conceptual framework of the influence of modifiable risk factors on key noncommunicable diseases**

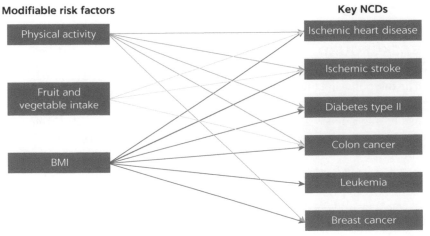

*Source:* World Bank data.
*Note:* BMI = body mass index; NCD = noncommunicable disease.

increasing overweight/obesity prevalence. Additionally, low intake of fruits and vegetables and low physical activity are modeled as separate modifiable risk factors, and their impact on the NCD burden in Saudi Arabia is illustrated. Annex 4A presents separate figures for female- and male-forecasted NCD burdens; annex 4B presents supplementary details for intervention assumptions.

## METHODS

This chapter forecasts several scenarios that assume changes to the prevalence of overweight/obesity, insufficient fruit and vegetable intake, and insufficient physical activity. These estimates are applied to the health and demographic situation in Saudi Arabia; several scenarios—of life expectancy, DALYs, deaths averted, and healthy life expectancy (HALE) that arise from changes in NCD burdens—are forecast. *HALE* is defined as the average years of life that a person can expect to live in "full health" (WHO 2020).

This chapter quantifies, from 2020 to 2050, disability and life years lost due to overweight- and obesity-related NCDs in Saudi Arabia. NCDs cause not only premature death (years of life lost, or YLLs) but also disability (years of life disabled, or YLDs). When summed, these two measures form the DALY value. This measure quantifies the health gap between an ideal health state—a theoretical state in which mortality is caused only by old age—and years of life spent disabled or injured, in subpar health due to disease. DALYs are often used as a basis for health policy making as well as for setting intervention priorities. The DALY calculation appears as follows:

$$DALY = YLL + YLD \qquad (4.1)$$

Minimizing premature death and disability is the equivalent of maximizing healthy life years. HALE represents a more intuitive way to think about reductions to disability and premature mortality. These reductions can be interpreted as a gain in healthy years lived, or a gain in HALE. This summary measure is adjusted for years that are lived with disease and injury:

$$HALE = ex_0 - YLD \qquad (4.2)$$

where $ex_0$ equals life expectancy at birth.

First, the baseline (2020) NCD burden estimates for males and females in Saudi Arabia were retrieved. The data source for these baseline estimates of the DALY burden for specific NCDs was the Global Burden of Disease (GBD) database (IHME 2018b). Next, a baseline scenario was assumed in which the DALY burden remains unchanged from 2020 to 2050—save for the fact that the Saudi population distribution shifts to older ages. The population size and age structure values for 2020, 2030, 2040, and 2050 were based on United Nations (UN) population estimates for Saudi Arabia (UN DESA 2019b). This population projection, combined with the 2017 GBD database, allowed forecasting to 2050 the DALY burden by NCD, sex, and age group. Table 4.1 shows the total DALYs for each of the key health conditions.

Demographic life tables were used to calculate baseline (2020) life expectancy, healthy life expectancy, and deaths averted. A *life table* is a tool used by demographers to quantify mortality and life expectancy at various ages.

TABLE 4.1 **Both sexes: Estimated disability-adjusted life years for each condition, 2020**

| NCD CONDITION | FEMALE | MALE | TOTAL |
|---|---|---|---|
| Ischemic heart disease | 203,178 | 535,065 | 738,242 |
| Stroke | 108,833 | 167,593 | 276,426 |
| Type 2 diabetes | 91,111 | 162,535 | 253,646 |
| Colon cancer | 15,279 | 36,468 | 51,747 |
| Leukemia | 18,020 | 29,651 | 47,671 |
| Breast cancer | 40,193 | — | 40,193 |
| Total | 476,614 | 931,311 | 1,407,925 |

*Sources:* Calculations for baseline data were obtained using population data (UN DESA 2019b), DALY rates (GBD 2017 DALYs and HALE Collaborators 2018), and estimates of relative risk (IHME 2018a).
*Note:* Ischemic heart disease, stroke, and diabetes are the three leading causes of DALYs among NCDs in Saudi Arabia. — = not available; NCDs = noncommunicable diseases.

Life tables are calculated separately for males and females because of their different patterns of mortality (UN DESA 2019a). *Life expectancy at birth*, which is often used to summarize a country's overall health, refers to the average number of years that an infant who is born today would be expected to live. There are two conceptual frameworks for the life table method—the period life table and the cohort life table. The *cohort life table* follows the actual mortality experience (as quantified by exact age of death) of a cohort of individuals throughout their lifetimes until their eventual deaths (Guillot and Kim 2011). By contrast, the *period life table* takes a cross-section of the current-day population and combines multiple birth cohorts' experiences to quantify age-specific mortality rates (Guillot and Kim 2011).

The more commonly used method to summarize life expectancy and mortality is the period life table. The period life table has two advantages over the cohort life table. First, cohort life tables are complete only for cohorts who are already extinct (that is, those born in and before 1920). Estimates of period life expectancy, however, can occur for contemporary populations who have not yet died. The assumption here is that births—for example, in 2020—will be subject over their entire lifetime to the age-specific mortality rates of the Saudi population in 2020. Second, period life expectancy uses up-to-date data and health statistics combined with current-day health knowledge to estimate future life expectancy. Whereas period life expectancy tends to underestimate cohort life expectancy, the two practical advantages described earlier make it the predominant choice among demographers in describing life expectancy.

In Saudi Arabia, the average period life expectancy at birth ($ex_0$, equation 4.2) is 76.51 years for females and 73.71 years for males. By 2050, this is projected to increase to 80.93 years for females and 78.22 years for males. This increase assumes no change in the NCD profile. Rather, these estimates come directly from UN Population Estimates forecasts (UN DESA 2019b). Table 4.2 lists an overview of assumptions for models 1–10 and corresponding risk factors.

## Overweight and obesity

Current estimates of the NCD burden associated with overweight/obesity prevalence were applied to the life tables to arrive at 2030, 2040, and 2050 forecasts

TABLE 4.2 **Overview of assumptions for models 1–10 and corresponding risk factors**

| MODELS | RISK FACTORS | CHANGE TO RISK FACTORS[a] | DESCRIPTION |
|---|---|---|---|
| 1 | Overweight. obesity | 0% | Baseline scenario of no change to risk factors; reference group for models 2 and 3 |
| 2 | Overweight, obesity | –10% | Moderate intervention of 10% reduction to risk factors |
| 3 | Overweight obesity | –20% | Ambitious scenario of 20% reduction to risk factors |
| 4 | Insufficient fruit and vegetable intake | 0% | Baseline scenario of no change to risk factors; reference group for model 5 |
| 5 | Insufficient fruit and vegetable intake | –10% | Moderate intervention of 10% reduction to risk factors |
| 6 | Insufficient physical activity | 0% | Baseline scenario of no change to risk factors; reference group for model 7 |
| 7 | Insufficient physical activity | –10% | Moderate intervention of 10% reduction to risk factors |
| 8[b] | Overweight, obesity | –1.4 to + 4.8% + 15.4 to 22.6% | Baseline scenario of increasing prevalence of risk factors; reference group for models 9 and 10. |
| 9 | Overweight, obesity | –10% | Moderate intervention of 10% reduction to risk factors |
| 10 | Overweight, obesity | –20% | Ambitious scenario of 20% reduction to risk factors |

*Source:* World Bank data.

a. corresponds to percent change per decade.

b. For model 8, we used sex-specific projections of overweight and obesity from 2013 to 2030 from Lo et al. (2014). We calculated a year over year rate to arrive at the 10-year change. See corresponding prevalence table 4.3 for increasing scenario for more details. Prevalence of obesity was projected to increase for both males and females. However, for overweight prevalence, there was a small decrease for males and an increase for females.

of NCD premature mortality and disability. Model 1 assumes no changes in risk factors, in that no interventions have occurred (that is, there has been no government intervention and no increase in prevalence). This model applies age-specific risks of disease for the key NCD conditions as a function of exposure to key risk factors—overweight and obesity. These age-specific risk estimates were used to arrive at DALYs, HALEs, $ex_0$ (calculation 4.2), and deaths by sex. All of the forecasts assume decreasing fertility trends, aging of the population, and decreases from mortality and morbidity from disease for all age groups, based on UN Population Estimates (UN DESA 2019b). Models 2 and 3 in this chapter are calculated as deviations from model 1, the baseline scenario.

Next, the NCD disability was forecasted to 2050 using different assumptions about modification in risk factors. Model 2 (moderate intervention) assumes that Saudi Arabia will adopt some governmental policy changes and that these changes will be mildly successful. *Moderate success* is considered to be a 10.0 percent reduction in the prevalence of overweight (BMI = 25.0–29.9 kg/m²) and obesity (BMI > 30) every 10 years. For example, the current overweight prevalence for women in Saudi Arabia in 2020 is estimated at 32.7 percent (MOH 2020). If a 10.0 percent reduction in obesity prevalence every 10 years is assumed, then a moderate intervention scenario forecasts the following obesity prevalence among women:

- 2030: 32.7% × 0.90 = 29.4%
- 2040: 32.7% × (0.90 x 0.90) = 26.5%
- 2050: 32.7% × (0.90 x 0.90 x 0.90) = 23.8%

Model 3, which is the ambitious scenario, assumes that policy interventions will aggressively target reducing both overweight and obesity prevalence. The ambitious scenario of model 3 assumes a 20 percent reduction in overweight and obese population every 10 years.

## Unhealthy diet (low fruit and vegetable intake)

The NCD burden associated with low fruit and vegetable intake was quantified using the life tables to obtain 2030, 2040, and 2050 forecasts of NCD premature mortality and disability. Model 4 assumes no changes to the population's fruit and vegetable intake. Age-specific risks were calculated for stroke, ischemic heart disease, and colon cancer as a function of exposure to insufficient fruit and vegetable intake. These age-specific risk estimates were used to arrive at DALYs and deaths averted by sex (UN DESA 2019a; WHO 2004).

NCD disability was forecasted into 2030, 2040, and 2050 assuming a 10 percent reduction in insufficient fruit and vegetable intake each decade. Model 5 (moderate intervention) assumes that Saudi Arabia will adopt some governmental policy changes and that these changes will focus on increasing fruit and vegetable intake in the population. *Moderate success* is considered to be a 10 percent increase in the prevalence of sufficient fruit and vegetable intake (five servings per day). Model 4 serves as the baseline scenario for model 5.

## Insufficient physical activity

Estimates of the NCD burden associated with the prevalence of insufficient physical activity was applied to the life tables to arrive at 2030, 2040, and 2050 forecasts of NCD premature mortality and disability. Model 6 is a no-change scenario that assumes that the prevalence of insufficient physical activity will remain unchanged from 2020. This model assumes that no interventions have occurred (that is, there has been no government intervention and no increase in the prevalence of risk factors). Age-specific risks of disease for stroke, ischemic heart disease, diabetes, breast cancer, and colon cancer were calculated as a function of exposure to insufficient physical activity (IMHE 2018a). These age-specific risk estimates were used to arrive at DALYs and deaths averted, by sex (UN DESA 2019a; WHO 2004).

NCD disability and premature mortality were forecasted for 2030–50 assuming a 10 percent increase in sufficient physical activity for each decade. Model 7 (moderate intervention) assumes that Saudi Arabia will adopt some governmental policy changes and that these changes will be mildly successful. Moderate success is considered to be a 10 percent increase in the prevalence of sufficient physical activity (150 minutes of exercise per week).

## Overweight and obesity, increasing prevalence

Models 8, 9, and 10 assume that overweight/obesity prevalence will increase by 1.2 percent and 19.6 percent, respectively (Lo et al. 2014). Model 8 assumes no changes in risk factors and that no interventions have occurred (that is, no government intervention and no increase in prevalence). Models 9 and 10 in this chapter are calculated as deviations from model 8, the increasing scenario.

The NCD burden due to premature death and disability was forecasted to 2050 using different assumptions about modification in risk factors. Model 9 (moderate intervention) assumes a moderate reduction of 10 percent to overweight (BMI = 25.0–29.9 kg/m$^2$) and obesity (BMI ≥ 30) prevalence every 10 years. The ambitious scenario, model 10, assumes a 20 percent reduction in overweight/obesity every 10 years.

## Defining the measures of health

Risk factors for at-risk populations were defined using the following terms. *Overweight* and *obesity* were defined as BMI 25.0–29.9 kg/m² and BMI ≥ 30.0 kg/m², respectively. *Insufficient fruit and vegetable intake* was defined as less than five servings of fruit and vegetables per day. *Insufficient physical activity* was defined as less than 150 minutes of moderate-intensity or less than 75 minutes of vigorous-intensity physical activity per week.

For key conditions (by age and sex), the population attributable risk fraction (PAF) was calculated for all risk factors for projected YLLs and YLDs to 2050 (see box 4.1 for an example). The population attributable risk summarizes the fraction of YLL and YLD due to the prevalence of the risk factor. Relative risks were obtained from GBD estimates (IHME 2018a) and the World Health Organization's Quantification of Health Risks (WHO 2004). The GBD estimates utilize a wide range of primary research from Saudi Arabia. The estimates for the causes of death and disability used for this chapter utilized 262 studies. For stroke, ischemic heart disease, and diabetes, Saudi Arabia–specific primary research studies are used. For cancers, the inputs included primary research studies and data from the Saudi Cancer Registry. Other data sources included national health surveys such as the Saudi Health Interview Survey 2013 and vital registration data.

Changes in the PAF (as observed via changes to age- and sex-specific risk factors) were used to calculate changes in mortality for the life table (UN DESA 2019a) and YLD.

---

**BOX 4.1**

## Examples of population attributable risk fraction

There are several formulas that can be used to estimate population attributable risk fractions (PAFs), depending on whether one is using unadjusted or adjusted relative risks (RRs), but a common formula that uses unadjusted RRs is the following:

$$PAF_1\ (\%) = \frac{p_1\left(RR_1 - 1\right)}{1 + p_1\left(RR_1 - 1\right) + p_2\left(RR_2 - 1\right)} \quad \text{(B4.1)}$$

$$PAF_2\ (\%) = \frac{p_2\left(RR_2 - 1\right)}{1 + p_1\left(RR_1 - 1\right) + p_2\left(RR_2 - 1\right)} \quad \text{(B4.2)}$$

where $p_1$ and $p_2$ represent the prevalence of overweight (25 kg/m² ≤ $BMI$ < 30 kg/m²) and obesity (BMI ≥ 30 kg/m²) in the population of interest (that is, Saudi Arabia's population) respectively; $RR_1$ represents the unadjusted RR of a particular NCD of interest for

overweight relative to normal weight individuals; and $RR_2$ represents the corresponding figure for obesity relative to normal weight individuals. RR estimates can be obtained from cohort studies and do not necessarily need to come from the population under study as long as excess weight can be assumed to influence the condition of interest equally across the two populations:

**2020 and 2030**

$$PAF_{1\,(2020)} = \frac{p_{1\,(2020)}\left(RR_x - 1\right)}{1 + p_{1\,(2020)}\left(RR_x - 1\right)} \quad \text{(B4.3)}$$

$$PAF_{2\,(2030)} = \frac{p_{2\,(2030)}\left(RR_x - 1\right)}{1 + p_{2\,(2030)}\left(RR_x - 1\right)} \quad \text{(B4.4)}$$

$$YLD * \left(PAF_1 - PAF_2\right) = YLD\ averted\ /\ saved \quad \text{(B4.5)}$$

*Note:* YLD = years of life-disabled. PAFs were calculated for each priority health condition.

Saudi Arabia's World Health Survey estimates (MOH 2020) were used to calculate baseline overweight/obesity prevalence. To estimate HALEs gained, the YLD-averted calculation B4.5 was used to derive the sex- and age-specific YLD saved and concordant reduction in mortality. The proportion of mortality attributable to the key NCDs was then calculated. For each disease, the difference in PAF and the YLD and PAF calculations was used to adjust mortality, YLL, and YLD.

Period life expectancy was recalculated using the modified life table (that is, where reductions in mortality were observed as a result of a change in the prevalence of risk factors). The survivorship and years of life that contributed to the censoring of the last age group (95 or more years) were not changed. The force of mortality was revised accordingly, since the YLDs were removed from the life table in the form of person-years. The gains in life expectancy were calculated using the updated age-specific mortality rates under the various scenarios of reduced prevalence of risk factors.

## RESULTS

In this section, the results from three risk factors are presented. The first assesses the effects of overweight/obesity, the second considers the effects of a low intake of fruits and vegetables, and the third the effects of insufficient activity.

### Overweight and obesity

As mentioned in the introduction, the burden of NCDs is expected to increase to 2050 as a result of changes in population distribution (that is, population aging), increasing life expectancy, and decreasing fertility rates. The aging of the population will result in an increase in the NCD burden to 2050 for key conditions in Saudi Arabia. Separate figures for female and male forecasted NCD burdens are presented in annex 4A. Model 1 estimates that NCD DALYs per 100,000 for females would increase from 3,246 in 2020 to 7,856 by 2050 (see annex figure 4A.1). For males, NCD DALYs would increase from 4,630 in 2020 to 10,832 per 100,000 by 2050 (figure 4A.2). Since DALYs resulting from the aforementioned priority NCDs are primarily concentrated among persons ages 40 and older (84.9 percent for females and 88.6 percent for males in 2020), it is no surprise that the growth of this age group as a fraction of the total population will increase the overall NCD burden. This baseline model takes into consideration the trends of declining fertility rates, decreasing mortality, and the aging of the Saudi population. Figure 4.2 shows this increase in NCD burden for both females and males over time.

If moderate reductions in overweight/obesity prevalence were achieved (that is, model 2, the moderate scenario), Saudi Arabia's NCD burden would decline by 115,012 DALYs for females and 221,790 for males from 2020 to 2050. This reduction equates to a 3.33 percent reduction in the burden for females and a 3.57 percent reduction for males from 2020 to 2050. Tables 4.4 and 4.5 describe the DALY reduction under the moderate scenario for females and males, respectively. In addition, table 4.6 shows that the majority (52.2 percent) of DALYs averted among the target NCDs would involve ischemic heart disease.

Males contribute to a higher number of DALYs averted for priority health conditions. After age 40, for the priority health conditions, males have a higher

FIGURE 4.2

## Both sexes: Model 1, forecasted noncommunicable diseases burden for key conditions in Saudi Arabia, 2020–50, baseline scenario of no change in risk factors

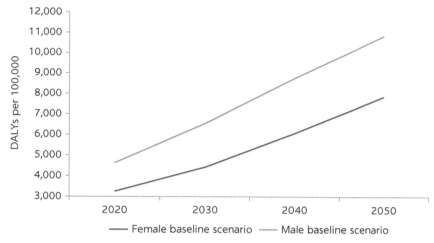

— Female baseline scenario — Male baseline scenario

*Sources:* Calculations for baseline data were obtained using population data (UN DESA 2019b) and DALY rates (GBD 2017 DALYs and HALE Collaborators 2018).
*Note:* DALYs = disability-adjusted life years; NCD = noncommunicable disease.

TABLE 4.3 **Both sexes: Baseline prevalence of overweight and obesity in 2020 for models 2–3 and 8–10**

| AGE GROUP (YEARS) | FEMALE BMI | | MALE BMI | |
|---|---|---|---|---|
| | 25.0–30.0 KG/M² | 30.0+ KG/M² | 25.0–30.0 KG/M² | 30.0+ KG/M² |
| 15–29 | 23.4% | 13.9% | 24.9% | 13.4% |
| 30–44 | 33.6% | 33.3% | 39.4% | 25.0% |
| 45–59 | 30.7% | 49.5% | 37.9% | 37.4% |
| 60–69 | 28.0% | 57.6% | 40.6% | 35.9% |
| 70–79 | 27.3% | 63.1% | 39.5% | 35.9% |
| 80+ | 33.6% | 43.6% | 38.3% | 27.8% |

*Source:* MOH 2020.
*Note:* BMI = body mass index; kg/m² = kilogram per square meter.

TABLE 4.4 **Females: Model 2, forecasted disability-adjusted life years for the baseline scenario of no change in overweight and obesity prevalence relative to the moderate scenario, 2020–50**

| FEMALE DALYS (1,000S) | 2020 | 2030 | 2040 | 2050 |
|---|---|---|---|---|
| Baseline | 477 | 747 | 1,131 | 1,574 |
| Moderate | 477 | 720 | 1,092 | 1,524 |
| Averted | n.a. | 27 | 39 | 50 |
| Percent change | n.a. | 3.58 | 3.41 | 3.16 |

*Sources:* Calculations for baseline data were obtained using population data (UN DESA 2019b), DALY rates (GBD 2017 DALYs and HALE Collaborators 2018), and estimates of relative risk (IHME 2018a).
*Note:* DALYs averted are not cumulative and represent the DALYs averted within the decade. DALYs = disability-adjusted life years; n.a. = not applicable.

TABLE 4.5 **Males: Model 2, forecasted disability-adjusted life years for the baseline scenario of no change in risk factors relative to the moderate scenario, 2020–50**

| MALE DALYS (1,000S) | 2020 | 2030 | 2040 | 2050 |
|---|---|---|---|---|
| Baseline | 932 | 1,466 | 2,087 | 2,657 |
| Moderate | 932 | 1,408 | 2,011 | 2,569 |
| Averted | n.a. | 58 | 76 | 88 |
| Percent change | n.a. | 3.94 | 3.65 | 3.31 |

*Sources:* Calculations for baseline data were obtained using population data (UN DESA 2019b), DALY rates (GBD 2017 DALYs and HALE Collaborators 2018), and estimates of relative risk (IHME 2018a).
*Note:* DALYs averted are not cumulative and represent the DALYs averted within the decade. DALYs = disability-adjusted life years; n.a. = not applicable.

TABLE 4.6 **Both sexes: Model 2, cumulative disability-adjusted life years averted by condition, baseline scenario of no change overweight and obesity prevalence relative to the moderate scenario, 2020–50**

| PRIORITY NCD CONDITION | FEMALE | MALE | TOTAL |
|---|---|---|---|
| Ischemic heart disease | 52,401 | 123,524 | 175,925 |
| Stroke | 28,194 | 42,930 | 71,124 |
| Type 2 diabetes | 26,339 | 43,882 | 70,221 |
| Colon cancer | 1,993 | 6,277 | 8,269 |
| Leukemia | 2,310 | 5,177 | 7,486 |
| Breast cancer | 3,777 | — | 3,777 |
| Total | 115,012 | 221,790 | 336,802 |

*Sources:* Calculations for baseline data were obtained using population data (UN DESA 2019b), DALY rates (GBD 2017 DALYs and HALE Collaborators 2018), and estimates of relative risk (IHME 2018a).
*Note:* DALYs = disability-adjusted life years; — = not available; NCD = noncommunicable diseases.

DALY rate than females. This is particularly stark when it comes to ischemic heart disease, where males ages 40–44 are almost twice as likely to be affected (2,100 per 100,000) than females (1,079 per 100,000).

HALEs would also increase under the moderate scenario. Figures 4.3 and 4.4 plot forecasted HALEs to 2050 under the moderate scenario for females and males, respectively. An additional 0.1353 year is gained for females and an additional 0.1359 year for males (above forecasted projections, assuming no change). Ischemic heart disease and stroke are the two conditions for which the largest reductions in mortality and disability are seen.

Deaths would decrease under the moderate scenario. Tables 4.7 and 4.8 show the forecasted deaths averted under the moderate scenario for females and males, respectively. By 2050, the total number of averted deaths under this scenario will be 18,986 for females and 32,560 for males.

Other scenarios of modest reduction in key risk factors also correspond to a forecasted reduction in the NCD burden. Model 3 simulates a larger decrease (−20.0 percent) for overweight/obesity. The overall NCD burden would decline by 222,006 DALYs for females and 427,290 for males from 2020 to 2050. This equates to a 6.43 percent reduction in the overall burden for females and a 6.88 percent reduction for males from 2020 to 2050. Table 4.9 and table 4.10

FIGURE 4.3

**Females: Model 2, forecasted healthy life expectancies in Saudi Arabia, 2020–50, baseline scenario of no change in overweight and obesity prevalence versus moderate scenario**

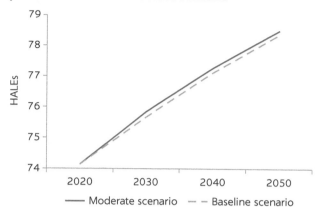

*Sources:* Calculations for baseline data were obtained using population data (UN DESA 2019b), HALE (IHME 2018b), and estimates of relative risk (IHME 2018a).
*Note:* HALEs averted are not cumulative and represent HALEs averted within the decade. HALE = healthy life expectancy.

FIGURE 4.4

**Males: Model 2, forecasted healthy life expectancies in Saudi Arabia, 2020–50: Baseline scenario of no change in overweight and obesity prevalence versus moderate scenario**

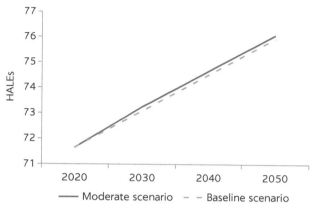

*Sources:* Calculations for baseline data were obtained using population data (UN DESA 2019b), HALE (IHME 2018b), and estimates of relative risk (IHME 2018a).
*Note:* HALEs averted are not cumulative and represent HALEs averted within the decade. HALE = healthy life expectancy.

TABLE 4.7 **Females: Model 2, forecasted deaths for the baseline scenario of no change in overweight/obesity relative to the moderate scenario, 2020–50**

| FEMALE DEATHS | 2020 | 2030 | 2040 | 2050 |
|---|---|---|---|---|
| Baseline | 91,514 | 130,903 | 200,233 | 299,587 |
| Moderate | 91,514 | 126,595 | 194,018 | 291,122 |
| Averted | n.a. | 4,308 | 6,214 | 8,464 |
| Percent change | n.a. | 3.29 | 3.10 | 2.83 |

*Sources:* Calculations for baseline data were obtained using population data (UN DESA 2019a), death rates (UN DESA 2019a), and estimates of relative risk (IHME 2018a).
*Note:* Deaths averted are not cumulative and represent the deaths averted within the decade.
n.a. = not applicable.

TABLE 4.8 **Males: Model 2, forecasted deaths for the baseline scenario of no change in overweight/obesity relative to the moderate scenario, 2020–50**

| MALE DEATHS | 2020 | 2030 | 2040 | 2050 |
|---|---|---|---|---|
| Baseline | 136,411 | 228,591 | 359,323 | 478,833 |
| Moderate | 136,411 | 220,791 | 348,026 | 465,369 |
| Averted | n.a. | 7,799 | 11,297 | 13,464 |
| Percent change | n.a. | 3.41 | 3.14 | 2.81 |

*Sources:* Calculations for baseline data were obtained using population data (UN DESA 2019b), death rates (UN DESA 2019a), and estimates of relative risk (IHME 2018a).
*Note:* Deaths averted are not cumulative and represent the deaths averted within the decade.
n.a. = not applicable.

TABLE 4.9 **Females: Model 3, forecasted disability-adjusted life years for the baseline scenario of no change in overweight and obesity prevalence relative to the ambitious scenario, 2020–50**

| FEMALE DALYS (1,000S) | 2020 | 2030 | 2040 | 2050 |
|---|---|---|---|---|
| Baseline | 477 | 747 | 1,131 | 1,574 |
| Ambitious | 477 | 692 | 1,055 | 1,483 |
| Averted | n.a. | 55 | 76 | 91 |
| Percent change | n.a. | 7.42 | 6.70 | 5.77 |

*Sources:* Calculations for baseline data were obtained using population data (UN DESA 2019b), DALY rates (GBD 2017 DALYs and HALE Collaborators 2018), and estimates of relative risk (IHME 2018a).
*Note:* DALYs averted are not cumulative and represent the DALYs averted within the decade. DALYs = disability-adjusted life years; n.a. = not applicable.

TABLE 4.10 **Males: Model 3, forecasted disability-adjusted life years for the baseline scenario of no change in overweight and obesity prevalence relative to the ambitious scenario, 2020–50**

| MALE DALYS (1,000S) | 2020 | 2030 | 2040 | 2050 |
|---|---|---|---|---|
| Baseline | 932 | 1,466 | 2,087 | 2,657 |
| Ambitious | 932 | 1,346 | 1,938 | 2,498 |
| Averted | n.a. | 120 | 149 | 159 |
| Percent change | n.a. | 8.16 | 7.12 | 5.99 |

*Sources:* Calculations for baseline data were obtained using population data (UN DESA 2019b), DALY rates (GBD 2017 DALYs and HALE Collaborators 2018), and estimates of relative risk (IHME 2018a).
*Note:* DALYs averted are not cumulative and represent the DALYs averted within the decade. DALYs = disability-adjusted life years; n.a. = not applicable.

TABLE 4.11 **Both sexes: Model 3, cumulative disability-adjusted life years averted by condition for the baseline scenario of no change in overweight and obesity prevalence relative to the ambitious scenario, 2020–50**

| PRIORITY NCD CONDITION | FEMALE | MALE | TOTAL |
|---|---|---|---|
| Ischemic heart disease | 99,672 | 235,182 | 334,853 |
| Stroke | 54,180 | 82,452 | 136,632 |
| Type 2 diabetes | 52,896 | 88,223 | 141,119 |
| Colon cancer | 3,749 | 11,764 | 15,513 |
| Leukemia | 4,355 | 9,670 | 14,025 |
| Breast cancer | 7,154 | — | 7,154 |
| Total | 222,006 | 427,290 | 649,296 |

*Sources:* Calculations for baseline data were obtained using population data (UN DESA 2019b), DALY rates (GBD 2017 DALYs and HALE Collaborators 2018), and estimates of relative risk (IHME 2018a).
*Note:* DALYs = disability-adjusted life years; — = not available; NCD = noncommunicable diseases.

describe the DALY reduction under the ambitious scenario. Table 4.11 shows the breakdown of the DALYs by condition, and once again, the majority (51.6 percent) of DALYs averted among the target NCDs would be in ischemic heart disease.

HALE is projected to increase under the ambitious scenario. Figure 4.5 shows the gains in HALEs for females. This represents an additional 0.242 year

FIGURE 4.5

**Females: Model 3, forecasted healthy life expectancies in Saudi Arabia, 2020–50, baseline scenario of no change in overweight and obesity prevalence versus ambitious scenario**

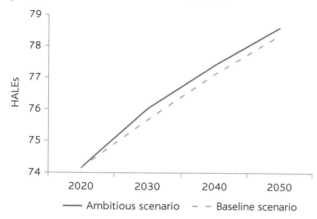

Sources: Calculations for baseline data were obtained using population data (UN DESA 2019b), HALE (IHME 2018b), and estimates of relative risk (IHME 2018a).
Note: HALEs averted are not cumulative and represent HALEs averted within the decade. HALE = healthy life expectancy.

FIGURE 4.6

**Males: Model 3, forecasted healthy life expectancies in Saudi Arabia, 2020–50, baseline scenario of no change in overweight and obesity prevalence versus ambitious scenario**

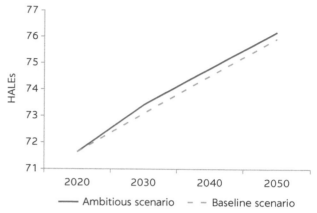

Sources: Calculations for baseline data were obtained using population data (UN DESA 2019b), HALE (IHME 2018b), and estimates of relative risk (IHME 2018a).
Note: HALEs averted are not cumulative and represent HALEs averted within the decade. HALE = healthy life expectancy.

gained for females in 2050. Figure 4.6 shows the gains for males. This represents an additional 0.245 year gained for males in 2050 (above forecasted projections assuming no change). Ischemic heart disease and stroke are the two conditions for which largest reductions in mortality and morbidity are seen in this scenario.

By 2050, total deaths would decrease by 35,828 for females and 62,040 for males under the ambitious scenario. Tables 4.12 and 4.13 show the forecasted deaths averted under the ambitious scenario for females and males, respectively.

## Unhealthy diet (insufficient fruit and vegetable intake)

If there is no change in population fruit and vegetable intake, the NCD burden for stroke, ischemic heart disease, and colon cancer in Saudi Arabia is forecasted to increase to 2050. Under model 4, the baseline scenario, the NCD burden as measured by DALYs will increase substantially for these three conditions (figure 4.7). Data for females and males are presented separately in the annex: for females, NCD DALYs per 100,000 will increase from 1,836 to 5,170 (figure 4A.3); for males, NCD DALYs will increase from 3,211 to 8,089 per 100,000 (figure 4A.4).

If moderate reductions (that is, 10 percent each decade) in insufficient fruit and vegetable intake were achieved (that is, model 5, the moderate scenario), Saudi Arabia's NCD burden would decline by 13,037 DALYs for females and 28,339 for males from 2020 to 2050. This averages a 0.60 percent reduction in the burden for females and a 0.62 percent reduction for males from 2020 to 2050. Tables 4.15 and 4.16 describe the DALY reduction under this moderate

TABLE 4.12 **Females: Model 3, forecasted deaths for the baseline scenario of no change in overweight and obesity relative to the ambitious scenario, 2020–50**

| FEMALE DEATHS | 2020 | 2030 | 2040 | 2050 |
|---|---|---|---|---|
| Baseline | 91,514 | 130,903 | 200,233 | 299,587 |
| Ambitious | 91,514 | 122,033 | 188,264 | 284,596 |
| Averted | n.a. | 8,870 | 11,968 | 14,991 |
| Percent change | n.a. | 6.78 | 5.98 | 5.00 |

*Sources:* Calculations for baseline data were obtained using population data (UN DESA 2019b), death rates (UN DESA 2019a), and estimates of relative risk (IHME 2018a).
*Note:* Deaths averted are not cumulative and represent the deaths averted within the decade.
n.a. = not applicable.

TABLE 4.13 **Males: Model 3, forecasted deaths for the baseline scenario of no change in overweight and obesity relative to the ambitious scenario, 2020–50**

| MALE DEATHS | 2020 | 2030 | 2040 | 2050 |
|---|---|---|---|---|
| Baseline | 136,411 | 228,591 | 359,323 | 478,833 |
| Ambitious | 136,411 | 212,490 | 337,438 | 454,779 |
| Averted | n.a. | 16,100 | 21,886 | 24,055 |
| Percent change | n.a. | 7.04 | 6.09 | 5.02 |

*Sources:* Calculations for baseline data were obtained using population data (UN DESA 2019b), death rates (UN DESA 2019a), and estimates of relative risk (IHME 2018a).
*Note:* Deaths averted are not cumulative and represent the deaths averted within the decade.
n.a. = not applicable.

FIGURE 4.7

**Both sexes: Model 4, forecasted noncommunicable diseases burden for stroke, ischemic heart disease, and colon cancer in Saudi Arabia, 2020–50, baseline scenario of no change in fruit and vegetable intake**

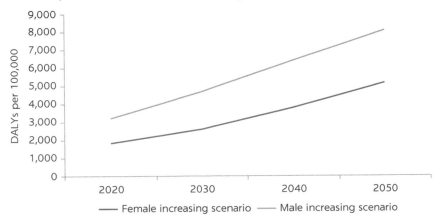

—— Female increasing scenario  —— Male increasing scenario

*Sources:* Calculations for baseline data were obtained using population data (UN DESA 2019b), DALY rates (GBD 2017 DALYs and HALE Collaborators 2018), and estimates of relative risk (WHO 2004).
*Note:* DALYs = disability-adjusted life years; NCD = noncommunicable disease.

scenario for females and males, respectively. Unsurprisingly, table 4.17 shows that the overwhelming majority (87.3 percent) of DALYs averted for insufficient fruit and vegetable intake among the three NCDs would involve ischemic heart disease.

TABLE 4.14 **Both sexes: Baseline prevalence of insufficient fruit and vegetable intake in 2020 for model 5**

| AGE GROUP (YEARS) | FEMALE (%) | MALE (%) |
|---|---|---|
| 15–29 | 93.9 | 94.3 |
| 30–44 | 92.4 | 92.8 |
| 45–59 | 91.6 | 92.0 |
| 60–69 | 93.5 | 93.9 |
| 70–79 | 93.9 | 94.3 |
| 80+ | 96.8 | 97.2 |

*Source:* MOH 2020.

TABLE 4.15 **Females: Model 5, forecasted disability-adjusted life years for the baseline scenario of no change in prevalence of insufficient fruit and vegetable intake relative to the moderate scenario, 2020–50**

| FEMALE DALYS (1,000S) | 2020 | 2030 | 2040 | 2050 |
|---|---|---|---|---|
| Baseline | 270 | 440 | 707 | 1,036 |
| Moderate | 270 | 437 | 703 | 1,030 |
| Averted | n.a. | 3 | 4 | 6 |
| Percent change | n.a. | 0.69 | 0.62 | 0.54 |

*Sources:* Calculations for baseline data were obtained using population data (UN DESA 2019b), DALY rates (GBD 2017 DALYs and HALE Collaborators 2018), and estimates of relative risk (WHO 2004). *Note:* DALYs averted are not cumulative and represent the DALYs averted within the decade. DALYs = disability-adjusted life years; n.a. = not applicable.

TABLE 4.16 **Males: Model 5, forecasted disability-adjusted life years for the baseline scenario of no change in prevalence of insufficient fruit and vegetable intake relative to the moderate scenario, 2020–50**

| MALE DALYS (1,000S) | 2020 | 2030 | 2040 | 2050 |
|---|---|---|---|---|
| Baseline | 646 | 1,049 | 1,529 | 1,984 |
| Moderate | 646 | 1,042 | 1,519 | 1,973 |
| Averted | n.a. | 8 | 10 | 11 |
| Percent change | n.a. | 0.73 | 0.64 | 0.55 |

*Sources:* Calculations for baseline data were obtained using population data (UN DESA 2019b), DALY rates (GBD 2017 DALYs and HALE Collaborators 2018), and estimates of relative risk (WHO 2004). *Note:* DALYs averted are not cumulative and represent the DALYs averted within the decade. DALYs = disability-adjusted life years; n.a. = not applicable.

TABLE 4.17 **Both sexes: Model 5, cumulative disability-adjusted life years averted by condition for the baseline scenario of no change in insufficient fruit and vegetable intake relative to the moderate scenario, 2020–50**

| PRIORITY NCD CONDITION | FEMALE | MALE | TOTAL |
|---|---|---|---|
| Ischemic heart disease | 10,970 | 25,148 | 36,119 |
| Stroke | 1,986 | 2,988 | 4,974 |
| Colon cancer | 81 | 202 | 282 |
| Total | 13,037 | 28,338 | 41,375 |

*Sources:* Calculations for baseline data were obtained using population data (UN DESA 2019b), DALY rates (GBD 2017 DALYs and HALE Collaborators 2018), and estimates of relative risk (WHO 2004). *Note:* DALYs = disability-adjusted life years; NCD = noncommunicable diseases.

Under the moderate scenario, by 2050 deaths would decrease by 954 for females and 1,857 for males. Tables 4.18 and 4.19 show the forecasted deaths averted under the moderate scenario for females and males, respectively.

## Insufficient physical activity

The NCD burden for stroke, ischemic heart disease, type 2 diabetes, breast cancer, and colon cancer in Saudi Arabia is forecasted to increase to 2050. Model 6 assumes no changes to population physical activity, and the NCD burden as measured by DALYs is expected to increase. Figure 4A.5 in the annex shows the expected increase for females from 2,731 to 6,807, and figure 4A.6 shows the projected NCD DALYs for males would increase from 4,023 to 9,614 per 100,000. Figure 4.8 shows the forecast for both females and males.

If a moderate (that is, 10 percent) increase in sufficient physical activity were achieved (that is, model 7, the moderate scenario), Saudi Arabia's NCD burden would decline by 41,795 DALYs for females and 82,635 for males from 2020 to 2050. This corresponds to a 1.41 percent reduction in the burden for females and a 1.51 percent reduction for males from 2020 to 2050. Table 4.20 and table 4.21 describe the DALY reduction under the moderate scenario for females and males, respectively. Table 4.22 shows the prevalence of the insufficient physical activity used for the baseline model. Table 4.23 shows the breakdown of DALYs averted by condition. The largest reductions are for ischemic heart disease and type 2 diabetes.

TABLE 4.18 **Females: Model 5, forecasted deaths for the baseline scenario of no change in prevalence of insufficient fruit and vegetable intake relative to the moderate scenario, 2020–50**

| FEMALE DEATHS | 2020 | 2030 | 2040 | 2050 |
|---|---|---|---|---|
| Baseline | 67,438 | 97,255 | 151,829 | 232,448 |
| Moderate | 67,438 | 97,022 | 151,489 | 232,067 |
| Averted | n.a. | 233 | 340 | 381 |
| Percent change | n.a. | 0.24 | 0.22 | 0.16 |

*Sources:* Calculations for baseline data were obtained using population data (UN DESA 2019b), death rates (UN DESA 2019a), and estimates of relative risk (WHO 2004).
*Note:* Deaths averted are not cumulative and represent the deaths averted within the decade.
n.a. = not applicable.

TABLE 4.19 **Males: Model 5, forecasted deaths for the baseline scenario of no change in prevalence of insufficient fruit and vegetable intake relative to the moderate scenario, 2020–50**

| MALE DEATHS | 2020 | 2030 | 2040 | 2050 |
|---|---|---|---|---|
| Baseline | 109,186 | 183,436 | 289,225 | 387,414 |
| Moderate | 109,186 | 182,963 | 288,573 | 386,682 |
| Averted | n.a. | 473 | 652 | 733 |
| Percent change | n.a. | 0.26 | 0.23 | 0.19 |

*Sources:* Calculations for baseline data were obtained using population data (UN DESA 2019b), death rates (UN DESA 2019a), and estimates of relative risk (WHO 2004).
*Note:* Deaths averted are not cumulative and represent the deaths averted within the decade.
n.a. = not applicable.

FIGURE 4.8

**Both sexes: Model 6, forecasted noncommunicable diseases burden for associated noncommunicable diseases in Saudi Arabia, 2020–50, baseline scenario of no change in physical inactivity**

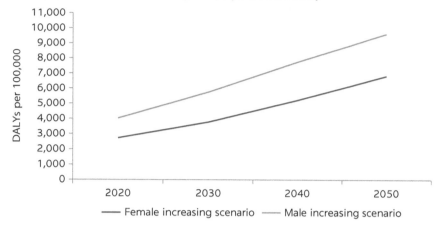

*Sources:* Calculations for baseline data were obtained using population data (UN DESA 2019b), DALY rates (GBD 2017 DALYs and HALE Collaborators 2018), and estimates of relative risk (WHO 2004).
*Note:* DALYs = disability-adjusted life years; NCD = noncommunicable disease.

TABLE 4.20 **Females: Model 7, forecasted disability-adjusted life years for the baseline scenario of no change in prevalence of insufficient physical activity relative to the moderate scenario, 2020–50**

| FEMALE DALYS (1,000S) | 2020 | 2030 | 2040 | 2050 |
|---|---|---|---|---|
| Baseline | 401 | 635 | 972 | 1,364 |
| Moderate | 401 | 626 | 958 | 1,346 |
| Averted | n.a. | 10 | 14 | 18 |
| Percent change | n.a. | 1.53 | 1.45 | 1.32 |

*Sources:* Calculations for baseline data were obtained using population data (UN DESA 2019b), DALY rates (GBD 2017 DALYs and HALE Collaborators 2018), and estimates of relative risk (WHO 2004).
*Note:* DALYs averted are not cumulative and represent the DALYs averted within the decade. DALYs = disability-adjusted life years; n.a. = not applicable.

TABLE 4.21 **Males: Model 7, forecasted disability-adjusted life years for the baseline scenario of no change in prevalence of insufficient physical activity relative to the moderate scenario, 2020–50**

| MALE DALYS (1,000S) | 2020 | 2030 | 2040 | 2050 |
|---|---|---|---|---|
| Baseline | 810 | 1,286 | 1,843 | 2,358 |
| Moderate | 810 | 1,265 | 1,814 | 2,325 |
| Averted | n.a. | 22 | 28 | 33 |
| Percent change | n.a. | 1.68 | 1.54 | 1.38 |

*Sources:* Calculations for baseline data were obtained using population data (UN DESA 2019b), DALY rates (GBD 2017 DALYs and HALE Collaborators 2018), and estimates of relative risk (WHO 2004).
*Note:* DALYs averted are not cumulative and represent the DALYs averted within the decade. DALYs = disability-adjusted life years; n.a. = not applicable.

By 2050, if a moderate increase in sufficient physical activity were achieved, then the total number of averted deaths would be 3,550 for females and 5,667 for males. Table 4.24 and table 4.25 show the forecasted deaths averted under the moderate scenario for females and males, respectively.

TABLE 4.22 **Both sexes: Baseline prevalence of insufficient physical activity in 2020 for model 7**

| AGE GROUP (YEARS) | FEMALE (%) | MALE (%) |
|---|---|---|
| 15–29 | 80.1 | 77.7 |
| 30–44 | 80.3 | 77.9 |
| 45–59 | 84.1 | 81.7 |
| 60–69 | 90.1 | 87.5 |
| 70–79 | 96.8 | 94.0 |
| 80+ | 100.0 | 98.1 |

*Source:* MOH 2020.

TABLE 4.23 **Both sexes: Model 7, cumulative disability-adjusted life years averted by condition for the baseline scenario of no change in physical inactivity relative to the moderate scenario, 2020–50**

| PRIORITY NCD CONDITION | FEMALE | MALE | TOTAL |
|---|---|---|---|
| Ischemic heart disease | 29,307 | 65,129 | 94,436 |
| Stroke | 2,575 | 3,772 | 6,347 |
| Type 2 diabetes | 7,195 | 11,346 | 18,541 |
| Colon cancer | 999 | 2,388 | 3,387 |
| Breast cancer | 1,718 | — | 1,718 |
| Total | 41,795 | 82,635 | 124,430 |

*Sources:* Calculations for baseline data were obtained using population data (UN DESA 2019b), DALY rates (GBD 2017 DALYs and HALE Collaborators 2018), and estimates of relative risk (WHO 2004).
*Note:* NCD = noncommunicable diseases; — = not available.

TABLE 4.24 **Females: Model 7, forecasted deaths for the baseline scenario of no change in prevalence of insufficient physical activity relative to the moderate scenario, 2020–50**

| FEMALE DEATHS | 2020 | 2030 | 2040 | 2050 |
|---|---|---|---|---|
| Baseline | 89,549 | 128,587 | 197,443 | 296,191 |
| Moderate | 89,549 | 127,774 | 196,265 | 294,631 |
| Averted | n.a. | 813 | 1,177 | 1,560 |
| Percent change | n.a. | 0.63 | 0.60 | 0.53 |

*Sources:* Calculations for baseline data were obtained using population data (UN DESA 2019b), death rates (UN DESA 2019a), and estimates of relative risk (WHO 2004).
*Note:* Deaths averted are not cumulative and represent the deaths averted within the decade.
n.a. = not applicable.

TABLE 4.25 **Males: Model 7, forecasted deaths for the baseline scenario of no change in prevalence of insufficient physical activity relative to the moderate scenario, 2020–50**

| MALE DEATHS | 2020 | 2030 | 2040 | 2050 |
|---|---|---|---|---|
| Baseline | 132,853 | 223,521 | 352,213 | 470,074 |
| Moderate | 132,853 | 222,098 | 350,233 | 467,810 |
| Averted | n.a. | 1,423 | 1,981 | 2,264 |
| Percent change | n.a. | 0.64 | 0.56 | 0.48 |

*Sources:* Calculations for baseline data were obtained using population data (UN DESA 2019b), death rates (GBD 2017 DALYs and HALE Collaborators 2018), and estimates of relative risk (WHO 2004).
*Note:* Deaths averted are not cumulative and represent the deaths averted within the decade.
n.a. = not applicable.

## Overweight and obesity, increasing prevalence

Model 8 assumes that prevalence in overweight/obesity will increase in Saudi Arabia. Under the increasing prevalence scenario, the NCD burden for key conditions is forecasted to increase substantially (figure 4.9). Therefore, the potential for DALYs averted via reduction in risk factors will be substantially larger than for models 2 and 3, which assume no change. NCD DALYs per 100,000 for females is expected to increase from 3,246 to 8,167. For males, NCD DALYs would increase from 4,630 to 11,349 per 100,000. Annex figures 4A.7 and 4A.8 show this increase in NCD burden for females and males, respectively, over time.

Under the increasing prevalence model (that is, model 9, the moderate scenario), if a 10 percent reduction in overweight/obesity prevalence were achieved, Saudi Arabia's NCD burden would decline by 250,597 DALYs for females and 512,785 for males from 2020 to 2050. This reduction equates to a 6.99 percent reduction in the burden for females and a 7.89 percent reduction for males from 2020 to 2050. Table 4.26 and table 4.27 show the expected DALY reduction

FIGURE 4.9

**Both sexes: Model 8, forecasted noncommunicable diseases burden for key conditions in Saudi Arabia, 2020–50, increasing scenario for overweight and obesity**

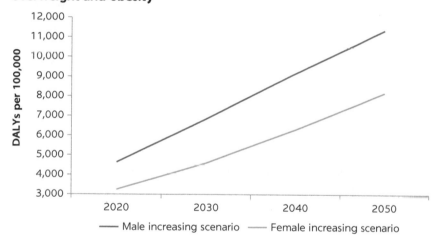

*Sources:* Calculations for baseline data were obtained using population data (UN DESA 2019b), DALY rates (GBD 2017 DALYs and HALE Collaborators 2018), and estimates of relative risk (IHME 2018a).
*Note:* DALYs = disability-adjusted life years; NCD = noncommunicable disease.

TABLE 4.26 **Females: Model 9, forecasted disability-adjusted life years for increasing prevalence in overweight and obesity prevalence relative to the moderate reduction scenario, 2020–50**

| FEMALE DALYS (1,000S) | 2020 | 2030 | 2040 | 2050 |
|---|---|---|---|---|
| Increasing | 477 | 776 | 1,175 | 1,636 |
| Moderate | 477 | 720 | 1,092 | 1,524 |
| Averted | n.a. | 55 | 83 | 112 |
| Percent change | n.a. | 7.14 | 7.07 | 6.85 |

*Sources:* Calculations for baseline data were obtained using population data (UN DESA 2019b), DALY rates (GBD 2017 DALYs and HALE Collaborators 2018), and estimates of relative risk (IHME 2018a).
*Note:* DALYs averted are not cumulative and represent the DALYs averted within the decade.
DALYs = disability-adjusted life years; n.a. = not applicable.

TABLE 4.27 **Males: Model 9, forecasted disability-adjusted life years for increasing prevalence in overweight and obesity relative to the moderate reduction scenario, 2020–50**

| MALE DALYS (1,000S) | 2020 | 2030 | 2040 | 2050 |
|---|---|---|---|---|
| Increasing | 932 | 1,533 | 2,185 | 2,783 |
| Moderate | 932 | 1,408 | 2,011 | 2,569 |
| Averted | n.a. | 124 | 174 | 214 |
| Percent change | n.a. | 8.12 | 7.96 | 7.70 |

*Sources:* Calculations for baseline data were obtained using population data (UN DESA 2019b), DALY rates (GBD 2017 DALYs and HALE Collaborators 2018), and estimates of relative risk (IHME 2018a).
*Note:* DALYs averted are not cumulative and represent the DALYs averted within the decade. DALYs = disability-adjusted life years; n.a. = not applicable.

TABLE 4.28 **Both sexes: Model 9, cumulative disability-adjusted life years averted by condition for increasing prevalence in overweight and obesity relative to the moderate reduction scenario, 2020–50**

| PRIORITY NCD CONDITION | FEMALE | MALE | TOTAL |
|---|---|---|---|
| Ischemic heart disease | 117,026 | 294,832 | 411,858 |
| Stroke | 61,473 | 99,647 | 161,120 |
| Type 2 diabetes | 51,438 | 85,306 | 136,745 |
| Colon cancer | 5,078 | 17,248 | 22,326 |
| Leukemia | 5,636 | 15,752 | 21,388 |
| Breast cancer | 9,945 | — | 9,945 |
| Total | 250,597 | 512,785 | 763,382 |

*Sources:* Calculations for baseline data were obtained using population data (UN DESA 2019b), DALY rates (GBD 2017 DALYs and HALE Collaborators 2018), and estimates of relative risk (IHME 2018a).
*Note:* NCD = noncommunicable diseases; — = not available.

TABLE 4.29 **Females: Model 9, forecasted deaths for increasing prevalence in overweight and obesity relative to the moderate reduction scenario, 2020–50**

| FEMALE DEATHS | 2020 | 2030 | 2040 | 2050 |
|---|---|---|---|---|
| Increasing | 91,514 | 130,903 | 200,233 | 299,587 |
| Moderate | 91,514 | 121,890 | 186,574 | 279,822 |
| Averted | n.a. | 9,013 | 13,658 | 19,765 |
| Percent change | n.a. | 6.89 | 6.82 | 6.60 |

*Sources:* Calculations for baseline data were obtained using population data (UN DESA 2019), death rates (UN DESA 2019a), and estimates of relative risk (IHME 2018a).
*Note:* Deaths averted are not cumulative and represent the deaths averted within the decade. n.a. = not applicable.

under the moderate scenario for females and males, respectively. In addition, table 4.28 shows that over half (54.0 percent) of DALYs averted would come from ischemic heart disease.

Assuming an increase in overweight/obesity prevalence, deaths for priority health conditions decrease substantially with moderate reductions to risk factors. Tables 4.29 and 4.30 show the forecasted deaths averted under the moderate scenario for females and males, respectively. By 2050, the total number of averted deaths would total 42,436 for females and 81,231 for males.

TABLE 4.30 **Males: Model 9, forecasted deaths for increasing prevalence in overweight and obesity relative to the moderate reduction scenario, 2020–50**

| MALE DEATHS | 2020 | 2030 | 2040 | 2050 |
|---|---|---|---|---|
| Increasing | 136,411 | 238,626 | 375,697 | 501,095 |
| Moderate | 136,411 | 220,791 | 348,026 | 465,369 |
| Averted | n.a. | 17,835 | 27,670 | 35,726 |
| Percent change | n.a. | 7.47 | 7.37 | 7.13 |

*Sources:* Calculations for baseline data were obtained using population data (UN DESA 2019b), death rates (UN DESA 2019a), and estimates of relative risk (IHME 2018a).
*Note:* Deaths averted are not cumulative and represent the deaths averted within the decade.
n.a. = not applicable.

TABLE 4.31 **Females: Model 10, forecasted disability-adjusted life years for increasing prevalence in overweight and obesity prevalence relative to the ambitious reduction scenario, 2020–50**

| FEMALE DALYS (1,000S) | 2020 | 2030 | 2040 | 2050 |
|---|---|---|---|---|
| Increasing | 477 | 776 | 1,175 | 1,636 |
| Ambitious | 477 | 692 | 1,055 | 1,483 |
| Averted | n.a. | 84 | 120 | 153 |
| % change | n.a. | 10.84 | 10.23 | 9.36 |

*Sources:* Calculations for baseline data were obtained using population data (UN DESA 2019b), DALY rates (GBD 2017 DALYs and HALE Collaborators 2018), and estimates of relative risk (IHME 2018a).
*Note:* DALYs averted are not cumulative and represent the DALYs averted within the decade.
DALYs = disability-adjusted life years; n.a. = not applicable.

TABLE 4.32 **Males: Model 10, forecasted disability-adjusted life years for increasing prevalence in overweight and obesity prevalence relative to the ambitious reduction scenario, 2020–50**

| MALE DALYS (1,000S) | 2020 | 2030 | 2040 | 2050 |
|---|---|---|---|---|
| Increasing | 932 | 1,533 | 2,185 | 2,783 |
| Ambitious | 932 | 1,346 | 1,938 | 2,498 |
| Averted | n.a. | 186 | 246 | 285 |
| Percent change | n.a. | 12.16 | 11.28 | 10.26 |

*Sources:* Calculations for baseline data were obtained using population data (UN DESA 2019b), DALY rates (GBD 2017 Collaborators 2018), and estimates of relative risk (IHME 2018a).
*Note:* DALYs averted are not cumulative and represent the DALYs averted within the decade.
DALYs = disability-adjusted life years; n.a. = not applicable.

Model 10 assumes an ambitious decrease (20 percent) for overweight/obesity. Assuming that overweight/obesity prevalence were to increase, an ambitious reduction in the current-day prevalence of risk factors would decrease the NCD burden by 357,590 DALYs for females and 718,285 for males from 2020 to 2050. Tables 4.31 and 4.32 describe the DALY reduction under the ambitious scenario for females and males, respectively. This represents a 9.97 percent reduction in the overall burden for females and a 11.0 percent reduction for males from 2020 to 2050. Table 4.33 shows the breakdown of the DALYs by condition. Ischemic heart disease represents over half (53.0 percent) of total DALYs averted among the target NCDs.

If an ambitious reduction in risk factors were achieved, relative to present day prevalence, then the total deaths would decrease by 59,279 for females and 110,712 for males under the ambitious scenario. Table 4.34 and table 4.35 show the forecasted deaths averted under the ambitious scenario for females and males, respectively.

TABLE 4.33 **Both sexes: Model 10, cumulative disability-adjusted life years averted by condition for increasing prevalence in overweight and obesity relative to the ambitious reduction scenario, 2020–50**

| PRIORITY NCD CONDITION | FEMALE | MALE | TOTAL |
|---|---|---|---|
| Ischemic heart disease | 164,297 | 406,490 | 570,787 |
| Stroke | 87,460 | 139,168 | 226,628 |
| Type 2 diabetes | 77,995 | 129,647 | 207,642 |
| Colon cancer | 6,834 | 22,735 | 29,569 |
| Leukemia | 7,681 | 20,245 | 27,926 |
| Breast cancer | 13,322 | — | 13,322 |
| Total | 357,590 | 718,285 | 1,075,875 |

*Sources:* Calculations for baseline data were obtained using population data (UN DESA 2019b), DALY rates (GBD 2017 Collaborators 2018), and estimates of relative risk (IHME 2018a).
*Note:* NCD = noncommunicable diseases; — = not available.

TABLE 4.34 **Females: Model 10, forecasted deaths for the baseline scenario of no change in overweight and obesity relative to the ambitious scenario, 2020–50**

| FEMALE DEATHS | 2020 | 2030 | 2040 | 2050 |
|---|---|---|---|---|
| Increasing | 91,514 | 135,608 | 207,677 | 310,887 |
| Ambitious | 91,514 | 122,033 | 188,264 | 284,596 |
| Averted | n.a. | 13,575 | 19,412 | 26,291 |
| Percent change | n.a. | 10.01 | 9.35 | 8.46 |

*Sources:* Calculations for baseline data were obtained using population data (UN DESA 2019b), death rates (UN DESA 2019a), and estimates of relative risk (IHME 2018a).
*Note:* Deaths averted are not cumulative and represent the deaths averted within the decade.
n.a. = not applicable.

TABLE 4.35 **Males: Model 10, forecasted deaths for the baseline scenario of no change in overweight and obesity relative to the ambitious scenario, 2020–50**

| MALE DEATHS | 2020 | 2030 | 2040 | 2050 |
|---|---|---|---|---|
| Increasing | 136,411 | 238,626 | 375,697 | 501,095 |
| Ambitious | 136,411 | 212,490 | 337,438 | 454,779 |
| Averted | n.a. | 26,136 | 38,259 | 46,317 |
| Percent change | n.a. | 10.95 | 10.18 | 9.24 |

*Sources:* Calculations for baseline data were obtained using population data (UN DESA 2019b), death rates (UN DESA 2019a), and estimates of relative risk (IHME 2018a).
*Note:* Deaths averted are not cumulative and represent the deaths averted within the decade.
n.a. = not applicable.

## CONCLUSIONS

The aim of this chapter was to provide an overview of the health burden of NCDs on Saudi Arabia associated with overweight/obesity, unhealthy diet, and low physical activity. Overweight/obesity are the largest risk factors for NCD DALYs in Saudi Arabia. The rise in excess weight in the population is driven by excess energy intake and sedentary lifestyle, as shown in chapter 3. From 2013 to 2019, the observed rate of insufficient physical activity and insufficient fruit and vegetable intake increased for both men and women (MOH 2020; MOH and IHME n.d.).

Reductions in overweight/obesity from 2020 to 2050 have the potential to substantially improve overall health and reduce the NCD burden. However, these complex issues need to be tackled at the individual consumer level (for example, food marketing restrictions) and systematically (for example, taxes on unhealthy foods). Research on interventions in schools, workplaces, and the health care system have been successful in changing public opinion on unhealthy diet in addition to improving access to healthier food and physical activity (Crespo et al. 2012; Lo et al. 2014; Mozaffarian et al. 2018).

The forecasts indicate that, under a modest scenario of changes in overweight/obesity, by 2050 Saudi Arabia may reduce the DALY burden due to NCDs by 3.3–3.8 percent. Men have the potential to show greater DALY reductions owing to their much higher prevalence of overweight/obesity relative to women. Men have the potential for greater health gains in this area. This DALY reduction by 2050, while appearing modest at first, represents a substantial gain in health given the demographic backdrop in which population aging in Saudi Arabia will occur over the next 30 years. In addition, more ambitious scenarios of change in overweight/obesity have the potential to lead to 5.9–7.9 percent reductions in the DALY burden.

The forecasts, while potentially useful for public health planning and development of national policy, rely on several assumptions. In order to achieve the forecasted impact, the reduction of obesity and overweight for each of the scenarios requires a sustained, consistent reduction over every decade-forecasted impact (that is, a 10.0 percent reduction for moderate scenarios and a 20.0 percent reduction for the ambitious scenarios). In addition, the HALE gains, DALY reductions, and deaths averted capture only the changes that are directly attributable to aforementioned risk factors. They do not capture the full potential of what could happen. The incremental structural and societal changes that will be necessary to curb the rise of obesity, unhealthy diet, and low physical activity will fundamentally change the environment in which current Saudis are living in addition to the one that future Saudis will inhabit. Such a future scenario would have to be more amenable to healthy food choices and provide more opportunities and social norms that increase physical activity. Such ambitious changes may contribute to a multiplicative effect that would further reduce the burden of NCDs and increase healthy life expectancy beyond what has been forecasted.

## ANNEX 4A: FEMALE AND MALE FORECASTED NONCOMMUNICABLE DISEASES BURDENS

Annex 4A contains supplementary figures for baseline models 1, 4, 6, and 8. The DALYs per 100,000 population estimates the burden of NCDs, from 2020 to 2050, under assumptions of no change or increasing prevalence of risk factors.

These estimates serve as the baseline for models 2, 3, 5, 7, 9, and 10, whereby we assume that government interventions will result in changes to risk factors. The difference between the baseline models (1, 4, 6, and 8) and the models assuming changes to risk factors (2, 3, 5, 7, 9, and 10) is the expected DALYs averted.

FIGURE 4A.1

**Females: Model 1, forecasted noncommunicable diseases burden for key conditions in Saudi Arabia, 2020–50, baseline scenario of no change in risk factors**

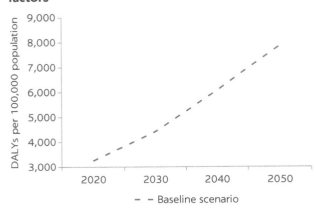

*Sources:* Calculations for baseline data were obtained using population data (UN DESA 2019b), DALY rates (GBD 2017 DALYs and HALE Collaborators 2018), and estimates of relative risk (IHME 2018a).
*Note:* DALYs = disability-adjusted life years.

FIGURE 4A.2

**Males: Model 1, forecasted noncommunicable diseases burden for key conditions in Saudi Arabia, 2020–50, baseline scenario of no change in risk factors**

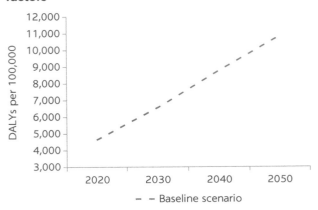

*Sources:* Calculations for baseline data were obtained using population data (UN DESA 2019b), DALY rates (GBD 2017 DALYs and HALE Collaborators 2018), and estimates of relative risk (IHME 2018a).
*Note:* DALYs = disability-adjusted life years.

FIGURE 4A.3

**Females: Model 4, forecasted noncommunicable diseases burden for stroke, ischemic heart disease, and colon cancer in Saudi Arabia, 2020–50, baseline scenario of no change in fruit and vegetable intake**

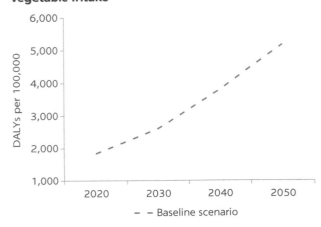

*Sources:* Calculations for baseline data were obtained using population data (UN DESA 2019b), DALY rates (GBD 2017 DALYs and HALE Collaborators 2018), and estimates of relative risk (WHO 2004).
*Note:* DALYs = disability-adjusted life years.

FIGURE 4A.4

**Males: Model 4, forecasted noncommunicable diseases burden for stroke, ischemic heart disease, and colon cancer in Saudi Arabia, 2020–50, baseline scenario of no change in fruit and vegetable intake**

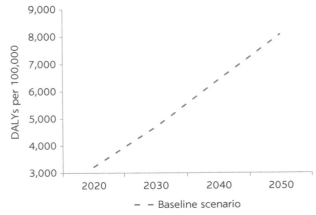

*Sources:* Calculations for baseline data were obtained using population data (UN DESA 2019b), DALY rates (GBD 2017 DALYs and HALE Collaborators 2018), and estimates of relative risk (WHO 2004).
*Note:* DALYs = disability-adjusted life years.

**FIGURE 4A.5**

**Females: Model 6, forecasted noncommunicable diseases burden for associated NCDs in Saudi Arabia, 2020–50, baseline scenario of no change in physical inactivity**

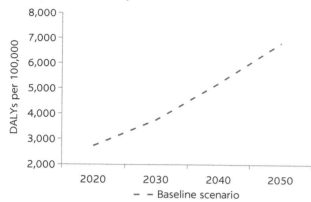

*Sources:* Calculations for baseline data were obtained using population data (UN DESA 2019b), DALY rates (GBD 2017 DALYs and HALE Collaborators 2018), and estimates of relative risk (WHO 2004).
*Note:* DALYs = disability-adjusted life years.

**FIGURE 4A.6**

**Males: Model 6, forecasted noncommunicable diseases burden for associated NCDs in Saudi Arabia, 2020–50, baseline scenario of no change in physical inactivity**

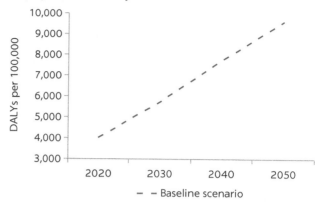

*Sources:* Calculations for baseline data were obtained using population data (UN DESA 2019b), DALY rates (GBD 2017 DALYs and HALE Collaborators 2018), and estimates of relative risk (WHO 2004).
*Note:* DALYs = disability-adjusted life years.

**FIGURE 4A.7**

**Females: Model 8, forecasted noncommunicable diseases burden for key conditions in Saudi Arabia, 2020–50, increasing scenario for overweight and obesity**

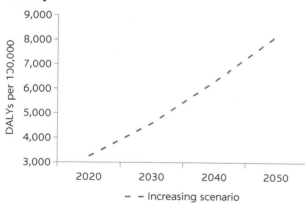

*Sources:* Calculations for baseline data were obtained using population data (UN DESA 2019b), DALY rates (GBD 2017 DALYs and HALE Collaborators 2018), and estimates of relative risk (IHME 2018a).
*Note:* DALYs = disability-adjusted life years.

**FIGURE 4A.8**

**Males: Model 8, forecasted noncommunicable diseases burden for key conditions in Saudi Arabia, 2020–50, increasing scenario for overweight and obesity**

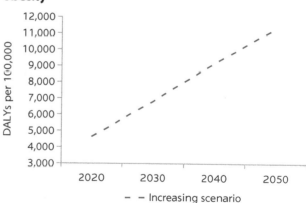

*Sources:* Calculations for baseline data were obtained using population data (UN DESA 2019b), DALY rates (GBD 2017 DALYs and HALE Collaborators 2018), and estimates of relative risk (IHME 2018a).
*Note:* DALYs = disability-adjusted life years.

## ANNEX 4B: SUPPLEMENTARY DETAILS FOR INTERVENTION ASSUMPTIONS

### Note on limitations of forecasting

The scenarios contained in this chapter represent conservative estimates of the potential DALYs and deaths averted as a result of population interventions. There are three reasons for this: the limitation of reviewing only six NCDs, the no change scenario, and the exclusion of widespread societal changes that could take place if population interventions aimed at reducing modifiable risk factors were to be successful.

This chapter includes only the top six NCDs that contribute to the largest proportion of DALYs (mortality and morbidity) and that can be directly impacted by modifications to prevalence of overweight, obesity, insufficient fruit and vegetable intake, and insufficient physical activity. There are more conditions that were not included in this analysis—for example, other types of cancers, where a reduction in DALYs would be expected if reductions to the aforementioned risk factors were to take place.

The no change scenario assumes that there will be no changes to the prevalence of risk factors and no changes to the DALY rate for the key conditions over time. This means that the rate of NCDs will freeze in place (per the 2017 Global Burden of Disease estimates) and that only the aging of the population will affect the DALY and death burden. Since the key NCDs in this chapter affect primarily the population age 40 and over, the overall burden will increase irrespective of the change in risk factors.

The limitation of the no change scenario is that it does not capture what would happen if these risk factors were to increase over time. This is why the increasing risk factors model was also included. If modifiable risk factors were to increase within the next decade and beyond, then the total DALYs and deaths attributable to NCDs would also be expected to increase. The increasing scenario assumes that risk factors, overweight, and obesity will increase over time. This means that the aging of the population and increasing risk factors will affect DALYs and deaths.

If population interventions are successful within the Saudi population and reductions in risk factors could be achieved, we could be looking at a much larger and longer lasting impact than can be captured. For example, childhood obesity is a known predictor of obesity in adulthood. If interventions can change not only populations at risk but also populations that are not yet at risk (in this case children), then the health gains would be expected to produce gains throughout Saudi society.

### Challenges to reducing population body mass index: Comments on unhealthy diet and physical activity as risk factors

Unhealthy diet and physical activity are risk factors for raised body mass index (BMI) and consequently are risk factors for NCDs. While it is possible to affect BMI via diet, no population-level interventions were found in the countries considered (that is, Australia, Canada, and the United States) that were successful in producing significant and long-term changes to overweight/obesity (Crespo et al. 2012; Millar et al. 2011; Raine et al. 2013). Participants in the

Australia intervention achieved a 740 gram average weight reduction, although there was no significant reduction in obesity prevalence (Millar et al. 2011). The community-level intervention in the United States showed success in changing some obesity-related behaviors (for example, fruit and vegetable consumption) in children but did not produce a significant change to BMI.

## Estimating age- and sex-specific changes using the Saudi Arabia world health survey 2019 data

Age- and sex-specific prevalence estimates of risk factors were obtained from the Saudi Arabia World Health Survey 2019 report (MOH 2020). Since the estimates were available only by sex or by age group (see table 4B.1), we used a weighted-average calculation to calculate age- and sex-specific prevalence for use in the life table calculation to estimate DALYs averted and HALEs.

## Example of weighted average calculation for overweight males ages 30–44

The prevalences of risk factors by sex and age-group were calculated using the weighted average formula. The percent of overweight males ages 30–44 was calculated by multiplying the total prevalence of overweight in the population by two. This value was divided by the percent overweight for males and females and then reweighted to arrive at the percent overweight for males ages 30–44:

$$\%Overweight_{Male\ (30-44)} = \frac{(\%Overweight_{30-44} \times 2)}{\%Overweight_{Male} + \%Overweight_{Female}} \times \%Overweight_{Male} \qquad (A4B.1)$$

$$21.1\% = \frac{(22.3\% \times 2)}{(19.2\% + 21.4\%)} \times 19.2\% \qquad (A4B.2)$$

TABLE 4B.1 **Both sexes: Prevalence estimates for overweight (BMI = 25.0–29.9 kg/m²) and obesity (BMI > 30.0 kg/m²) by age and sex**

| DEMOGRAPHICS | BMI | |
| --- | --- | --- |
| | 25.0–29.9 | > 30.0 |
| Sex | | |
| Female | 32.7% | 21.4% |
| Male | 42.7% | 19.2% |
| Age group | | |
| 18–29 | 30.4% | 10.2% |
| 30–44 | 43.2% | 22.3% |
| 45–59 | 40.1% | 32.7% |
| 60–69 | 38.2% | 32.5% |
| 70–79 | 47.0% | 29.1% |
| >80 | 41.0% | 22.0% |

*Source:* Calculations used data from MOH 2020.
*Note:* BMI = body mass index; kg/m² = kilogram per square meter.

## Estimates of overweight and obesity by age and sex using the weighted average formula

Table 4B.2, table 4B.3, and table 4B.4 show the detailed data used to construct the tables in the subsequent section.

TABLE 4B.2 **Both sexes: Estimates for overweight (BMI = 25.0–29.9 kg/m² ) and obesity (BMI > 30.0 kg/m² ) by age and sex using the weighted average formula**

| AGE GROUP (YEARS) | FEMALE BMI | | MALE BMI | |
|---|---|---|---|---|
| | 25.0–29.9 | > 30.0 | 25.0–29.9 | > 30.0 |
| 18–29 | 26.4% | 10.8% | 34.4% | 9.6% |
| 30–44 | 37.5% | 23.5% | 48.9% | 21.1% |
| 45–59 | 34.8% | 34.5% | 45.4% | 30.9% |
| 60–69 | 33.1% | 34.3% | 43.3% | 30.7% |
| 70–79 | 40.8% | 30.7% | 53.2% | 27.5% |
| > 80 | 35.6% | 23.2% | 46.4% | 20.8% |

*Source:* Calculations used data from MOH 2020.
*Note:* BMI = body mass index; kg/m² = kilogram per square meter.

TABLE 4B.3 **Females: UN population estimates and projections by age, 2020–50**

| AGE GROUP (YEARS) | 2020 POPULATION (1,000S) | 2030 POPULATION (1,000S) | 2040 POPULATION (1,000S) | 2050 POPULATION (1,000S) |
|---|---|---|---|---|
| 0–4 | 1,467,625 | 1,268,792 | 1,182,144 | 1,201,286 |
| 5–9 | 1,467,381 | 1,377,065 | 1,198,480 | 1,198,258 |
| 10–14 | 1,300,660 | 1,453,228 | 1,267,715 | 1,181,950 |
| 15–19 | 1,089,822 | 1,453,330 | 1,370,178 | 1,192,927 |
| 20–24 | 1,105,071 | 1,306,934 | 1,456,716 | 1,272,652 |
| 25–29 | 1,357,837 | 1,141,580 | 1,487,990 | 1,406,059 |
| 30–34 | 1,417,027 | 1,194,180 | 1,365,245 | 1,515,367 |
| 35–39 | 1,332,808 | 1,409,684 | 1,182,519 | 1,528,308 |
| 40–44 | 1,283,693 | 1,397,485 | 1,187,639 | 1,358,713 |
| 45–49 | 969,318 | 1,282,971 | 1,373,895 | 1,151,070 |
| 50–54 | 606,771 | 1,226,417 | 1,356,255 | 1,152,625 |
| 55–59 | 426,374 | 916,062 | 1,235,320 | 1,328,554 |
| 60–64 | 286,771 | 562,436 | 1,154,745 | 1,287,152 |
| 65–69 | 239,327 | 381,549 | 826,611 | 1,132,075 |
| 70–74 | 142,030 | 236,020 | 474,286 | 998,856 |
| 75–79 | 99,235 | 169,917 | 284,294 | 640,797 |
| 80–84 | 56,036 | 79,854 | 142,934 | 305,570 |
| 85–89 | 24,394 | 37,972 | 72,448 | 132,912 |
| 90–94 | 8,321 | 11,999 | 19,769 | 40,160 |
| 95+ | 2,058 | 2,881 | 5,230 | 11,405 |

*Source:* Calculations used data from UN DESA 2019b.

TABLE 4B.4 **Males: UN population estimates and projections by age, 2020–50**

| AGE GROUP (YEARS) | 2020 POPULATION (1,000S) | 2030 POPULATION (1,000S) | 2040 POPULATION (1,000S) | 2050 POPULATION (1,000S) |
|---|---|---|---|---|
| 0–4 | 1,510,712 | 1,305,993 | 1,216,901 | 1,236,901 |
| 5–9 | 1,510,498 | 1,417,282 | 1,233,350 | 1,233,464 |
| 10–14 | 1,340,839 | 1,495,259 | 1,304,136 | 1,216,204 |
| 15–19 | 1,128,960 | 1,491,637 | 1,406,322 | 1,224,616 |
| 20–24 | 1,228,060 | 1,448,606 | 1,561,693 | 1,325,750 |
| 25–29 | 1,663,792 | 1,539,815 | 1,765,995 | 1,551,184 |
| 30–34 | 2,020,910 | 1,777,969 | 1,875,086 | 1,856,995 |
| 35–39 | 2,209,618 | 2,015,546 | 1,814,774 | 2,012,770 |
| 40–44 | 2,293,870 | 1,988,073 | 1,767,998 | 1,885,700 |
| 45–49 | 1,861,908 | 1,915,334 | 1,867,161 | 1,685,073 |
| 50–54 | 1,284,975 | 1,891,528 | 1,755,181 | 1,604,644 |
| 55–59 | 898,452 | 1,542,430 | 1,646,314 | 1,689,762 |
| 60–64 | 532,166 | 1,123,975 | 1,652,164 | 1,583,502 |
| 65–69 | 315,257 | 751,925 | 1,309,012 | 1,440,904 |
| 70–74 | 151,011 | 397,191 | 866,573 | 1,327,276 |
| 75–79 | 101,580 | 193,260 | 491,151 | 906,049 |
| 80–84 | 50,137 | 71,436 | 205,176 | 485,815 |
| 85–89 | 20,619 | 32,558 | 69,474 | 196,963 |
| 90–94 | 6,603 | 9,829 | 15,973 | 52,202 |
| 95+ | 1,341 | 2,334 | 4,182 | 10,014 |

*Source:* Calculations used data from UN DESA 2019b.

## Supplemental tables and figures

The data sources described in table 4B.2, table 4B3, and table 4B.4 were used to calculate figure 4B.1 and figure 4B.2 and table 4B.5 and table 4B.6.

FIGURE 4B.1

**Females: Forecasted DALYs in Saudi Arabia, 2020–50, no change in risk factors versus ambitious scenario**

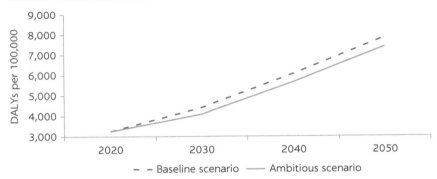

*Sources:* Calculations for baseline data were obtained using population data (UN DESA 2019b), DALY rates (GBD 2017 DALYs and HALE Collaborators 2018), and estimates of relative risk (IHME 2018a).
*Note:* DALYs = disability-adjusted life years.

FIGURE 4B.2

**Males: Forecasted disability-adjusted life years, 2020–50, no change in risk factors versus ambitious scenario**

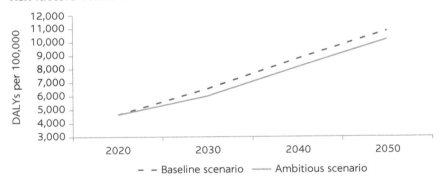

*Sources:* Calculations for baseline data were obtained using population data (UN DESA 2019b), DALY rates (GBD 2017 DALYs and HALE Collaborators 2018), and estimates of relative risk (IHME 2018a).
*Note:* DALYs = disability-adjusted life years.

**TABLE 4B.5 Females: Disability-adjusted life years (per 100,000) for the baseline scenario versus ambitious scenario**

| FEMALE DALYs (Per 100,000) | 2020 | 2030 | 2040 | 2050 |
|---|---|---|---|---|
| Baseline | 3,246 | 4,415 | 6,064 | 7,856 |
| Ambitious | 3,246 | 4,087 | 5,658 | 7,403 |
| Averted | n.a. | 328 | 407 | 453 |

*Sources:* Calculations for baseline data were obtained using population data (UN DESA 2019b), DALY rates (GBD 2017 DALYs and HALE Collaborators 2018), and estimates of relative risk (IHME 2018a).
*Note:* DALYs = disability-adjusted life years; n.a. = not applicable.

TABLE 4B.6 **Males: DALYs (per 100,000) for the baseline scenario versus ambitious scenario**

| MALE DALYS (Per 100,000) | 2020 | 2030 | 2040 | 2050 |
|---|---|---|---|---|
| Baseline | 4,630 | 6,541 | 8,758 | 10,832 |
| Ambitious | 4,630 | 6,007 | 8,134 | 10,183 |
| Averted | n.a. | 534 | 624 | 649 |

*Sources:* Calculations for baseline data were obtained using population data (UN DESA 2019b), DALY rates (GBD 2017 DALYs and HALE Collaborators 2018), and estimates of relative risk (IHME 2018a).
*Note:* DALYs = disability-adjusted life years; n.a. = not applicable.

## NOTES

1. The value for total DALYs (9,151,937) represents the age-standardized all-cause DALYs for Saudi Arabia. This value was obtained by multiplying all-cause DALY rates (per 100,000) by the population (per 100,000) for each five-year age group. These values were summed to arrive at the total all-cause DALY burden for Saudi Arabia. The value for 5,964,386 NCD DALYs was obtained in the same way as for all-cause DALYs. The rates for all-cause DALYs and NCD DALYs were obtained from the Global Burden of Disease (IHME 2018a, 2018b) estimates and the population estimates were obtained from the UN DESA (2019b) population estimates.
2. The etiology of men's breast cancer is not well understood (Auvinen, Curtis, and Ron 2002). This uncertainty is reflected in the estimates of risk (IMHE 2018a). Therefore, the interventions presented in this chapter exclude breast cancer in men.

## REFERENCES

Auvinen, A., R. E. Curtis, and E. Ron. 2002. "Risk of Subsequent Cancer Following Breast Cancer in Men." *Journal of the National Cancer Institute* 94 (17): 1330–32. doi:10.1093/jnci/94.17.1330.

Catenacci, V. A., and H. R. Wyatt. 2007. "The Role of Physical Activity in Producing and Maintaining Weight Loss." *Nature Clinical Practice Endocrinology and Metabolism* 3 (7): 518–29. doi:10.1038/ncpendmet0554.

Crespo, N. C., J. P. Elder, G. X. Ayala, D. J. Slymen, N. R. Campbell, J. F. Sallis, T. L. McKenzie, B. Baquero, and E. M. Arredondo. 2012. "Results of a Multi-Level Intervention to Prevent and Control Childhood Obesity among Latino Children: The *Aventuras Para Niños* Study." *Annals of Behavioral Medicine* 43 (1): 84–100.

GBD 2017 DALYs and HALE Collaborators. 2018. "Global, Regional, and National Disability-Adjusted Life-Years (DALYs) for 359 Diseases and Injuries and Healthy Life Expectancy (HALE) for 195 Countries and Territories, 1990–2017: A Systematic Analysis for the Global Burden of Disease Study 2017." *Lancet* 392: (10159): 1923–94. doi:10.1016/S0140-6736(18)32225-6.

Guillot, M., and H. S. Kim. 2011. "On the Correspondence between CAL and Lagged Cohort Life Expectancy." *Demographic Research* 24: 611–32. https://www.ncbi.nlm.nih.gov/pmc/articles/PMC3328313/.

IHME (Institute for Health Metrics and Evaluation). 2018a. Global Burden of Disease Study 2017 (GBD 2017), Burden by Risk 1990–2017, database. Seattle IHME. http://ghdx.healthdata.org/gbd-results-tool.

IHME (Institute for Health Metrics and Evaluation). 2018b. Global Burden of Disease Study 2017 (GBD 2017), Results, database. Seattle: IHME. http://ghdx.healthdata.org/gbd-results-tool.

Lo, E., D. Hamel, P. Lamontagne, S. Martel, C. Steensma, C. Blouin, and R. Steele. 2014. "Projection Scenarios for Body Mass Index (2013–2030) for Public Health Planning in Quebec." *BMC Public Health* 14: 996.

Millar, L., P. Kremer., A. de Silva-Sanigorski, M. P. McCabe, H. Mavoa, M. Moodie, J. Utter, C. Bell, M. Malakellis, L. Mathews, G. Roberts, N. Robertson, and B. A. Swinburn. 2011. "Reduction in Overweight/Obesity from a 3-Year Community-Based Intervention in Australia: The 'It's Your Move!' Project." *Obesity Reviews* 12 (s2): 20–28. doi:10.1111/j.1467-789X.2011.00904.x.

MOH (Ministry of Health). 2020. *Kingdom of Saudi Arabia World Health Survey 2019 Report*. Riyadh: Ministry of Health.

MOH (Ministry of Health) and IHME (Institute for Health Metrics and Evaluation). n.d. *Saudi Health Interview Survey Results*. Seattle: University of Washington. http://www.healthdata.org/sites/default/files/files/Projects/KSA/Saudi-Health-Interview-Survey-Results.pdf.

Mozaffarian, D., S. Y. Angell, T. Lang, and J. A. Rivera. 2018. "Role of Government Policy in Nutrition: Barriers to and Opportunities for Healthier Eating." *British Medical Journal* 361: k2426. doi:10.1136/bmj.k2426.

Raine, K. D., R. Plotnikoff, D. Schopflocher, E. Lytvyak, C. I. J. Nykiforuk, K. Storey, A. Ohinmaa, L. Purdy, P. Veugelers, and C. T. Wild. 2013. "Healthy Alberta Communities: Impact of a Three-Year Community-Based Obesity and Chronic Disease Prevention Intervention." *Preventive Medicine* 57 (6): 955–62.

Samdal, G. B., G. E. Eide, T. Barth, G. Williams, and E. Meland. 2017. "Effective Behaviour Change Techniques for Physical Activity and Healthy Eating in Overweight and Obese Adults: A Systematic Review and Meta-Regression Analysis." *International Journal of Behavioral Nutrition and Physical Activity* 14 (1): 42. doi:10.1186/s12966-017-0494-y.

UN DESA (United Nations Department of Economic and Social Affairs). 2019a. World Population Prospects 2019, database. "Mortality Data: Deaths by Age Groups—Both Sexes." New York: UN DESA. https://population.un.org/wpp/Download/Standard/Mortality/.

UN DESA (United Nations Department of Economic and Social Affairs). 2019b. World Population Prospects 2019, database. "Population Dynamics: Annual Population by Age Groups." New York: UN DESA. https://population.un.org/wpp/Download/Standard/Population/.

WHO (World Health Organization). 2004. *Comparative Quantification of Health Risks: Global and Regional Burden of Disease Attributable to Selected Major Risk Factors*, vol. 1. Geneva: WHO. https://apps.who.int/iris/handle/10665/42770.

WHO (World Health Organization). 2020. *Health Status Statistics: Mortality*. Geneva: WHO. https://www.who.int/healthinfo/statistics/indhale/en/.

# 5 The Economic Burden of Overweight and Obesity in Saudi Arabia

ERIC FINKELSTEIN, DRISHTI BAID, MOHAMMED ALLUHIDAN,
REEM F. ALSUKAIT, DI DONG, ABDULLAH ALFRAIH,
HANA ALABDULKARIM, TAGHRED ALGHAITH,
ABDULAZIZ ALTOWAIJRI, AND CHRISTOPHER H. HERBST

## KEY MESSAGES

- Overweight and obesity impose a tremendous economic burden of direct and indirect costs.
- There are three main ways to estimate the costs discussed in this chapter: the cost-of-illness method, the value-of-a-statistical-life method, and the economic growth approach method.
- Each takes a different perspective, includes different cost components, focuses on different timeframes, and relies on different data and assumptions.
- Results from these methods cannot be directly compared and are not completely independent. However, each can provide a different picture of the economic burden of overweight and obesity.
- Direct costs of overweight and obesity are found to exceed 7 percent of total annual health expenditures in Saudi Arabia. Overweight- and obesity-attributable absenteeism may reduce gross domestic product by 1.42 percent annually. This does not include presenteeism and other indirect costs.
- These estimated costs, however, are uncertain because data are incomplete and each method makes many assumptions. Moreover, several cost categories are not even included, suggesting that the actual costs are likely to be much larger.
- Better estimates can be made available through greater access to the most recent 2019 World Health Survey and other local data sources, such as health care utilization and claims databases.
- Better data will improve these estimates, but they will not change the primary conclusion that overweight and obesity, without interventions, will continue to take a significant health and economic toll on the people of Saudi Arabia and the broader economy.
- Interventions to reduce this burden are sorely needed. Saudi-specific economic growth and other models that allow for quantifying the health and economic benefits of these interventions will bolster the case for implementing the most promising interventions.

## BACKGROUND

The economic burden of excess weight comprises both direct and indirect costs. Direct costs include the medical costs for diagnosis and treatment of obesity and for the conditions it causes. Direct costs also extend to ancillary costs associated with treatment, such as transportation. Indirect costs often focus on human capital losses, including the value of lost productivity due to absenteeism (workdays missed due to illness or injury), presenteeism (reduced productivity while working), reduced labor force participation of the individual and/or his or her caregivers, and premature mortality. Other, less tangible costs include the monetary value of pain and suffering and opportunity costs resulting from lower economic output. These are summarized in table 5.1.

The direct and indirect costs of excess weight are often quantified using a prevalence-based approach. An example would be the per capita or total medical and absenteeism costs in 2020 resulting from excess weight in the population. Results from the prevalence-based approach should be interpreted as a determination of how much less the burden would be had the risk factor never existed. For example, how many fewer cases of diabetes would exist if no one had obesity? Although *burden* is often interpreted to mean how many cases or dollars can be saved by eliminating the risk factor, this assumes that the total burden is fully reversible, which is not necessarily the case. Just as a former smoker does not necessarily have the same risk profile as a never smoker, the same is likely true for the formerly obese. Some damage is irreversible. Thus, a prevalence-based approach likely overestimates how many dollars could be saved by eliminating a risk factor. The prevalence-based approach applied to economic burden is useful for understanding how resources are being allocated and for drawing attention to the costs imposed by a risk factor or condition. It is less relevant for economic evaluations of interventions aimed at reducing a risk factor or condition of interest. For such evaluations, an incidence-based approach is appropriate.

The incidence-based approach quantifies the burden of new (or incident) cases. This approach typically takes a longitudinal perspective and can be used to quantify, for example, the lifetime medical costs of new cases of obesity in 2020, or the value of current and future lost output resulting from those who are newly obese or from obesity-attributable deaths in a given year. This approach is more appropriate for economic evaluations of interventions because the costs are often immediate or recurring, but the benefits of improved health or lower incidence of disease often do not materialize until well into the future, as would

TABLE 5.1 **Summary of types of economic costs incurred by obesity and overweight**

| DIRECT COSTS | INDIRECT COSTS | INTANGIBLE COSTS | OPPORTUNITY COSTS |
|---|---|---|---|
| • Medical<br>　○ Medications<br>　○ Lab tests<br>　○ Radiology<br>　○ Inpatient hospitalizations<br>　○ Durable medical equipment<br>　○ Physician fees<br>　○ Personnel fees<br>　○ Medical supplies<br>• Nonmedical<br>　○ Transportation<br>　○ Food<br>　○ Home help | • Lost wages<br>• Lost income due to premature death<br>• Loss of livelihood<br>• Loss of life<br>• Loss of productivity | • Pain<br>• Suffering<br>• Grief<br>• Inconvenience | • Lost opportunity<br>• Revenue forgone |

*Source:* Original table for this publication.

occur in a childhood obesity intervention, for example. For this reason, the lifetime perspective is recommended for economic evaluations of obesity and related interventions. Economic growth models tend to take this perspective, as does the disability-adjusted life year, which is commonly used to evaluate the health benefits in cost-effectiveness analyses of public health interventions.

Regardless of whether the estimates are prevalence or incidence based, they are often quantified using one of three common approaches: (1) the cost-of-illness method, (2) the value-of-a-statistical-life method (incidence-based costs only), or (3) dynamic economic growth models. This chapter reviews the existing evidence on the burden of excess weight in Saudi Arabia, including both prevalence- and incidence-based approaches, based on these three methods. Where data permit, new evidence is also generated.

## ESTIMATING THE ECONOMIC BURDEN USING THE COST-OF-ILLNESS METHOD

Cost-of-illness estimates for excess weight are often quantified using either an epidemiologic or an econometric (regression-based) approach. The epidemiologic approach estimates the proportion of each condition that is attributed to overweight and/or obesity. This is implemented using a population attributable fraction (PAF) approach described in chapter 4. Using local prevalence data and relative risks from the literature, a PAF can be calculated for each condition of interest. This fraction can then be multiplied by an estimate of total burden (for example, total number of cases, total costs, and so on) to quantify the value of the total burden that is attributable to the risk factor. For a given condition, summing the burden across overweight and obesity (hereafter overweight/obesity, when considered together) yields the total burden attributable to excess weight for that condition and summing across conditions yields the total burden.

The underlying assumption behind this approach is that having the risk factor increases the likelihood of having the condition, but conditional on having the condition, the burden is the same. In other words, the PAF approach assumes that, despite individuals with obesity being more likely to develop diabetes, the costs of diabetes treatment are the same for the two groups conditional on a positive diagnosis. This is likely to be a conservative assumption.

Using the epidemiologic approach, the direct medical costs resulting from excess weight in Saudi Arabia in 2018 were quantified for six noncommunicable diseases (NCDs): coronary heart disease, stroke, diabetes mellitus, breast cancer in women, colon cancer, and asthma. These six are the most costly and prevalent NCDs in Saudi Arabia (UN Interagency Task Force on NCDs 2018). As shown in table 5.2, table 5.3, and table 5.4, assuming a population size of 33,699,947 (World Bank 2018b), obesity prevalence estimates from the 2019 Saudi Arabia World Health Survey (MOH 2020), and disease cost and relative risk estimates extrapolated from publicly available sources (Ding et al. 2016; Guh et al. 2009), it is estimated that

- the direct medical cost of excess weight in 2018 was $11.3 billion (2018 international dollars), and
- this estimate represents 7.00 percent of annual health expenditure and 0.42 percent of gross domestic product (GDP) in 2018 (World Bank 2018a).

As shown in table 5.2, table 5.3, and table 5.4, the estimated PAFs are in the range of those reported in the literature. These studies suggest that overweight/

TABLE 5.2 **Direct medical costs attributable to overweight**

| DISEASE | RELATIVE RISK[a] | | POPULATION ATTRIBUTABLE FRACTION[b,c,d] | | TOTAL COST OF DISEASE (2018 INTERNATIONAL $)[e] | SEX-SPECIFIC COST OF DISEASE (2018 INTERNATIONAL $)[e] | | COST ATTRIBUTABLE TO OVERWEIGHT (PAF × TOTAL COST OF DISEASE) | | COST ATTRIBUTABLE TO OVERWEIGHT (2018 INTERNATIONAL $) |
|---|---|---|---|---|---|---|---|---|---|---|
| | MALES | FEMALES | MALES | FEMALES | | MALE | FEMALE | MALE | FEMALE | |
| Coronary heart disease | 1.29 | 1.80 | 0.10 | 0.16 | 656,071,600 | 395,556,706 | 260,514,894 | 39,101,008 | 40,840,815 | 79,941,822 |
| Stroke | 1.23 | 1.15 | 0.08 | 0.04 | 35,243,400 | 16,773,139 | 18,470,261 | 1,387,242 | 796,756 | 2,183,998 |
| Type 2 diabetes[f] | 2.40 | 3.92 | 0.22 | 0.23 | 15,973,711,980 | 8,764,619,537 | 7,209,092,441 | 1,959,556,177 | 1,636,207,244 | 3,595,763,421 |
| Breast cancer, postmenopausal | n.a. | 1.08 | n.a. | 0.03 | 13,029,500 | n.a. | 13,029,500 | n.a. | 326,852 | 326,852 |
| Colorectal cancer | 1.51 | 1.45 | 0.16 | 0.12 | 16,993,600 | 10,111,733 | 6,881,867 | 1,584,157 | 798,092 | 2,382,249 |
| Asthma | 1.20 | 1.25 | 0.07 | 0.07 | 429,906,240 | 202,366,442 | 227,539,796 | 14,904,097 | 30,061,169 | 30,061,169 |
| | | | | | | | **Total cost attributable to overweight (2018 international $)** | | | **$3,710,659,511** |

*Data sources:*
a. Relative risks of comorbidities were obtained from Guh et al. 2009.
b. Population attributable fractions (PAFs) for overweight and obesity are calculated using the formula $PAF_1 (\%) = [p_1(RR_1 - 1)]/[1 + p_1(RR_1 - 1) + p_2(RR_2 - 1)]$ and $PAF_2 (\%) = [p_2(RR_2 - 1)]/[1 + p_1(RR_1 - 1) + p_2(RR_2 - 1)]$, respectively, where 1 and 2 represent the overweight and obesity groups, respectively; $p$ = prevalence rate; $RR$ = relative risk.
c. Prevalence estimates for overweight (male, 43 percent; female, 33 percent) and obesity (male, 19 percent; female, 20 percent) are obtained from preliminary findings for the 2019 Saudi Arabia World Health Survey (MOH 2020).
d. The 2017 estimates for sex-specific prevalence rates are obtained from the Global Burden of Disease Results Tool, http://ghdx.healthdata.org/gbd-results-tool.
e. Total cost of disease is obtained from the table 5A.1 in annex 5A. Sex-specific cost of disease is obtained by multiplying the ratio of sex-specific disease prevalence rates to prevalence rates for both sexes, times the total cost of disease.
f. Total cost estimates account for both type 1 and type 2 diabetes, as prevalence figures for each type were not available.
*Note:* n.a. = not applicable.

TABLE 5.3 **Direct medical costs attributable to obesity**

| DISEASE | RELATIVE RISK[a] | | POPULATION ATTRIBUTABLE FRACTION[b,c,d] | | TOTAL COST OF DISEASE (2018 INTERNATIONAL $)[e] | SEX-SPECIFIC COST OF DISEASE (2018 INTERNATIONAL $)[e] | | COST ATTRIBUTABLE TO OBESITY (PAF × TOTAL COST OF DISEASE) | | COST ATTRIBUTABLE TO OBESITY (2018 INTERNATIONAL $) |
|---|---|---|---|---|---|---|---|---|---|---|
| | MALES | FEMALES | MALES | FEMALES | | MALE | FEMALE | MALE | FEMALE | |
| Coronary heart disease | 1.72 | 3.10 | 0.11 | 0.25 | 656,071,600 | 395,556,706 | 260,514,894 | 42,895,091 | 64,974,024 | 107,869,115 |
| Stroke | 1.51 | 1.49 | 0.08 | 0.09 | 35,243,400 | 16,773,139 | 18,470,261 | 1,359,188 | 1,577,417 | 2,936,605 |
| Type 2 diabetes | 6.74 | 12.41 | 0.41 | 0.54 | 15,973,711,980 | 8,764,619,537 | 7,209,092,441 | 3,549,986,655 | 3,874,870,207 | 7,424,856,862 |
| Breast cancer, postmenopausal | n.a. | 1.13 | n.a. | 0.02 | 13,029,500 | n.a. | 13,029,500 | n.a. | 321,899 | 321,899 |
| Colorectal cancer | 1.95 | 1.66 | 0.13 | 0.10 | 16,993,600 | 10,111,733 | 6,881,867 | 1,303,878 | 709,415 | 2,013,293 |
| Asthma | 1.43 | 1.78 | 0.07 | 0.13 | 429,906,240 | 202,366,442 | 227,539,796 | 14,158,892 | 42,819,537 | 42,819,537 |
| | | | | | | | **Total cost attributable to Obesity (2018 international $)** | | | **$7,580,817,310** |

*Data sources:*

a. Relative risks of comorbidities were obtained from Guh et al. 2009.

b. Population attributable fractions (PAFs) for overweight and obesity are calculated using the formula $PAF_1 (\%) = [p_1(RR_1 - 1) + p_2(RR_2 - 1)]/[1 + p_1(RR_1 - 1) + p_2(RR_2 - 1)]$ and $PAF_2 (\%) = [p_2(RR_2 - 1)]/[1 + p_1(RR_1 - 1) + p_2(RR_2 - 1)]$, respectively, where 1 and 2 represent the overweight and obesity groups, respectively; $p$ = prevalence rate; $RR$ = relative risk.

c. Prevalence estimates for overweight (male, 43 percent; female, 33 percent) and obesity (male, 19 percent; female, 20 percent) are obtained from preliminary findings for the 2019 Saudi Arabia World Health Survey (MOH 2020).

d. The 2017 estimates for sex-specific prevalence rates are obtained from the Global Burden of Disease Results Tool, http://ghdx.healthdata.org/gbd-results-tool.

e. Total cost of disease is obtained from the table 5A.1 in annex 5A. Sex-specific cost of disease is obtained by multiplying the ratio of sex-specific disease prevalence rates to prevalence rates for both sexes, times the total cost of disease.

*Note:* n.a. = not applicable.

TABLE 5.4 **Summary of findings: Direct medical costs attributable to overweight and obesity**

| | |
|---|---|
| Current health expenditure (CHEs) as percentage of gross domestic product (GDP) in 2017[a] | 6% |
| GDP in 2018 (2018 international $)[a] | $2,714,546,976,703.24 |
| Current health expenditure (2018 international $) (CHEs (%) × GDP) | $173,731,006,509 |
| Overweight/obesity burden | $11,291,476,821 |
| Overweight/obesity burden as a % of current health expenditure | 7% |
| Overweight/obesity burden as a % of GDP | 0.42% |

*Sources:* Table 5.2 and table 5.3. Original table for this publication.
a. Current health expenditure (percent) estimates were obtained from National Health Accounts, Saudi Arabia, 2018, obtained from the Saudi Health Council.

obesity account for as much as 83 percent of cases of type 2 diabetes (Flegal, Panagiotou, and Graubard 2015), 44 percent of coronary heart disease (Birmingham et al. 1999; Flegal, Panagiotou, and Graubard 2015), 10 percent of ischemic stroke (Asia Pacific Cohort Studies Collaboration 2007; Birmingham et al. 1999), 10 percent of asthma (Dal Grande et al. 2009; Tonorezos et al. 2008), 13 percent of breast cancer (Birmingham et al. 1999; Flegal, Panagiotou, and Graubard 2015), and 15 percent of colon cancer incidence (Arnold et al. 2015; Birmingham et al. 1999; Flegal, Panagiotou, and Graubard 2015). However, these total cost estimates are conservative, since costs for hypertension, dyslipidemia, endometrial cancer, and several other NCDs are not included because of a lack of available data. By comparison, a recently published Organisation for Economic Co-operation and Development (OECD) report using an alternative method reported that Saudi Arabia will spend about 7 percent of its annual health expenditure on overweight/obesity between 2020 and 2050 (Cecchini and Vuik 2019). The United Nations (UN) Interagency Task Force on NCDs (2018) for Saudi Arabia reports a direct cost burden of 0.84 percent of GDP, which is slightly greater than the estimate here of 0.42 percent. Both the OECD and the UN reports rely on dynamic models that are further discussed in this chapter's section "Estimating the Economic Burden Using the Economic Growth Approach Method."

An alternative to using the epidemiologic approach is to use an econometric model. However, this requires individual-level data on both the outcome of interest and a person's BMI. As shown in equation 5.1, if these data are available, the model can be estimated using the outcome of interest (for example, days missed from work) as the dependent variable and indicators for overweight and obesity as the key independent variables, with controls for other variables that may influence the outcome and be correlated with a person's weight, such as age, education, or sex:

$$days\ absent\ from\ work = \alpha + \beta_1\ (Overweight) + \beta_2\ (Obese) + \varepsilon \qquad (5.1)$$

In equation 5.1, $\alpha$ represents days missed from work for normal-weight individuals, and the coefficients on the overweight ($\beta_1$ and obesity ($\beta_2$) variables represent the incremental burden imposed by the average individual in these weight classes relative to normal-weight individuals. This approach can be applied to multiple categories of direct and indirect costs, from different types of medical expenditure to various aspects of human capital losses, such as absenteeism or presenteeism. Compared to the epidemiological approach, the econometric approach relies on fewer assumptions. However, it requires more granular data that are not easily accessible in Saudi Arabia. For this reason, published estimates for the costs of medical care in Saudi Arabia using this approach could not be found in the published literature.

As an example of what is possible, using the 2013 Saudi Health Interview Survey (MOH and IHME 2013), the econometric approach was applied to estimate the increase in absenteeism days (that is, workdays missed due to illness or injury) resulting from excess weight. The 2013 Saudi Health Interview Survey (Saudi nationals only) includes questions on height and weight (to quantify BMI) and on days missed from work over the past 12 months because of illness or injury. These questions were used to quantify the incremental costs of absenteeism. Using responses to the days-missed question as the dependent variables in an individual level regression analysis allowed for quantifying the increase in days missed from work for those with excess weight.

The data set excluded underweight individuals and defined a normal-weight reference group based on World Health Organization (WHO) definitions: *normal weight* (18.5 kg/m² ≤ BMI < 25 kg/m²), *overweight* (25 kg/m² ≤ BMI < 30 kg/m²), and *obesity* (BMI ≥ 30 kg/m²). A linear regression model (ordinary least squares) was then used to estimate the incremental days missed at work per year by respondents within each BMI category while controlling for demographics. Finally, the estimates were monetized based on the average wage of full-time workers (estimated to be $214 per day for Saudi nationals, in 2018 international dollars) and the number of overweight and obese employees in the population. The regression results are presented in table 5.5.

TABLE 5.5 **Absenteeism costs for overweight and obese employees in Saudi Arabia, 2018**

| BMI CLASS[a] | SAMPLE SIZE (N = 4,030) | | INCREMENTAL DAYS MISSED, ADJUSTED (OLS ESTIMATES) (N = 3,148)[c,d] | | INDIRECT COSTS ASSOCIATED WITH DISEASE CATEGORY (2018 INTERNATIONAL $) | |
|---|---|---|---|---|---|---|
| | N | PERCENT[b] | COEFF | 95% CI | COST PER CASE[e] | TOTAL COST[f] |
| Normal weight: 18.5 ≤ BMI < 25 | 976 | 24.2 | *Reference category* | | *Reference category* | |
| Overweight: 25 ≤ BMI < 30 | 1,517 | 37.6 | 0.13 | −0.84 1.11 | $28.64 | **$3,321,626,300** |
| Obese: BMI ≥ 30 | 1,339 | 33.2 | 1.07 | 0.06 2.08 | $229.68 | **$23,511,460,330** |
| **Total cost** | | | | | | **$26,833,086,630** |

*Data sources:*
a. MOH and IHME 2013. One hundred thirty-six individuals (3.3 percent) had missing or out-of-range weight or height information. *Reported weight* of < 35 kg or > 400 kg and *reported height* of <110 cm were defined as out of range.
b. MOH and IHME 2013. Percentages were calculated with respect to the total number of employed individuals ages 15–64 years (*n* = 4,030). Percentages do not total to 100 percent because of the presence of underweight individuals and missing and out-of-range height and weight observations.
c. MOH and IHME 2013. Sixty-two individuals (1.5 percent) were underweight and were excluded from the analysis.
d. MOH and IHME 2013. Adjusted models include the following covariates: age, gender, education level, and marital status.
e. Average wage of full-time workers is estimated to be $214 per day for Saudi Nationals in 2018 international $. This is based on (1) wage data reported by General Statistics Authority (Bulletin, Labour Market Q1 2019), www.stats.gov.sa/sites/default/files/labour_market_q1_2019_en.pdf, and (2) country-specific inflation rates and purchasing power parity exchange rates reported by the World Bank, https://data.worldbank.org/indicator/PA.NUS.PPP?locations=SA.
f. Total cost = cost per case × prevalence rate × number of employed Saudis in the age group 15–64 years as of Q1 2019. The number of employed persons was obtained from General Statistics Authority (Bulletin, Labour Market Q1 2019), www.stats.gov.sa/sites/default/files/labour_market_q1_2019_en.pdf.
*Note:* CI = confidence interval; OLS = ordinary least squares; BMI = body mass index.

Monetizing the days missed and multiplying by the number of employees in each weight category yields the following findings:

- The average employee with a normal BMI reported missed 1.78 days per year due to illness or injury.
- Overweight/obesity increased reported annual absenteeism by 0.13 and 1.07 days, respectively. However, only the estimate for obesity was statistically significant.
- Based on these estimates and the prevalence of overweight/obesity, total annual absenteeism costs due to excess weight are estimated to be $26.8 billion (2018 international $), which represented 1.42 percent of GDP in 2018.

Comparable estimates from Saudi Arabia are not available. However, our estimates are broadly consistent with previous published estimates in the United States. Finkelstein et al. (2010), for example, found that overweight employees in the United States miss up to 1.1 days more per year and obese individuals miss between 0.5 and 9.4 days more, depending on the degree of excess weight. The findings of this chapter are also consistent with two studies that found that obesity, but not overweight, is significantly associated with greater absenteeism among full-time male employees in the United States (Cawley, Rizzo, and Haas 2007; Finkelstein, Fiebelkorn, and Wang 2005).

Note that these estimates do not take into account presenteeism (that is, reduced productivity while working) or other productivity-related expenses that may result from excess weight, such as those due to disability or inability to work. For obese full-time employees in the United States, presenteeism costs are estimated to be US$30 billion (2010 dollars) or 41 percent of total costs attributable to obesity annually (Finkelstein et al. 2010). Thus, these estimates understate the total indirect costs attributable to excess weight.

## ESTIMATING THE ECONOMIC BURDEN USING THE VALUE-OF-A-STATISTICAL-LIFE METHOD

Burden-of-illness studies such as those described earlier tend to use market rates for forgone earnings. An alternative paradigm is to apply a value of a statistical life (VSL). A VSL is quantified based on the marginal rate of substitution between income (or wealth) and mortality risk. Using the VSL method, the value of premature death is inferred from real or hypothetical trade-offs that people willingly make (how much individuals are willing to pay to reduce the risk of death). These trade-offs typically entail taking on greater health risks in exchange for something of value, such as trading off the risk of working in a smoke-filled bar or on a deep sea fishing vessel, both risky occupations, in exchange for a higher salary. This higher salary can be interpreted as a risk premium and can be used to estimate the VSL.

The main advantage of this approach is that it is most consistent with economic theory (that is, utility maximization). The cost-of-illness approach accurately quantifies the burden of disease from an accounting perspective but does not take into account the changes in utility (value) that individuals may accrue from, say, not having to diet and exercise or the intrinsic value that people place on being alive. An additional advantage of the VSL approach is that, unlike the cost-of-illness approach, it can be used to generate unique estimates that each individual or set of individuals places on a particular risky scenario. These estimates, if aggregated across individuals, can be interpreted as the total statistical value of the loss due to a condition (for example, diabetes) and may include all direct, indirect, and intangible costs not easily measured, such as pain and suffering and premature mortality.

The logic of the VSL approach can be illustrated through the following thought experiment (US EPA 2020). Suppose each person in a sample of 100,000 people were asked how much they would be willing to pay for a reduction in their individual risk of dying of 1 in 100,000, or 0.001 percent, over the next year. Since this reduction means we would expect one fewer death among the sample over the next year, this is sometimes described as "one statistical life saved." Now suppose that the average response to this hypothetical question was $100. Then the total dollar amount that the group would be willing to pay to save one statistical life in a year would be $100 per person times 100,000 people, or $10 million. This is an estimate of the VSL.

Although this approach is intuitively appealing and has been used in policy analyses in a range of fields, from environment to transportation to health, it has several limitations. Weaknesses include problems with stated preference questions, such as the one posed above, where responses are skewed by people's inability to differentiate between changes in small risks, framing issues, and hypothetical bias, as well as oversimplification.

An alternative to eliciting information through survey questions is to observe behavior in real-world situations, such as the wage premia required by workers who engage in risky occupations, as compared to similar workers who engage in lower-risk occupations. This approach, known as *revealed preference*, avoids many of the problems of the survey-based approach, but it suffers from other methodological issues such as possible selection bias and the variation in risk perceptions across individuals. For these reasons, results of the VSL vary greatly across studies, with estimates ranging between $45,000 and $18.3 million (Viscusi and Masterman 2017).

A recent OECD report indicates that the societal cost of overweight/obesity using the VSL method is $3,000 (US$ purchasing power parity, or PPP) per capita per year on average between 2020 and 2050 (Cecchini and Vuik 2019). Based on population estimates, obesity prevalence, and 2018 GDP (US$ PPP) (World Bank 2018a, 2018b) (current international $), this suggests an annual societal cost of obesity of 5.42 percent of GDP worldwide.

Although no direct measures of VSL attributable to obesity in Saudi Arabia were identified, a published estimate of the US VSL converted to Saudi Arabia, after adjusting for PPP, indicates a Saudi Arabia VSL of $4.05 million (2015 US$) per statistical life saved (Viscusi and Masterman 2017). Published estimates indicate that, globally, obesity contributes to 7.1 percent of deaths from all causes (GBD 2015 Obesity Collaborators 2017). Given this figure, the Saudi population count of 31.72 million for 2015 and an overall death rate of 0.35 percent (IHME 2019), taken together, suggest that, in 2015, 7,684 premature deaths ($= 0.071 \times 0.003412 \times 31,717,667$) were attributable to obesity. Multiplying the obesity-attributable deaths in Saudi Arabia times the Saudi Arabia VSL ($4.05 million in 2015 US$) suggests that the value of premature mortality resulting from obesity is $31.1 billion (2015 US$) or 4.76 percent of GDP in 2015 (World Bank 2018a), which is in line with the OECD estimate.

## ESTIMATING THE ECONOMIC BURDEN USING THE ECONOMIC GROWTH APPROACH METHOD

A complementary approach for assessing the economic burden of excess weight is to look at its effect on economic growth. This dynamic approach extends the static cost-of-illness and VSL methodologies by also considering how excess weight depletes the labor supply—not just through absenteeism, presenteeism, and premature mortality but also through reduced labor force participation. Dynamic models consider how current and future NCDs impact all of these factors over time and thus their impact on the available mix of labor and capital in the economy and, ultimately, economic output. Four dynamic models that have been used to quantify the burden of obesity and the benefits of prevention are the Foresight Obesity System Map, OECD Strategic Public Health Planning for NCDs (SPHeP-NCDs) model, WHO's Environmental Policy Integrated Climate (EPIC) model, and the United Nations Children's Fund/United Nations Development Programme (UNICEF/UNDP) OneHealth tool.

The Foresight Obesity System Map provides insight into the complexity of and interrelationships between the biological and social determinants of obesity and suggests possible intervention points (Butland et al. 2007). Although the burden of excess weight in Saudi Arabia has not yet been estimated using this model, possibly because of the limited Saudi-specific data available, country-specific estimates are available for the United Kingdom and Ireland. In the United Kingdom, assuming that all variables other than BMI remain at current levels, the total annual direct cost attributable to overweight/obesity by 2050 is estimated to be £9.7 billion (Butland et al. 2007), or 0.45 percent of 2018 GDP (World Bank n.d.). If the ratio of total costs of overweight/obesity (which include indirect costs) to health service costs of obesity remains similar to that of 2001 (that is, 7 to 1), by 2050 an overall total cost of overweight/obesity per annum of £49.9 billion (Butland et al. 2007), 2.33 percent of 2018 GDP (World Bank n.d.) at today's prices can be anticipated. In Ireland, the Foresight model indicates that, by 2030, obesity-related prevalence of coronary heart disease and stroke will increase by 97 percent, cancers by 61 percent, and type 2 diabetes by 21 percent. Direct health care costs associated with these increases will amount to €5.4 billion by 2030 (Keaver et al. 2013), equivalent to 1.67 percent of 2018 GDP (World Bank n.d.). Application of the Foresight model to Saudi Arabia may be possible in the future, by combining prevalence data from the 2019 Saudi Arabia World Health Survey, health care utilization data from the Saudi Health Interview Survey 2013, survival data from national disease-specific registries, and detailed costing data from the Ministry of Health or other sources.

The OECD SPHeP-NCDs model is a tool for public health policy and strategic planning. It is used to predict the health and economic outcomes of the population of a country or a region up to 2050 (OECD Public Health Explorer 2019). The model uses a case-based microsimulation approach to create synthetic life histories of individuals representative of a country's population while accounting for a comprehensive set of demographic factors and key behavioral and physiological risk factors (for example, obesity, physical activity, blood pressure, and so on) and their associated NCDs. Data inputs include demographic and risk factor characteristics by age as well as gender-specific population subgroups from international databases, relative risk estimates from the Global Burden of Disease study (GBD 2015 Obesity Collaborators 2017), and estimates of health care costs of disease treatment extrapolated from national health-related expenditure data (Cecchini and Vuik 2019). A recent study based on this model reports that Saudi Arabia will incur a loss of 4.4 percent of GDP due to excess weight on average between 2020 and 2050 (Cecchini and Vuik 2019). This model has also been used to assess the impact on health and health care expenditure of public health policies to promote physical activity in Italy (Goryakin et al. 2019) and France (Devaux et al. 2019).

The WHO's EPIC model has been used to simulate the macroeconomic consequences of NCDs by linking NCDs and subsequent morbidity and mortality to economic output (Abegunde and Stanicole 2006). This is done by modeling changes in labor and capital requirements as a function of changes in the incidence of NCDs (Bloom et al. 2011). EPIC estimates that global lost economic output from five conditions: cancers, cardiovascular disease, chronic respiratory diseases, diabetes, and mental health—all conditions linked to excess weight—over the period 2011–30 is nearly US$47 trillion (Bloom et al. 2011). For high-income countries only, this estimate is US$25.5 trillion (Bloom et al. 2011). Only two published studies were found that use this model to estimate the economic burden of NCDs for specific countries and none for obesity (Bloom et al. 2013; Bloom, Chen, and McGovern 2018). This suggests the model may have a limited reach, perhaps because of researchers' inability to easily access the model and underlying documentation.

A more popular economic growth model for examining risk factors for NCDs is the UNICEF/UNDP OneHealth tool (WHO, n.d.). This tool can be used to quantify economic burden but is designed for evaluating the costs and benefits of interventions. The tool is primarily intended to inform strategic planning purposes as it aims to answer the following questions: "(I) What would be the health system resources needed to implement strategic health plans, which may include a combination of policy initiatives, prevention, screening and treatment programs? (II) How much would the strategic plan cost, by year, by input, and by health system levels? (III) What is the estimated health impact of a group of interventions (including public health, policy, and medical intervention)? And (IV) How do costs compare with estimated available financing?" (WHO n.d.). The tool provides health care planners with a framework for quantifying the costs and benefits of selected NCD interventions. This tool was used in a prior analysis specifically for analyzing the return on investment of selected NCD interventions in Saudi Arabia using data from national and international databases, as well as local data on the direct and indirect cost of NCDs where possible (UN Interagency Task Force on NCDs 2018). As part of that effort, the tool estimated that the indirect costs of diabetes and cardiovascular disease, two conditions caused by excess weight, cost the Saudi economy US$13.0 billion annually, or 2 percent of GDP, with presenteeism responsible for 1.2 percent, replacement costs accounting for 0.6 percent, and absenteeism totaling 0.2 percent.

## SUMMARY AND CONCLUSIONS

This chapter presents three methods for quantifying the economic burden of excess weight in Saudi Arabia: the cost-of-illness method, the value-of-a-statistical-life method, and application of economic growth models such as the OECD SPHeP-NCDs model. Each takes a different perspective, includes different cost components, focuses on different timeframes, and relies on different data and assumptions. Therefore, results are neither directly comparable nor completely independent. However, each can provide a different picture of the economic burden that overweight/obesity imposes.

The chapter shows that direct costs of overweight/obesity exceed 7 percent of total annual health expenditures in Saudi Arabia. Overweight- and obesity-attributable absenteeism may reduce GDP by 1.42 percent annually—an estimate that does not include presenteeism and other indirect costs. These costs, however, are estimated with great uncertainty because of incomplete data and many assumptions. Moreover, they exclude several cost categories, suggesting that the actual costs are likely to be much larger.

Better estimates can be made available through greater access to the most recent 2019 World Health Survey and other local data sources, such as health care utilization and claims databases. The VSL approach would benefit from Saudi-specific estimates of the VSL and from up-to-date estimates of premature mortality resulting from NCDs associated with overweight/obesity. However, although access to better data will improve these estimates, it will not change the primary conclusion that overweight/obesity, without interventions, will continue to take a significant health and economic toll on the people of Saudi Arabia and the broader economy. Interventions to reduce this burden are sorely needed. Saudi-specific economic growth and other models that allow for quantifying the health and economic benefits of these interventions will bolster the case for implementing the most promising interventions.

## ANNEX 5A

TABLE 5A.1 **Direct costs of selected noncommunicable diseases in Saudi Arabia**

| COST CATEGORY | CORONARY HEART DISEASE | STROKE | TYPE 2 DIABETES | BREAST CANCER | COLON CANCER | COPD | ASTHMA |
|---|---|---|---|---|---|---|---|
| **Estimated annual health care cost per case (2019 international $)[a,d]** | 958 | 2,331 | 1,936 | 891 | 2,655 | 5,854 | 376 |
| **Prevalence rate (2019)[b] (%)** | 2.43 | 1.40 | 7.23 | 0.14 | 0.05 | 1.26 | 2.48 |
| **Total annual cases (population × prevalence rate)[c]** | 832,725 | 479,759 | 2,477,615 | 47,976 | 17,134 | 431,783 | 849,859 |
| **Total annual cost by disease: total cases × cost per case (2019 international $)[d]** | 797,720,686 | 1,118,451,375 | 4,795,817,529 | 42,740,651 | 45,489,279 | 2,527,502,138 | 319,483,424 |
| **Total annual cost: sum across all diseases (2019 international $)[d]** | | | | 9,647,205,082 | | | |
| **Current health expenditure as percentage of GDP in 2017[e]** | 5.2 | | | | | | |
| **GDP in 2019 (2019 international $)[f]** | 1,676,000,000,000 | | | | | | |
| **Current health expenditure (2019 Int $)** | 87,152,000,000 | | | | | | |
| **NCD burden as a % of current health expenditure** | 11 | | | | | | |
| **NCD burden as a % of 2018 GDP** | 0.6 | | | | | | |

*Data sources:*
a. Prevalence data are from the Institute for Health Metrics and Evaluation's Global Burden of Disease database, accessed November 5, 2020, http://vizhub.healthdata.org/gbd-compare. Cost data for coronary heart disease, stroke, type 2 diabetes, breast cancer, and colon cancer are from Ding et al. 2016. Cost data for COPD are from the United States (Dalal et al. 2010), Germany (Wacker et al. 2016), and Greece (Souliotis et al. 2017). Cost data for asthma are from Abu Dhabi in the United Arab Emirates (Alzaabi, Alseiari, and Mahboub 2014).

b. Prevalence data are from the Institute for Health Metrics and Evaluation's Global Disease Burden database, accessed November 5, 2020, http://vizhub.healthdata.org/gbd-compare.

c. Total annual cases are calculated using population estimates from World Population Review, https://worldpopulationreview.com/countries/saudi-arabia-population.

d. Monetary figures in local currency were updated to 2019 figures using country-specific annual inflation rates from World Bank data, https://data.worldbank.org/indicator/PA.NUS.PPP?locations=SA. These figures were then converted to 2019 international dollars by dividing the estimate by the purchasing power parity exchange rate reported in the World Bank databank, https://data.worldbank.org/indicator/PA.NUS. PPP?locations=SA.

e. Current health expenditure estimates were obtained from the WHO Global Health Observatory data repository, https://apps.who.int/gho/data/node.main.GHEDCHEGDPSHA2011?lang=en.

f. GDP (current PPP international dollars) estimates were obtained from World Bank data, https://data.worldbank.org/indicator/NY.GDP.MKTP.PP.CD?end=2019&locations=SA&start=2011.

*Note:* COPD = chronic obstructive pulmonary disease; GDP = gross domestic product; IHME = Institute for Health Metrics and Evaluation; NCD = noncommunicable disease.

# REFERENCES

Abegunde, D., and A. Stanciole. 2006. "An Estimation of the Economic Impact of Chronic Noncommunicable Diseases in Selected Countries." Department of Chronic Diseases and Promotion Working Paper, World Health Organization, Geneva. https://www.who.int/chp/working_paper_growth%20model29may.pdf.

Alzaabi, A., M. Alseiari, and B. Mahboub. 2014. "Economic Burden of Asthma in Abu Dhabi: A Retrospective Study." *ClinicoEconomics and Outcomes Research* 6: 445–50. https://pubmed.ncbi.nlm.nih.gov/25378938/.

Arnold, M., N. Pandeya, G. Byrnes, A. G. Renehan, G. A. Stevens, M. Ezzati, J. Ferlay, J. J. Miranda, I. Romieu, R. Dikshit, D. Forman, and I. Soergomataram. 2015. "Global Burden of Cancer Attributable to High Body-Mass Index in 2012: A Population-Based Study." *Lancet Oncology* 16 (1): 36–46. doi:10.1016/S1470-2045(14)71123-4.

Asia Pacific Cohort Studies Collaboration. 2007. "The Burden of Overweight and Obesity in the Asia–Pacific Region." *Obesity Review* 8 (3): 191–96. doi:10.1111/j.1467-789X.2006.00292.x.

Birmingham, C. L., J. L. Muller, A. Palepu, J. J. Spinelli, and A. H. Anis. 1999. "The Cost of Obesity in Canada." *Canadian Medical Association Journal* 160 (4): 483–88.

Bloom, D. E., E. T. Cafiero, E. Jané-Llopis, S. Abrahams-Gessel, L. R. Bloom, S. Fathima, A. B. Feigl, T. Gaziano, M. Mowafi, A. Pandya, K. Prettner, L. Rosenberg, B. Seligman, A. Z. Stein, and C. Weinstein. 2011. *The Global Economic Burden of Non-Communicable Diseases.* Geneva: World Economic Forum.

Bloom, D. E., E. T. Cafiero, M. E. McGovern, K. Prettner, A. Staniciole, J. Weiss, S. Bakkila, and L. Rosenberg. 2013. "The Economic Impact of Non-Communicable Disease in China and India: Estimates, Projections, and Comparisons." IZA Discussion Paper 7563, Institute of Labor Economics, Bonn. http://ftp.iza.org/dp7563.pdf.

Bloom, D. E., A. Chen, and M. E. McGovern. 2018. "The Economic Burden of Non-Communicable Diseases and Mental Health Conditions: Results for Costa Rica, Jamaica, and Peru." *Pan American Journal of Public Health* 42 (e18). https://scholar.harvard.edu/mcgovern/publications/economic-burden-non-communicable-diseases-and-mental-health-conditions-results.

Butland, B., S. Jebb, P. Kopelman, K. McPherson, S. Thomas, J. Mardell, and V. Parry. 2007. *Foresight—Tackling Obesities: Future Choices, Project Report.* London: UK Department of Innovation, Universities and Skills. https://assets.publishing.service.gov.uk/government/uploads/system/uploads/attachment_data/file/287937/07-1184x-tackling-obesities-future-choices-report.pdf.

Cawley, J., J. A. Rizzo, and K. Haas. 2007. "Occupation-Specific Absenteeism Costs Associated with Obesity and Morbid Obesity." *Journal of Occupational and Environmental Medicine* 49 (12): 1317–24. doi:10.1097/JOM.0b013e31815b56a0.

Cecchini, M., and S. Vuik. 2019. "The Heavy Burden of Obesity," in *The Heavy Burden of Obesity: The Economics of Prevention.* Paris: OECD. https://doi.org/10.1787/3c6ec454-en.

Dal Grande, E., T. Gill, L. Wyatt, C. R. Chittleborough, P. J. Phillips, and A. W. Taylor. 2009. "Population Attributable Risk (PAR) of Overweight and Obesity on Chronic Diseases: South Australian Representative, Cross-Sectional Data, 2004–2006." *Obesity Research and Clinical Practice* 3 (3): 159–68. doi:10.1016/j.orcp.2009.03.004.

Dalal, A. A., L. Christensen, F. Liu, and A. A. Reidel. 2010. "Direct Costs of Chronic Obstructive Pulmonary Disease among Managed Care Patients." *International Journal of Chronic Obstructive Pulmonary Disease* 5: 341–40. https://www.ncbi.nlm.nih.gov/pmc/articles/PMC2962300/.

Devaux, M., A. Lerouge, B. Ventelou, Y. Goryakin, A. Feigl, S. Vuik, and M. Cecchini. 2019. "Assessing the Potential Outcomes of Achieving the World Health Organization Global Non-Communicable Diseases Targets for Risk Factors by 2025: Is There Also an Economic Dividend?" *Public Health* 169: 173–79. doi:10.1016/j.puhe.2019.02.009.

Ding, D., K. D. Lawson, T. L. Kolbe-Alexander, E. A. Finkelstein, P. T. Katzmarzyk, W. van Mechelen, M. Pratt, and the Lancet Physical Activity Series 2 Executive Committee. 2016. "The Economic Burden Of Physical Inactivity: A Global Analysis of Major Non-Communicable Diseases." *Lancet* 388 (10051): 1311–24. doi:10.1016/S0140-6736(16)30383-X.

Finkelstein, E. A., M. daCosta DiBonaventura, S. M. Burgess, and B. C. Hale. 2010. "The Costs of Obesity in the Workplace." *Journal of Occupational and Environmental Medicine* 52 (10): 971–76. doi:10.1097/JOM.0b013e3181f274d2.

Finkelstein, E., I. C. Fiebelkorn, and G. Wang. 2005. "The Costs of Obesity among Full-Time Employees." *American Journal of Health Promotion* 20: 45–51. doi:10.4278 /0890-1171-20.1.45.

Flegal, K. M., O. A. Panagiotou, and B. I. Graubard. 2015. "Estimating Population Attributable Fractions to Quantify the Health Burden of Obesity." *Annals of Epidemiology* 25: 201–07. doi:10.1016/j.annepidem.2014.11.010.

GBD 2015 Obesity Collaborators. 2017. "Health Effects of Overweight and Obesity in 195 Countries over 25 Years." *New England Journal of Medicine* 377 (1): 13–27. doi:10.1056/ NEJMoa1614362.

Goryakin, Y., A. Aldea, A. Lerouge, V. Romano Spica, N. Nante, S. Vuik, M. Devaux, and M. Cecchini. 2019. "Promoting Sport and Physical Activity in Italy: A Cost-Effectiveness Analysis of Seven Innovative Public Health Policies." *Annali di igiene: medicina preventiva e di comunita* 31 (6): 614–25. doi:10.7416/ai.2019.2321.

Guh, D. P., W. Zhang, N. Bansback, Z. Amarsi, C. L. Birmingham, and A. H. Anis. 2009. "The Incidence of Co-Morbidities Related to Obesity and Overweight: A Systematic Review and Meta-Analysis." *BMC Public Health* 9: 88. doi:10.1186/1471-2458-9-88.

IHME (Institute for Health Metrics and Evaluation). 2019. Global Burden of Disease database. Seattle: University of Washington. http://www.healthdata.org/gbd/2019.

Keaver, L., L. Webber, A. Dee, F. Shiely, T. Marsh, K. Balanda, and I. Perry. 2013. "Application of the UK Foresight Obesity Model in Ireland: The Health and Economic Consequences of Projected Obesity Trends in Ireland." *PLoS One* 8 (12). doi:10.1371/journal.pone.0079827.

MOH (Ministry of Health). 2020. *Kingdom of Saudi Arabia World Health Survey 2019 Report.* Riyadh: Ministry of Health.

MOH and IHME (Ministry of Health and Institute for Health Metrics and Evaluation). 2013. *Saudi Health Interview Survey Results.* Seattle: University of Washington. http://www .healthdata.org/sites/default/files/files/Projects/KSA/Saudi-Health-Interview-Survey -Results.pdf.

OECD Public Health Explorer. 2019. *SPHeP-NCDs Documentation, Modelling the Burden of Disease.* Paris: Organisation for Economic Co-operation and Development. http:// oecdpublichealthexplorer.org/ncd-doc/_2_1_Modelling_Principles.html#.

Souliotis, K., H. Kousoulakou, G. Hillas, N. Tzanakis, M. Toumbis, and T. Vassilakopoulos. 2017. "The Direct and Indirect Costs of Managing Chronic Obstructive Pulmonary Disease in Greece." *International Journal of Chronic Obstructive Pulmonary Disease* 12: 1395–400. https://pubmed.ncbi.nlm.nih.gov/28546747/.

Tonorezos, E. S., A. M. Karpati, Y. Wang, and R. G. Barr. 2008. "Does the Relationship between Asthma and Obesity Differ by Neighborhood?" *Respiratory Medicine* 102 (12): 1797–804. doi:10.1016/j.rmed.2008.06.018.

UN Interagency Task Force on NCDs (United Nations Interagency Task Force on the Prevention and Control of Noncommunicable Diseases). 2018. *The Investment Case for Noncommunicable Disease Prevention and Control in the Kingdom of Saudi Arabia: Return on Investment Analysis and Institutional and Context Analysis, August 2017.* Geneva: World Health Organization. https://www.undp.org/content/dam/saudi_arabia/docs/Publications /180326%20MOH%20KSA%20NCDs%202017.pdf.

US EPA (United States Environmental Protection Agency). 2020. *Mortality Risk Valuation.* Updated November 20. Washington, DC: US EPA. https://www.epa.gov/environmental -economics/mortality-risk-valuation#means.

Viscusi, W. K., and C. J. Masterman. 2017. "Income Elasticities and Global Values of a Statistical Life." *Journal of Benefit-Cost Analysis* 8 (2): 226–50. doi:10.1017/bca.2017.12.

Wacker, M. E., R. A. Jörres, H. Schulz, J. Heinrich, S. Karrasch, A. Karch, A. Koch, A. Peters, R. Leidl, C. Vogelmeier, R. Holle, and the COCSYNCONET-Consortium. 2016. "Direct and Indirect Costs of COPD and Its Comorbidities: Results from the German COSYCONET Study." *Respiratory Medicine* 111: 39–46. https://pubmed.ncbi.nlm.nih.gov/26725462/.

WHO (World Health Organization). n.d. *Cost Effectiveness and Strategic Planning (WHO-CHOICE)*. OneHealth Tool. Geneva: WHO. https://www.who.int/choice/onehealthtool /en/.

World Bank. 2018a. *GDP, PPP (Current International $)—Saudi Arabia*. World Bank data, accessed May 20, 2020. https://data.worldbank.org/indicator/NY.GDP.PCAP.PP .KD?locations=SA.

World Bank. 2018b. Population, Total—Saudi Arabia. World Bank data, accessed May 20, 2020. https://data.worldbank.org/indicator/SP.POP.TOTL?locations=SA&display=graph.

World Bank. n.d. World Bank Open Data, accessed May 20, 2020. https://data.worldbank.org/.

# 6 Impact of Obesity on COVID-19

## A REVIEW OF THE EVIDENCE

SHUFA DU, MELINDA A. BECK, BARRY M. POPKIN, TAGHRED ALGHAITH,
CHRISTOPHER H. HERBST, WILLIAM D. GREEN, REEM F. ALSUKAIT,
MOHAMMED ALLUHIDAN, MEERA SHEKAR, AND NAHAR ALAZEMI

## KEY MESSAGES

- Overweight and obesity have been found to be critical drivers of the COVID-19 pandemic, increasing the chance and severity of infection.
- The containment policies linked to the COVID-19 response are likely to have had a detrimental effect on overweight and obesity.
- Further research is critical to obtain additional evidence on the links between obesity and COVID-19—both the impact of obesity on the severity and prognosis of COVID-19 and the impact of COVID-19-related policies on overweight and obesity rates.
- Existing evidence indicates that efforts to develop and roll out vaccines and treatment should closely monitor the impact of obesity on the efficacy of such interventions.
- Obesity could lower the effectiveness of vaccines—as observed with the influenza vaccine—thereby making it essential to explicitly control for this condition in any upcoming vaccine trial.
- For longer-term strategies, the reduction of obesity should be central to government efforts to reduce the impact of current and future pandemics. Obesity is already a priority area for governments to reduce the burden of noncommunicable diseases.

## INTRODUCTION

In late 2019, a novel coronavirus (SARS-CoV-2, a severe acute respiratory syndrome coronavirus that causes the disease COVID-19) started to spread from Wuhan, the capital of China's Hubei province. By January 30, 2020, the World Health Organization (WHO) declared the coronavirus outbreak a "Public Health Emergency of International Concern." On March 11, 2020, WHO declared it a pandemic. Since then, COVID-19 has touched more than 216 countries and territories with millions infected and hundreds of thousands of deaths. By June 23, 2021, Saudi Arabia had reported 161,005 cases and 1,307 deaths. Efforts to "flatten the curve" in order to contain the virus and maintain health care system capabilities were affecting economic growth. Strict containment policies, as introduced in Saudi Arabia and elsewhere, have a high direct economic impact across the economy, particularly on the services component. From both a health and an economic perspective, the reduction of COVID-19 infection and severity rates became a priority concern of both government and industry.

The containment policies linked to the COVID-19 response are likely to have had a detrimental effect on overweight and obesity. Policy responses for mitigating COVID-19 are likely to have caused food system problems, including changes in food availability and consumption patterns. Increases in physical inactivity and remote telework environments may exacerbate current trends in obesity prevalence. In high- and middle-income countries, the demand for packaged processed foods, which are linked to overweight and obesity and other health complications, has increased, particularly in the ready-to-eat and -drink categories (Kantar 2020; Euromonitor Passport 2020). These changes could have long-lasting implications beyond the mitigation of the current SARS-CoV-2 spread and may be detrimental to people's health.

Furthermore, overweight and obesity have been found to be critical drivers of the COVID-19 pandemic, increasing the chance and severity of the infection. Globally, for persons with COVID-19, there appears to be a strong relationship between having overweight or obesity and the risks of hospitalization and needing treatment in intensive care units (ICUs). A small body of literature even suggests that adults with obesity under the age of 60 are more likely to be hospitalized than those without obesity (Lighter et al. 2020).

This chapter explores the global evidence on the link between obesity and COVID-19 to further emphasize the need for investment in obesity prevention and intervention. Considering the exponential rise in obesity prevalence in Saudi Arabia and globally, understanding the links between obesity and COVID-19 and how obesity increases the risk for severe COVID-19 is critical to ensure the development of appropriate responses to the novel coronavirus.

The chapter is organized as follows: The next section highlights the epidemiological data that provide insight into the link between overweight and obesity and COVID-19, undertaking when possible metanalyses of the published data. The subsequent section provides an overview of the current understanding of how obesity affects the immunological and physiological response to SARS-CoV-2. The final section summarizes the main conclusions.

## THE IMPACT OF OBESITY ON COVID-19

This section summarizes the findings of a literature review on the evidence of the link between obesity and COVID-19. The findings look first at the risk of COVID-19, then at the link between obesity and severity of COVID-19, and finally at the link between obesity and COVID-19 prognosis.

The literature search identified 25 relevant publications on the link between obesity and COVID-19. PubMed, Google Scholar, MedRxiv, BioRxiv, China National Knowledge Infrastructure Data (for Chinese literature), and other literature search engines were used to systematically review all publications in Chinese or English that include data on COVID-19 and body mass index (BMI) or obesity. Abstracts and results available by May 9, 2020, that presented data on the BMI or BMI categories of diagnosed COVID-19 patients were reviewed. Literature in other languages was excluded. In total, 813 unduplicated studies were found, 25 of which, as noted, provided data used in this review. One was a case-control study, three were retrospective cohort or prospective cohort studies, and all the others were observational cross-sectional studies. All were conducted between January and April 2020, and sample sizes varied from 24 to 16,749 diagnosed patients in more than 10 countries in Asia, Europe, and North America. In total, 52,246 diagnosed patients were included in this study, 60 percent of whom were male.

Six out of the 25 relevant publications found reviewed the actual relationship between obesity and COVID-19. Whereas much of the literature reported on the broader links between obesity and COVID-19, three studies were identified that specifically assessed the association between obesity and COVID-19, all of which showed that obesity significantly increases the risk of COVID-19 (table 6.1). Another three studies were identified that examined the relationship between obesity and the severity of COVID-19.

## Obesity and the risk of COVID-19

Evidence from Mexico and the United Kingdom found that individuals who had obesity were more than 60 percent more likely to have COVID-19 than individuals without obesity. The study from Mexico tested 71,103 patients with fever, cough, and other COVID-19-like symptoms and diagnosed 15,529 (21.8 percent) with COVID-19. The odds of patients with obesity having COVID-19 were 61.0 percent higher than those among patients without obesity (odds ratio [OR] = 1.61 with 95 percent confidence interval [CI] of 1.53–1.68: $p$ [probability] < 0.0001) (Bello-Chavolla et al. 2020). Similarly, a case-controlled study from the United Kingdom showed that overweight and obesity increased the risk by 51.0 percent (OR = 1.51 with 95 percent CI of 1.13–2.02; $p$ = 0.0100) and 67.0 percent (OR = 1.67 with 95 percent CI of 1.24–2.26; $p$ < 0.0001), respectively (Darling et al. 2020).

Another study from the United Kingdom using biobank data confirmed a strong relationship between obesity and COVID-19 infection. The study used United Kingdom Biobank data ($n$ = 285,817) to show that overweight increased the risk of COVID-19 by 44.0 percent (relative risk [RR] = 1.44, 95 percent CI of 1.08–1.92, $p$ = 0.0100) and obesity almost doubled the risk (RR = 1.97, 95 percent CI of 1.46–2.65, $p$ < 0.0001), adjusted for age, sex, ethnicity, and socioeconomic deprivation as measured by unemployment, assets, and household density (Ho et al. 2020). The authors tested only a small portion of individuals (0.5 percent)

TABLE 6.1 **Association between obesity and COVID-19**

| STUDY'S FIRST AUTHOR | NUMBER | PERCENT OBESITY (%) | | OR (95% CI) | P |
|---|---|---|---|---|---|
| | | NON-COVID-19 | COVID-19 | | |
| Bello-Chavolla | 15,529 | 14.0 | 20.7 | 1.61 (1.53–1.68) | <0.0001 |
| Darling | 574 | 33.2 | 40.2 | 1.67 (1.24–2.26) | <0.0001 |
| Ho | 340 | 23.3 | 34.1 | 1.97 (1.46–2.65) | <0.0001 |
| Pooled data | 16,443 | — | — | 1.69 (1.45–1.96) | <0.0001 |

*Source:* Original table for this publication. See chapter references for full study information.
*Note:* OR = odds ratio; CI = confidence interval; — = not available; $p$ = probability.

for COVID-19, a key limitation of this study. A better way to calculate OR for this study would be to compare the odds between subjects who tested positive and those who tested negative. The pooled data analysis showed the odds of people with obesity being COVID-19 positive were 69.0 percent (OR = 1.69 with 95 percent CI of 1.45–1.96; $p < 0.0001$) higher than those of people without obesity (figure 6.1).

## Obesity and COVID-19 illness severity

Among diagnosed COVID-19 patients, the prevalence of obesity has been shown to be much higher in hospitalized patients than in nonhospitalized patients. A report that included 5,700 patients in New York City showed that 41.7 percent of COVID-19 hospitalized patients had obesity (Richardson et al. 2020), while the average prevalence of obesity in New York City was 22.0 percent (NYC Department of Health and Mental Hygiene 2020). Table 6.2 presents the results from six studies that examined the relationship between obesity and hospitalization (Ebinger et al. 2020; Garg et al. 2020; Lighter et al. 2020; Petrilli et al. 2020; Richardson et al. 2020; Wollenstein-Betec, Cassandras, and Paschalidis 2020). All showed a significantly higher prevalence of obesity among hospitalized

**FIGURE 6.1**

## Metanalysis of obesity and risk of COVID-19

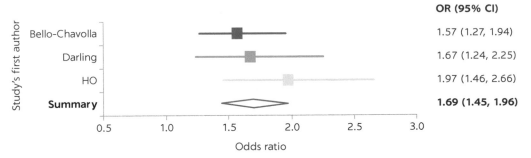

*Source:* Original figure for this publication. See chapter references for full study information.
*Note:* CI = confidence interval; OR = odds ratio.

TABLE 6.2 **Prevalence of overweight and obesity and risk of hospitalization of COVID-19 patients**

| STUDY'S FIRST AUTHOR | NUMBER | PERCENT OBESITY | | OR (95% CI) | P |
| --- | --- | --- | --- | --- | --- |
| | | NONHOSPITALIZED | HOSPITALIZED | | |
| Petrilli | 4,103 | 14.4 | 39.8 | 3.92 (3.37–4.56) | <0.0001 |
| Lighter | 3,615 | 33.5 | 41.1 | 1.38 (1.20–1.60) | <0.0001 |
| Ebinger | 424 | 11.8 | 20.6 | 2.04 (1.14–3.65) | 0.02 |
| Garg | 159 | — | 48.3 | — | — |
| Wollenstein-Betec | 20,734 | — | 33.7 | — | — |
| Richardson | 4,170 | — | 41.7 | — | — |
| Pooled data | 8,178 | 23.4 | 40.6 | 2.24 (2.18–4.26) | <0.0001 |

*Source:* Original table for this publication. See chapter references for full study information.
*Note:* OR = odds ratio; CI = confidence interval; — = not available; *p* = probability.

patients than among patients not hospitalized or the general population. The pooled OR was 2.24 (95 percent CI of 2.18–4.26, *p* < 0.0001) (figure 6.2).

Patients with severe or critical symptoms have been shown to have much higher obesity prevalence than the normal population or patients who were COVID-19 negative (Bhatraju et al. 2020; Chen et al. 2020; Ho et al. 2020; Li et al. 2020; Liao et al. 2020; Liu et al. 2020; Peng et al. 2020; Simonnet et al. 2020; Wu et al. 2020). Two studies showed that the odds of having COVID-19 increased by 30 percent (OR = 1.30 with 95 percent CI of 1.09–1.54; *p* = 0.0030) (Wu et al. 2020) and by 38 percent (OR = 1.38; *p* < 0.0001) (Ho et al. 2020), respectively, among those with obesity (table 6.3).

Among those diagnosed, patients who had obesity—especially those with morbid obesity—have been shown to be more likely to be admitted to ICUs (Bello-Chavolla et al. 2020; Cai et al. 2020; Ebinger et al. 2020; ICNARC 2020; Kalligeros et al. 2020; Lighter et al. 2020). Some of the effects in the studies with smaller sample sizes were not statistically significant (Cai et al. 2020; Ebinger et al. 2020; Kalligeros et al. 2020). In the studies that found that obesity did not significantly increase the odds of being admitted to the ICU, morbid obesity

**FIGURE 6.2**

## Metanalysis of obesity and COVID-19 hospitalization

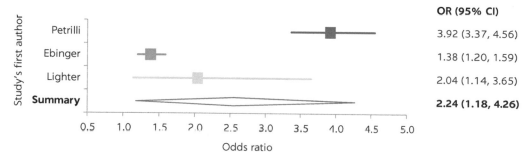

| | OR (95% CI) |
|---|---|
| Petrilli | 3.92 (3.37, 4.56) |
| Ebinger | 1.38 (1.20, 1.59) |
| Lighter | 2.04 (1.14, 3.65) |
| **Summary** | **2.24 (1.18, 4.26)** |

*Source:* Original figure for this publication. See chapter references for full study information.
*Note:* CI = confidence interval; OR = odds ratio.

**TABLE 6.3 Body mass index distributions among COVID-19 patients (mean with 95% CI or median with interquartile range)**

| STUDY'S FIRST AUTHOR | NUMBER | BMI (KG/M²) | | | NATIONAL (MEAN BMI DATA FROM THE COUNTRY OF THE STUDY) |
|---|---|---|---|---|---|
| | | MILD | CRITICAL | AVERAGE | |
| Chen | 145 | 23.2 (21.7–25.7) | 24.8 (23.1–27.0) | 23.7 (21.7–27.0) | 23.9 (Zhang et al. 2020) |
| Peng | 112 | 22.0 (20.0–24.0) | 25.5 (23.0–27.5) | 22.0 (20.0–25.0) | 23.9 (Zhang et al. 2020) |
| Liao | 81 | 24.5 (22.3–27.7) | 23.9 (20.0–27.3) | 24.0 (21.5–7.3) | 23.9 (Zhang et al. 2020) |
| Wu | 280 | 23.6± 3.2 | 25.8 ± 1.8 | 24.1 ± 3.0 | 23.9 (Zhang et al. 2020) |
| Liu | 30 | 22.0 ± 1.3 | 27.0 ± 2.5 | 22.7 ± 2.3 | 23.9 (Zhang et al. 2020) |
| Li | 182 | — | — | 24.8 ± 4.1 | 23.9 (Zhang et al. 2020) |
| Bhatraju | 24 | — | — | 33.2 ± 7.2 | 28.8 (WHO 2014) |
| Simonnet | 124 | — | — | 29.6 (26.4–36.4) | 25.3 (WHO 2014) |
| Ho | 340 | — | — | 29.0 ± 5.3 | 27.3 (Ho et al. 2020) |

*Source:* Original table for this publication. See chapter references for full study information.
*Note:* BMI = body mass index (kilogram per square meter); CI = confidence ratio; — = not available.

(defined as BMI ≥ 35) did significantly increase the odds of ICU admittance. The pooling of data finds that obesity increased the odds of being admitted to the ICU by 26 percent (OR = 1.26 with 95 percent CI of 1.21–1.31; $p$ < 0.0001) (table 6.4 and figure 6.3).

Finally, obesity has been shown to increase the odds of needing invasive mechanical ventilation (IMV) over that of patients without obesity. Reports with small sample sizes from the United Kingdom and other countries found that patients with obesity had higher but insignificant odds of IMV than patients without obesity (Cai et al. 2020; Caussy et al. 2020; Ebinger et al. 2020; ICNARC 2020). Reports from Mexico and some US cities showed significantly higher odds of IMV in patients with obesity than in patients without obesity (Bello-Chavolla et al. 2020; Caussy et al. 2020; Kalligeros et al. 2020; Simonnet et al. 2020). The pooled data showed a 24 percent increase in IMV in patients with obesity (OR = 1.50 with 95 percent CI of 1.17–1.91; $p$ < 0.0001) (table 6.5, figure 6.4).

TABLE 6.4 **The association between obesity and admission to intensive care unit**

| STUDY'S FIRST AUTHOR | NUMBER | PERCENT OBESITY | | ODDS RATIO (95% CI) | P |
| | | NOT ADMITTED TO ICU | ADMITTED TO ICU | | |
|---|---|---|---|---|---|
| Bello-Chavolla | 15,529 | 10.5 | 13.2 | 1.29 (1.15–1.45) | <0.0001 |
| Ebinger | 442 | 19.7 | 22.1 | 1.26 (0.62–2.57) | 0.52 |
| Kalligeros | 103 | 40.6 | 56.8 | 1.63 (0.67–3.94) | 0.28 |
| Cai | 383 | 10.3 | 14.3 | 1.62 (0.56–4.71) | 0.37 |
| Lighter | 3,615 | 36.7 | 46.9 | 1.52 (1.24–1.86) | 0.0035 |
| ICNARC | 7,594 | 37.7 | 38.9 | 1.05 (0.95–1.17) | 0.32 |
| Pooled data | 27,666 | — | — | 1.27 (1.07–1.52) | <0.0001 |

*Source:* Original table for this publication. See chapter references for full study information.
*Note:* ICU = intensive care unit; OR = odds ratio; — = not available; $p$ = probability.

FIGURE 6.3
**Metanalysis of obesity and COVID-19 intensive care unit**

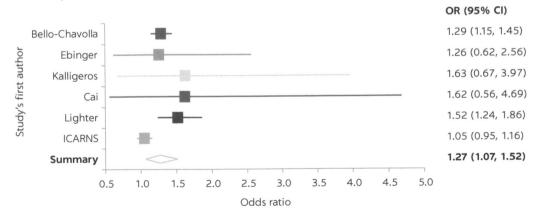

*Source:* Original figure for this publication. See chapter references for full study information.
*Note:* CI = confidence interval; ICARNS = Intensive Care National Audit and Research Centre; OR = odds ratio.

TABLE 6.5 **The association between obesity and the need for invasive mechanical ventilation**

| STUDY'S FIRST AUTHOR | NUMBER | PERCENT OBESITY | | OR (95% CI) | P |
|---|---|---|---|---|---|
| | | NON-IMV | IMV | | |
| Bello-Chavolla | 15,529 | 10.3 | 13.1 | 1.31 (1.17–1.48) | <0.0001 |
| Ebinger | 442 | — | 16.1 | 1.57 (0.72–3.41) | 0.26 |
| Kalligeros | 103 | 40.5 | 65.5 | 2.79 (1.14–6.82) | 0.022 |
| Caussy | 291 | 26.9 | 37.2 | 1.61 (0.97–2.68) | 0.066 |
| Goyal | 380 | 31.9 | 43.4 | 1.64 (1.06–2.54) | 0.026 |
| Simonnet | 124 | 28.2 | 56.5 | 3.30 (1.46–7.49) | 0.0034 |
| Cai | 383 | 10.3 | 14.3 | 1.62 (0.56–4.71) | 0.37 |
| ICNARC | 7,594 | 37.9 | 39.2 | 1.05 (0.96–1.15) | 0.32 |
| Pooled data | 24,846 | — | — | 1.50 (1.17–1.91) | <0.0001 |

*Source:* Original calculations for this publication. See chapter references for full study information.
*Note:* CI = confidence interval; IMV = invasive mechanical ventilation; OR = odds ratio; *p* = probability; — = not available.

FIGURE 6.4

**Metanalysis of obesity and COVID-19 invasive mechanical ventilation**

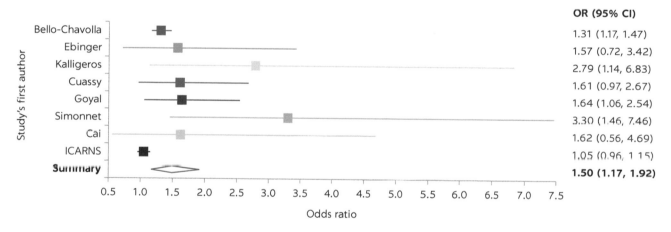

| | OR (95% CI) |
|---|---|
| Bello-Chavolla | 1.31 (1.17, 1.47) |
| Ebinger | 1.57 (0.72, 3.42) |
| Kalligeros | 2.79 (1.14, 6.83) |
| Cuassy | 1.61 (0.97, 2.67) |
| Goyal | 1.64 (1.06, 2.54) |
| Simonnet | 3.30 (1.46, 7.46) |
| Cai | 1.62 (0.56, 4.69) |
| ICARNS | 1.05 (0.96, 1.15) |
| **Summary** | **1.50 (1.17, 1.92)** |

*Source:* Original figure for this publication. See chapter references for full study information.
*Note:* CI = confidence interval; ICARNS = Intensive Care National Audit and Research Centre; OR = odds ratio.

## Obesity and COVID-19 prognosis

Obesity has been shown to increase the odds of death among COVID-19 patients. The data from this section include data from Gaibazzi et al. 2020, which has since been withdrawn. However, this has no material effect on the conclusions or the general findings. A UK study showed 13 percent lower mortality odds among COVID-19 patients with obesity (OR = 0.87 with 95 percent CI of 0.78–0.97; *p* = 0.010), while a New York City study showed 3 percent lower odds (OR = 0.97 with 95 percent CI of 0.78–1.19; *p* = 0.740) (ICNARC 2020; Petrilli et al. 2020). All the other studies showed that obesity significantly increased the odds of death among COVID-19 patients. The pooled data showed that patients with

TABLE 6.6 **The association between obesity and prognosis of COVID-19**

| STUDY'S FIRST AUTHOR | NUMBER | PERCENT OBESITY | | OR (95% CI) | P |
|---|---|---|---|---|---|
| | | DISCHARGED ALIVE | DIED | | |
| Liao | 81 | 19.7 | 10.0 | 1.45 (0.14–15.21) | 0.76 |
| Docherty | 16,749 | — | — | 1.37 (1.16–1.63) | <0.0001 |
| Gaibazzi | 279 | 8.0 | 15.0 | 2.08 (0.96–4.51) | 0.065 |
| Reyes Gil | 217 | — | — | 1.04 (0.98–1.04) | 0.18 |
| Borobia | 2,226 | 10.0 | 14.3 | 1.51 (1.12–2.05) | 0.0007 |
| Bello-Chavolla | 15,529 | 6.7 | 30.3 | 1.77 (1.57–1.99) | <0.0001 |
| Hu | 323 | 2.9 | 10.7 | 3.96 (1.28–12.29) | 0.01 |
| ICNARC | 5,714 | 40.0 | 36.7 | 0.87 (0.78–0.97) | 0.01 |
| Petrilli | 4,103 | 42.9 | 42.0 | 0.97 (0.78–1.19) | 0.74 |
| Peng | 112 | 18.9 | 88.2 | 32.08 (6.73–153.0) | <0.0001 |
| Pooled data | 45,333 | — | — | 1.30 (1.03–1.64) | <0.0001 |

*Source:* Original table for this publication. See chapter references for full study information.
*Note:* The Gaibazzi article has been withdrawn by the authors. CI = confidence interval; OR = odds ratio; — = not available; *p* = probability.

FIGURE 6.5

**Metanalysis of obesity and COVID-19 death**

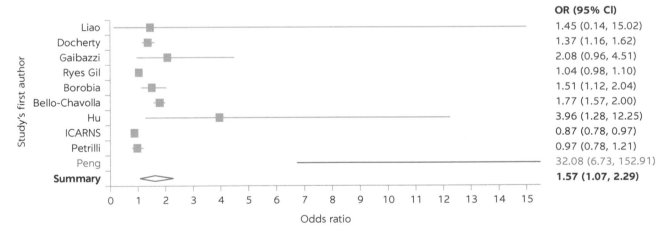

*Source:* Original figure for this publication. See chapter references for full study information.
*Note:* The Gaibazzi article has been withdrawn by the authors. The Peng study, which appears in red, had a very large OR and a very wide CI. CI = confidence interval; OR = odds ratio.

obesity were more likely to have unfavorable outcomes, with a 30 percent increase in deaths (OR = 1.30 with 95 percent CI of 1.03–1.64; *p* < 0.001) (table 6.6, figure 6.5) (Bello-Chavolla et al. 2020; Borobia et al. 2020; Docherty et al. 2020; Gaibazzi et al. 2020; Hu et al. 2020; Liao et al. 2020; Peng et al. 2020).

## HOW OBESITY AFFECTS THE IMMUNOLOGICAL RESPONSE

Although obesity is closely related to a number of risk factors that negatively impact COVID-19, obesity may also independently increase the risk for and

FIGURE 6.6

**Obesity-related comorbidities and mechanisms related to a severe course of COVID-19**

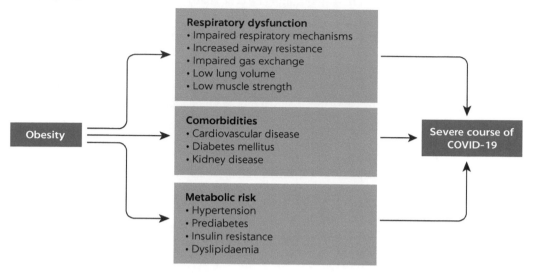

*Source:* Stefan et al. 2020.

severity of COVID-19. Obesity is associated with numerous underlying risk factors for COVID-19, including hypertension, dyslipidemia, type 2 diabetes, and chronic kidney or liver disease. Figure 6.6 shows how respiratory disease, comorbidities, and metabolic risks are all closely associated with obesity; in turn, each of these risk factors has been shown to substantially affect COVID-19. At the same time, the growing evidence detailed in the previous subsections demonstrates that obesity increases the risks of hospitalization, severity, and in some cases death with SARS-CoV-2 infections, thus escalating the likelihood that, as noted, obesity may also independently increase the risk and severity of COVID-19.

This section provides an overview of the current understanding of how obesity affects the immunological response to SARS-CoV-2. The subsections review the metabolic impairments linked to COVID-19, consider obesity's effect on the immune response to COVID-19, look at inflammatory considerations of COVID-19 and obesity, and consider obesity's impairment of treatment and vaccination strategies.

## Obesity's metabolic impairments are linked to COVID-19

As shown with other conditions, obesity can impact the body's response to infection. Obesity is a major risk factor for severe cases of certain infectious diseases, such as influenza, hepatitis, and nosocomial infections (Huttunen and Syrjanen 2010, 2013). As with influenza infections, obesity appears to increase COVID-19's severity. Obesity is inherently a metabolic disease characterized by alterations in systemic metabolism, including insulin resistance, elevated serum glucose, altered adipokines (for example, increased leptin, decreased adiponectin), and chronic low-grade inflammation (Rasouli and Kern 2008; Singla, Bardoloi, and Parkash 2010). Strong evidence demonstrates how hormone and nutrient dysregulation in obesity can impair the response to infection.

Hyperglycemia, associated with diabetes, is closely linked to obesity. Importantly, uncontrolled serum glucose has been shown to significantly increase COVID-19 mortality (Zhu et al. 2020). During times of infection, uncontrolled serum glucose can impair immune cell function either directly or indirectly via generation of oxidants and glycation products (Sheetz and King 2002). Similarly, both insulin and leptin signaling are critical in the inflammatory effector response of T cells by upregulating cellular glycolysis (Saucillo et al. 2014; Tsai et al. 2018), supporting the production of effector cytokines such as IFN-$\gamma$ and TNF-$\alpha$. These metabolic factors combine to influence immune cell metabolism (Ganeshan and Chawla 2014), which dictates the functional response to pathogens, such as SARS-CoV-2.

Dietary consumption of fatty acids can also influence inflammatory responses. Prostaglandins, the derivatives of long chain fatty acids, are acute phase pyrogens that initiate the local inflammatory response during infection. Omega-3 polyunsaturated fatty acids can induce anti-inflammatory responses through cyclooxygenase activity, whereas omega-6 fatty acids mediate the pro-inflammatory cyclooxygenase production of prostaglandins (Calder 2006a, 2006b; Norris and Dennis 2012). Current dietary intakes favor omega-6 fatty acids over omega-3s, with US consumption currently in a 10-to-1 ratio because of the widespread consumption of vegetable oils (Kris-Etherton et al. 2000). Fatty acid derivatives can directly influence COVID-19 in obesity. Crouch, Al-Shaer, and Shaikh (2020) find that "[p]reclinical data suggest a role for fatty acid derived pro-resolving lipid mediators, as they can be deficient in individuals with obesity and thus are not able to appropriately resolve inflammatory responses during infection."

Other fatty acids, such as cholesterol, are essential in the spread of enveloped RNA viruses such as respiratory syncytial viruses and influenza. SARS-CoV, the nearest relative to SARS-CoV-2, uses cholesterol to facilitate viral budding following S protein binding of cellular ACE2 receptors, allowing the spread to neighboring cells. Depletion of cholesterol in ACE2-expressing cells results in markedly reduced viral S protein binding (Glende et al. 2008). Obesity also increases the risk of COVID-19 severity among patients with metabolic-associated fatty liver disease, where adults with obesity had a greater than sixfold higher risk for severe COVID-19 regardless of age, sex, or comorbidities, such as hypertension, diabetes, and dyslipidemia (Zheng et al. 2020).

Physical features of obesity also likely increase COVID-19 severity and risk. Obstructive sleep apnea and other respiratory dysfunctions in those with obesity often increase the risk of hypoventilation-associated pneumonia, pulmonary hypertension, and cardiac stress (Stefan et al. 2020). Large waist circumference and greater BMI increase the difficulty of care in hospital settings for supportive therapies, such as intubation, mask ventilation, and prone positioning to help reduce abdominal tension and increase diaphragm capacity (Sattar, McInnes, and McMurray 2020). Thus the prognoses of COVID-19 patients with obesity may be complicated by the increased clinical care burden among this already vulnerable group.

## Obesity impairs the immune response to COVID-19

Obesity has modulatory effects on key immune cell populations critical in the response to SARS-CoV-2. Specifically, increased BMI is associated with greater frequency of the anti-inflammatory CD4 T cell subsets Th2 and T regulatory cells (van der Weerd et al. 2012). Increased anti-inflammatory cells may inhibit the ability to reduce the infection, as inflammatory responses are needed to control viral spread. Regulatory T cells (Tregs) primarily resolve immune cell–mediated inflammation following infection. Tregs from hyperinsulinemic mice with obesity have reduced IL-10 (interleukin 10) production (Han et al. 2014) and, despite being in higher abundance in the lungs during influenza infections, are 40 percent less suppressive (Milner et al. 2013). Functional responses to RNA viruses, such as SARS-CoV-2, rely on type 1 inflammatory responses by Th1 cells for protection with optimal anti-inflammatory Treg responses for immune resolution following infection. Thus any imbalance in these T cell subsets or functions is likely to impair the immune response to SARS-CoV-2.

A further imbalance in immune cell subsets occurs with the accumulation of pro-inflammatory cells—including macrophages, dendritic cells, cytotoxic T cells, and Th1 cells—in the adipose tissue of individuals with obesity. This influx of immune cells contributes to the development of insulin resistance and chronic inflammation (McLaughlin et al. 2017). These pro-inflammatory immune cells, along with hypertrophic adipocytes, are responsible for increased serum inflammatory cytokines such as IL-6, C-reactive protein, and type I and type III interferons (Jagannathan-Bogdan et al. 2011; McLaughlin et al. 2014). This immune phenotype can be further distinguished between nondiabetic and diabetic people with obesity through increased Th17 inflammation driven by impaired immune cell oxidation of fatty acid metabolites (Ip et al. 2016; Nicholas et al. 2019).

These changes in systemic immune cell populations and their accumulation in adipose tissue have been proposed as key mediators of COVID-19 severity in obesity (Ryan and Caplice 2020). Recently, mice with obesity that were infected with lymphocytic choriomeningitis virus (LCMV) were shown to have increased LCMV viral titers and LCMV-specific immune cells in white adipose tissue, which, upon secondary infection, resulted in greater inflammation and mortality in mice with obesity than lean mice (Misumi et al. 2019). Accumulation of adipocytes and adipocyte-like cells can increase immune activation and cytokine production during coronavirus infection (Kruglikov and Scherer 2020). In addition to being nutrient-rich storage pools, lipid accumulation and adipocyte hypertrophy might be an immune reservoir that, in obesity, becomes saturated with pro-inflammatory immune cell subsets.

Alterations in immune cell frequencies in obesity have been proposed for SARS-CoV-2, which uses the angiotensin-converting enzyme 2 (ACE2) for viral entry and is highly expressed in both vascular tissue, like the lungs, and adipose tissue (Kruglikov and Scherer 2020). Viral entry via ACE2 cleavage by the serine protease TMRPSS2 spike protein allows viral replication in the respiratory tract but also in other tissues expressing ACE2, including the intestinal enterocytes, liver, heart, and kidneys (Hoffmann et al. 2020; Vabret et al. 2020). This mechanism is thought to drive increased incidence of ischemic and coagulopathy conditions in COVID-19 patients.

## Inflammatory considerations of COVID-19 in obesity

Adults with obesity are more likely to develop acute respiratory distress syndrome (ARDS) and acute lung injury (ALI), which are two of the primary causes of morbidity and mortality among adults infected with SARS-CoV-2 (Ruan et al. 2020). Currently, adults with obesity infected with SARS-CoV-2 have higher burdens of mechanical respiratory therapy support and ARDS development (Simonnet et al. 2020). A retrospective multicenter study in Wuhan, China, found higher ARDS-related mortality among COVID-19 patients, which was predicted by elevated serum IL-6 (Ruan et al. 2020). Presentation of ARDS and ALI is characterized by respiratory failure due to excessive pro-inflammatory cytokine production. This inflammatory state leads to extensive lung damage, hypoxemic respiratory failure regardless of oxygen administration, and pulmonary edema not caused by congestive heart failure (Fanelli and Ranieri 2015). Patients who develop ARDS are typically administered mechanical ventilation with positive end-expiratory pressure and high fraction of inspired oxygen ($FiO_2$).

Males with obesity experience a higher burden of COVID-19 than females with obesity (Garg et al. 2020), which could be explained by hormonal differences. In men, obesity increases aromatase activity, which can convert testosterone to estradiol (Cohen 2008). Estrogen receptor signaling can subsequently downregulate IL-6 expression through inhibition of nuclear factor kappa-light-chain-enhancer of activated B cells (NF-κB) (Liu, Liu, and Bodenner 2005), which has been shown to confer protective effects against influenza A virus in women through stimulation of neutrophil and virus-specific CD8 T cell responses (Robinson et al. 2014). Interestingly, however, men with obesity have impaired estrogen receptor signaling, which leads to increased androgenic hormones and elevated estrogen production from adipose tissue (Schneider et al. 1979). Recently, androgen depletion therapy has been shown to protect against COVID-19 in male prostate cancer patients (Montopoli et al. 2020). Adequate control of pro- and anti-inflammatory responses during SARS-CoV-2 infections is critical to limit nonspecific tissue damage and subsequent development of ARDS, which has a higher burden among COVID-19 cases with obesity.

## Impairment of treatment and vaccination strategies

Obesity may also impair therapeutic treatments during COVID-19 infections. ACE inhibitors, which are commonly used to treat hypertension, may increase COVID-19 severity in type 2 diabetes patients, especially those with poorly controlled blood glucose (Cure and Cure 2020). While discontinuing the use of ACE inhibitors is not advisable at this time because of offsetting cardiovascular benefits (Mehta et al. 2020), current clinical trials are investigating mitigation of the spread of SARS-CoV-2 through the inhibition of ACE2 binding. How these treatments in patients with obesity contribute to COVID-19 severity, however, will be a key question in their overall effectiveness. In addition, the IL-6R (IL-6 receptor) antagonist tocilizumab may reduce IL-6 signaling in severe COVID-19 cases where cytokine release syndrome is a major factor of mortality (Moore and June 2020). As noted, chronic inflammation is a hallmark of obesity and includes elevated levels of IL-6. Preliminary data suggest tocilizumab treatment can reduce fever and oxygen requirement (Xu et al. 2020). However, subjects with obesity with chronically elevated IL-6 may not benefit from acute treatment. Limited information exists to date on other treatments, such as statins, nonsteroidal anti-inflammatory drugs, angiotensin receptor blockers, and the promising antiviral Remdesivir regarding their effectiveness against COVID-19 in those with obesity. It will be critical to factor in obesity for any treatment strategy.

In addition, a future COVID-19 vaccine may be less effective in a population with obesity. Obesity has been shown to impair the development of immunological memory. Influenza vaccination in adults with obesity results in equivalent influenza-specific antibody titers at 30 days postvaccination, but antibody titers wane significantly more in adults with obesity than lean adults at one year postvaccination (Sheridan et al. 2012). Compared with influenza-vaccinated lean adults, vaccinated adults with obesity have impaired CD4 and CD8 T cell production of key inflammatory cytokines IFN-γ and Granzyme B (Paich et al. 2013). Adults with obesity also have two times greater odds of influenza or influenza-like illness despite a robust antibody response (Neidich et al. 2017). Preclinical evidence demonstrates that adjuvant vaccines confer less protection against influenza viruses in diet-induced mice with obesity (Karlsson et al. 2016). Similar impairments in vaccine effectiveness have been reported in those with obesity for tetanus (Eliakim et al. 2006), hepatitis A and B, and rabies (Painter, Ovsyannikova, and Poland 2015). This suggests that a future COVID-19 vaccine may be less effective in a population with obesity. Therefore, it is urgent that vaccine trials and studies include BMI as a potential confounder for vaccine effectiveness and protection.

## CONCLUSIONS

This chapter has reviewed the global evidence on the link between obesity and COVID-19. While physical distancing and stay-at-home policies may have exacerbated adverse weight and health situations, the population with overweight and obesity faces a greater risk of severe consequences from COVID-19, including hospitalization, intensive clinical care requirements, and death. Moreover, obesity is likely to reduce the effectiveness of treatment as well as vaccines through mechanisms similar to those responsible for greater primary infection risk. The immunological impairments from obesity demonstrate the convergence of chronic and infectious disease risks. They expose a large portion of the world population to greater risk of pulmonary viral infections like COVID-19.

Further research is critical to obtain additional evidence on the links between obesity and COVID-19. This includes both the impact of obesity on COVID-19 and the impact of COVID-19-related policies on overweight and obesity rates. Additional evidence from different segments of the population could help us better understand the mechanism by which obesity increases COVID-19 infection rates, severity, and prognosis. The literature is fast accumulating but was limited by being observational and having potential sampling bias, small sample sizes, and potential confounding issues. This is an opportunity to step up research and collect more high-quality data on the relationship between BMI and COVID-19 in areas such as Saudi Arabia that have a relatively young population.

At the same time, the existing evidence already indicates that efforts to develop and roll out vaccines and treatment should closely monitor the impact of obesity on the efficacy of such interventions. There are currently multiple trials on different treatments such as ACE inhibitors, tocilizumab treatment, and others such as the promising antiviral Remdesivir. It is important to monitor how obesity can mediate or hinder the effectiveness of these treatments. Additionally, obesity could lower the effectiveness of vaccines, as observed with the influenza vaccine, thereby making it essential to explicitly control for it in any upcoming vaccine trial.

And for longer-term strategies, the reduction of obesity should be central to government efforts to reduce the impact of current and future pandemics. Obesity is already a priority area for governments to reduce the burden of noncommunicable diseases. High BMI is currently the second-highest risk factor for morbidity in Saudi Arabia. This chapter further emphasizes the importance of addressing obesity beyond noncommunicable disease prevention to reducing the impact of COVID-19 and other potential infectious diseases. Reducing overweight and obesity requires implementing comprehensive multicomponent national strategies, as described in chapters 7 and 8. The effort includes using fiscal policies to reduce ultraprocessed food consumption, employ front-of-package food labeling, and implement marketing regulations, especially in school settings.

## REFERENCES

Bello-Chavolla, O. Y., J. P. Bahena-Lopez, N. E. Antonio-Villa, A. Vargas-Vázquez, A. González-Díaz, A. Márquez-Salinas, C. A. Fermín-Martínez, J. J. Naveja, and C. A. Aguilar-Salinas. 2020. "Predicting Mortality due to SARS-CoV-2: A Mechanistic Score Relating Obesity and Diabetes to COVID-19 Outcomes in Mexico." *Journal of Clinical Endocrinology and Metabolism* 105 (8): 2752–61. doi:10.1210/clinem/dgaa346.

Bhatraju, P. K., B. J. Ghassemieh, M. Nichols, R. Kim, K. R. Jerome, A. K. Nalla, A. L. Greninger, S. Pipavath, M. M. Wurfel, L. Evans, P. A. Kritek, T. E. West, A. Luks, A. Gerbino, C. R. Dale, J. D. Goldman, S. O'Mahony, and C. Mikacenic. 2020. "COVID-19 in Critically Ill Patients in the Seattle Region—Case Series." *New England Journal of Medicine* 382: 2012–22.

Borobia, A. M., A. J. Carcas, F. Arnalich, R. Alvarez-Sala, J. Montserrat, M. Quintana, J. C. Figueira, R. M. Torres Santos-Olmo, J. Garcia-Rodriguez, A. Martin-Vega, E. Ramirez, A. Buno, G. Martinez-Ales, N. Garcia-Arenzana, C. Nunez Lopez, M. Marti de Gracia, F. Moreno, F. Reinoso-Barbero, A. Martin-Quiros, A. Rivera, J. Mingorance, C. C. Carpio, D. Prieto Arribas, E. Rey Cuevas, M. C. Prados, J. J. Rios, M. Hernan, J. Frias, and J. R. Arribas. 2020. "A Cohort of Patients with COVID-19 in a Major Teaching Hospital in Europe." *Journal of Clinical Medicine* 9 (6): 1733. doi:0.3390/jcm9061733.

Cai, Q., F. Chen, T. Want, F. Luo, X. Liu, Q. Wu, Q. He, Z. Wang, Y. Liu, J. Chen, and L. Xu. 2020. "Obesity and COVID-19 Severity in a Designated Hospital in Shenzhen, China." *Diabetes Care* 43 (7): 1392–98. doi:10.2337/dc20-0576.

Calder, P. C. 2006a. "n-3 Polyunsaturated Fatty Acids, Inflammation, and Inflammatory Diseases." *American Journal of Clinical Nutrition* 83 (6 suppl): 1505S–19S.

Calder, P. C. 2006b. "Polyunsaturated Fatty Acids and Inflammation." *Prostaglandins Leukot Essent Fatty Acids* 75 (3): 197–202.

Caussy, C., F. Wallet, M. Laville, and E. Disse. 2020. "Obesity Is Associated with Severe Forms of COVID-19." *Obesity* 28 (7): 1175. doi:10.1002/oby.22842.

Chen, Q., Z. Zheng, C. Zhang, X. Zhang, H. Wu, J. Wang, S. Wang, and C. Zheng. 2020. "Clinical Characteristics of 145 Patients with Corona Virus Disease 2019 (COVID-19) in Taizhou, Zhejiang, China." *Infection* 48 (4): 543–51. doi:10.1007/s15010-020-01432-5.

Cohen, P. G. 2008. "Obesity in Men: The Hypogonadal–Estrogen Receptor Relationship and Its Effect on Glucose Homeostasis." *Medical Hypotheses* 70 (2): 358–60.

Crouch, M., A. Al-Shaer, and S. R. Shaikh. 2020. "Hormonal Dysregulation and Unbalanced Specialized Pro-Resolving Mediator Biosynthesis Contribute toward Impaired B Cell Outcomes in Obesity." *Molecular Nutrition and Food Research* 65 (1): e1900924.

Cure, E. and M. C. Cure. 2020. "Angiotensin-Converting Enzyme Inhibitors and Angiotensin Receptor Blockers May Be Harmful in Patients with Diabetes during COVID-19 Pandemic." *Diabetes & Metabolic Syndrome: Clinical Research & Reviews* 14 (4): 349–50. doi:10.1016/j.dsx.2020.04.019.

Darling, A. L., K. R. Ahmadi, K. A. Ward, N. C. Harvey, A. Couto Alves, D. K. Dunn-Waters, S. A. Lanham-New, C. Cooper, and D. J. Blackbourn. 2020. "Vitamin D Status, Body Mass Index, Ethnicity and COVID-19: Initial Analysis of the First-Reported UK Biobank COVID-19 Positive Cases (n 580) Compared with Negative Controls (n 723)." *medRxiv.* doi: 10.1101/2020.04.29.20084277.

Docherty, A. B., E. M. Harrison, C. A. Green, H. E. Hardwick, R. Pius, L. Norman, K. A. Holden, J. M. Read, F. Dondelinger, G. Carson, L. Merson, J. Lee, D. Plotkin, L. Sigfrid, S. Halpin, C. Jackson, C. Gamble, P. W. Horby, J. S. Nguyen-Van-Tam, J. Dunning, P. J. M. Openshaw, J. K. Baillie, and M. G. Semple. 2020. "Features of 16,749 Hospitalised UK Patients with COVID-19 Using the ISARIC WHO Clinical Characterisation Protocol." *BMJ* 369: m1985.

Ebinger, J. E., N. Achamallah, H. Ji, B. L. Claggett, N. Sun, P. Botting, T.-T. Nguyen, E. Luong, E. H. Kim, E. Park, Y. Liu, R. Rosenberry, Y. Matusov, S. Zhao, I. Pedraza, T. Zaman, M. Thompson, K. Raedschelders, A. H. Berg, J. D. Grein, P. W. Noble, S. S. Chugh, C. N. Bairey Merz, E. Marbán, J. E. Van Eyk, S. D. Solomon, C. M. Albert, P. Chen, and S. Cheng. 2020. "Pre-Existing Characteristics Associated with COVID-19 Illness Severity." *PLoS One* 15 (7): e0236240. doi:10.1371/journal.pone.0236240.

Eliakim, A., C. Schwindt, F. Zaldivar, P. Casali, and D. M. Cooper. 2006. "Reduced Tetanus Antibody Titers in Overweight Children." *Autoimmunity* 39 (2): 137–41.

Euromonitor Passport. 2020. *The Impact of Coronavirus on Packaged and Fresh Food.* London: Euromonitor International. https://www.euromonitor.com/the-impact-of-coronavirus-on-packaged-and-fresh-food/report.

Fanelli, V., and V. M. Ranieri. 2015. "Mechanisms and Clinical Consequences of Acute Lung Injury." *Annals of the American Thoracic Society* 12 (suppl 1): S3–8.

Gaibazzi, N., C. Martini, M. Mattioli, D. Tuttolomondo, A. Guidorossi, S. Suma, D. Dey, A. Palumbo, and M. De Filippo. 2020. "Lung Disease Severity, Coronary Artery Calcium, Coronary Inflammation and Mortality in Coronavirus Disease 2019." *medRxiv:* 2020.2005.2001.20087114. This article has been withdrawn by the authors.

Ganeshan, K., and A. Chawla. 2014. "Metabolic Regulation of Immune Responses." *Annual Review of Immunology* 32: 609–34.

Garg, S, L. Kim, A. Whitaker, M. O'Halloran, C. Cummings, R. Holstein, M. Prill, S. J. Chai, P. D. Kirley, N. B. Alden, B. Kawasaki, K. Yousey-Hindes, L. Niccolai, E. J. Anderson, K. P. Openo, A. Weigel, M. L. Monroe, P. Ryan, J. Henderson, S. Kim, K. Como-Sabetti, R. Lynfield, D. Sosin, S. Torres, A. Muse, N. M. Bennett, L. Billing, M. Sutton, N. West, W. Schaffner, H. K. Talbot, C. Aquino, A. George, A. Budd, L. Brammer, G. Langley, A. J. Hall, and A. Fry. 2020. "Hospitalization Rates and Characteristics of Patients Hospitalized with Laboratory-Confirmed Coronavirus Disease 2019—COVID-NET, 14 States, March 1–30, 2020." *MMWR Morbidity and Mortality Weekly Report* 69 (15): 458–64.

Glende, J., C. Schwegmann-Wessels, M. Al-Falah, S. Pfefferle, X. Qu, H. Deng, C. Drosten, H. Y. Naim, and G. Herrler. 2008. "Importance of Cholesterol-Rich Membrane Microdomains in the Interaction of the S Protein of SARS-Coronavirus with the Cellular Receptor Angiotensin-Converting Enzyme 2." *Virology* 381 (2): 215–21.

Goyal, P., J. J. Choi, L. C. Pinheiro, E. J. Schenck, R. Chen, A. Jabir, M. J. Satlin, T. R. Campion Jr., M. Nahid, J. B. Ringel, K. L. Hoffman, M. N. Alshak, H. A. Li, G. T. Wehmeyer, M. Rajan, E. Reshetnyak, N. Hupert, E. M. Horn, F.J . Martinez, R. M. Gulick, and M. M. Safford. 2020. "Clinical Characteristics of Covid-19 in New York City." *New England Journal of Medicine* 382 (24): 2372–74. doi:10.1056/NEJMc2010419.

Han, J. M., S. J. Patterson, M. Speck, J. A. Ehses, and M. K. Levings. 2014. "Insulin Inhibits IL-10-Mediated Regulatory T Cell Function: Implications for Obesity." *Journal of Immunology* 192 (2): 623–29.

Ho, F. K., C. A. Celis-Morales, S. R. Gray, S. V. Katikireddi, C. L. Niedzwiedz, C. Hastie, D. M. Lyall, L. D. Ferguson, C. Berry, D. F. Mackay, J. M. R. Gill, J. P. Pell, N. Sattar, and P. I. Welsh. 2020. "Modifiable and Non-Modifiable Risk Factors for COVID-19: Results from UK Biobank." *medRxiv.* doi:10.1101/2020.04.28.20083295.

Hoffmann, M., H. Kleine-Weber, S. Schroeder, N. Kruger, T. Herrler, S. Erichsen, T. S. Schiergens, G. Herrler, N. H. Wu, A. Nitsche, M. A. Muller, C. Drosten, and S. Pohlmann. 2020.

"SARS-CoV-2 Cell Entry Depends on ACE2 and TMPRSS2 and Is Blocked by a Clinically Proven Protease Inhibitor." *Cell* 181 (2): 271–80.e278.

Hu, L., S. Chen, Y. Fu, Z. Gao, H. Long, J.-M. Wang, H.-W. Ren, Y. Zuo, H. Li, J. Wang, Q.-B. Xu, W.-X. Yu, J. Liu, C. Shao, J.-J. Hao, C.-Z. Wang, Y. Ma, Z. Wang, R. Yanagihara, and Y. Deng. 2020. "Risk Factors Associated with Clinical Outcomes in 323 COVID-19 Hospitalized Patients in Wuhan, China." *Clinical Infectious Diseases* 71 (16): 2089–98. doi:10.1093/cid/ciaa539.

Huttunen, R., and J. Syrjanen. 2010. "Obesity and the Outcome of Infection." *Lancet* 10: 442–43.

Huttunen, R., and J. Syrjanen. 2013. "Obesity and the Risk and Outcome of Infection." *International Journal of Obesity* 37 (3): 333–40.

ICNARC (Intensive Care National Audit and Research Centre). 2020. *ICNARC Report on COVID-19 in Critical Care: 08 May 2020.* London: ICNARC.

Ip, B., N. A. Cilfone, A. C. Belkina, J. DeFuria, M. Jagannathan-Bogdan, M. Zhu, R. Kuchibhatla, M. E. McDonnell, Q. Xiao, T. B. Kepler, C. M. Apovian, D. A. Lauffenburger, and B. S. Nikolajczyk. 2016. "Th17 Cytokines Differentiate Obesity from Obesity-Associated Type 2 Diabetes and Promote TNFalpha Production." *Obesity* 24 (1): 102–12.

Jagannathan-Bogdan, M., M. E. McDonnell, H. Shin, Q. Rehman, H. Hasturk, C. M. Apovian, and B. S. Nikolajczyk. 2011. "Elevated Proinflammatory Cytokine Production by a Skewed T Cell Compartment Requires Monocytes and Promotes Inflammation in Type 2 Diabetes." *Journal of Immunology* 186 (2): 1162–72.

Kalligeros, M., F. Shehadeh, E. K. Mylona, G. Benitez, C. G. Beckwith, P. A. Chan, and E. Mylonakis. 2020. "Association of Obesity with Disease Severity among Patients with COVID-19." *Obesity* 28 (7): 1200–04. https://doi.org/10.1002/oby.22859.

Kantar. 2020. "Covid-19: Wave 2, 27–30 March, among Connected South African Consumers." Kantar World Panel: Johannesburg.

Karlsson, E. A., T. Hertz, C. Johnson, A. Mehle, F. Krammer, and S. Schultz-Cherry. 2016. "Obesity Outweighs Protection Conferred by Adjuvanted Influenza Vaccination." *MBio* 7 (4): e01144–16.

Kris-Etherton, P. M., D. S. Taylor, S. Yu-Poth, P. Huth, K. Moriarty, V. Fishell, R. L. Hargrove, G. Zhao, and T. D. Etherton. 2000. "Polyunsaturated Fatty Acids in the Food Chain in the United States." *American Journal of Clinical Nutrition* 71 (1 suppl): 179S–88S.

Kruglikov, I. L., and P. E. Scherer. 2020. "The Role of Adipocytes and Adipocyte-Like Cells in the Severity of COVID-19 Infections." *Obesity* 28 (7): 1187–90. doi:10.1002/oby.22856.

Li, T., Y. Zhang, C. Gong, J. Wang, B. Liu, L. Shi, and J. Duan. 2020. "Prevalence of Malnutrition and Analysis of Related Factors in Elderly Patients with COVID-19 in Wuhan, China." *European Journal of Clinical Nutrition* 74 (6). doi:10.1038/s41430-020 -0642-3.

Liao, X., H. Chen, B. Wang, Z. Li, Z. Zhang, W. Li, Z. Liang, J. Tang, J. Wang, R. Shi, X. Zhen, M. Wang, Y. Lei, Y. Gong, S. Lv, C. Jia, L. Chen, J. Shang, M. Yang, H. Wei, Y. Zhang, X. Yang, H. Shen, X. Xiao, J. Yang, Q. Wu, W. Wang, J. Yang, C. Liu, W. Yin, X. Xie, Y. Tian, H. Liu, B. Shuai, W. Zhang, X. Song, X. Jin, and Y. Kang. 2020. "Critical Care for Severe COVID-19: A Population-Based Study from a Province with Low Case-Fatality Rate in China." *Chinese Medical Journal* 134 (1): 98–100.

Lighter, J., M. Phillips, S. Hochman, S. Sterling, D. Johnson, F. Francois, and A. Stachel. 2020. "Obesity in Patients Younger than 60 Years Is a Risk Factor for Covid-19 Hospital Admission." *Clinical Infectious Diseases* 71 (15): 896–97. https://doi.org/10.1093/cid/ciaa415.

Liu, H., K. Liu, and D. L. Bodenner. 2005. "Estrogen Receptor Inhibits Interleukin-6 Gene Expression by Disruption of Nuclear Factor Kappab Transactivation." *Cytokine* 31 (4): 251–57.

Liu, M., P. He, H. Liu, X. Wang, F. Li, S. Chen, J. Lin, B. Chen, J. Liu, and C. Li. 2020. "Clinical Characteristics of 30 Medical Workers Infected with New Coronavirus Pneumonia." *Zhonghua Jie He Hu Xi Za Zhi* 43: E016.

McLaughlin, T., S. E. Ackerman, L. Shen, and E. Engleman. 2017. "Role of Innate and Adaptive Immunity in Obesity-Associated Metabolic Disease." *Journal of Clinical Investigation* 127 (1): 5–13.

McLaughlin, T., L. F. Liu, C. Lamendola, L. Shen, J. Morton, H. Rivas, D. Winer, L. Tolentino, O. Choi, H. Zhang, M. Hui Yen Chng, and E. Engleman. 2014. "T-Cell Profile in Adipose Tissue Is Associated with Insulin Resistance and Systemic Inflammation in Humans." *Arteriosclerosis, Thrombosis, and Vascular Biology* 34 (12): 2637–43.

Mehta, N., M. Mazer-Amirshahi, N. Alkindi, and A. Pourmand. 2020. "Pharmacotherapy in COVID-19: A Narrative Review for Emergency Providers." *American Journal of Emergency Medicine* 38 (7): 1488–93. doi:10.1016/j.ajem.2020.04.035.

Milner, J. J., P. A. Sheridan, E. A. Karlsson, S. Schultz-Cherry, Q. Shi, and M. A. Beck. 2013. "Diet-Induced Obese Mice Exhibit Altered Heterologous Immunity during a Secondary 2009 Pandemic H1N1 Infection." *Journal of Immunology* 191 (5): 2474–85.

Misumi, I., J. Starmer, T. Uchimura, M. A. Beck, T. Magnuson, and J. K. Whitmire. 2019. "Obesity Expands a Distinct Population of T Cells in Adipose Tissue and Increases Vulnerability to Infection." *Cell Reports* 27 (2): 514–24.e515.

Montopoli, M., S. Zumerle, R. Vettor, M. Rugge, M. Zorzi, C. V. Catapano, G. M. Carbone, A. Cavalli, F. Pagano, E. Ragazzi, T. Prayer-Galetti, and A. Alimonti. 2020. "Androgen-Deprivation Therapies for Prostate Cancer and Risk of Infection by SARS-CoV-2: A Population-Based Study (n=4532)." *Annals of Oncology* 31 (8): 1040–45. doi:10.1016/j.annonc.2020.04.479.

Moore, B. J. B., and C. H. June. 2020. "Cytokine Release Syndrome in Severe COVID-19." *Science* 368 (6490): 473–74. doi:10.1126/science.abb8925.

Neidich, S. D., W. D. Green, J. Rebeles, E. A. Karlsson, S. Schultz-Cherry, T. L. Noah, S. Chaklader, M. G. Hudgens, S. S. Weir, and M. A. Beck. 2017. "Increased Risk of Influenza among Vaccinated Adults Who Are Obese." *International Journal of Obesity* 41: 1324–30.

Nicholas, D. A., E. A. Proctor, M. Agrawal, A. C. Belkina, S. C. Van Nostrand, L. Panneerseelan-Bharath, A. R. T. Jones, F. Raval, B. C. Ip, M. Zhu, J. M. Cacicedo, C. Habib, N. Sainz-Rueda, L. Persky, P. G. Sullivan, B. E. Corkey, C. M. Apovian, P. A. Kern, D. A. Lauffenburger, and B. S. Nikolajczyk. 2019. "Fatty Acid Metabolites Combine with Reduced Beta Oxidation to Activate Th17 Inflammation in Human Type 2 Diabetes." *Cell Metabolism* 30 (3): 447–61.e445.

Norris, P. C., and E. A. Dennis. 2012. "Omega-3 Fatty Acids Cause Dramatic Changes in TLR4 and Purinergic Eicosanoid Signaling." *Proceedings of the National Academy of Sciences of the United States of America* 109 (22): 8517–22.

NYC Department of Health and Mental Hygiene. 2020. "Obesity," accessed May 12, 2020. https://www1.nyc.gov/site/doh/health/health-topics/obesity.page.

Paich, H. A., P. A. Sheridan, J. Handy, E. A. Karlsson, S. Schultz-Cherry, M. G. Hudgens, T. L. Noah, S. S. Weir, and M. A. Beck. 2013. "Overweight and Obese Adult Humans Have a Defective Cellular Immune Response to Pandemic H1N1 Influenza A Virus." *Obesity* 21 (11): 2377–86.

Painter, S. D., I. G. Ovsyannikova, and G. A. Poland. 2015. "The Weight of Obesity on the Human Immune Response to Vaccination." *Vaccine* 33 (36): 4422–29.

Peng, Y. D., K. Meng, H. Q. Guan, L. Leng, R. R. Zhu, B. Y. Wang, M. A. He, L. X. Cheng, K. Huang, and Q. T. Zeng. 2020. "Clinical Characteristics and Outcomes of 112 Cardiovascular Disease Patients Infected by 2019-nCoV." *Zhonghua Xin Xue Guan Bing Za Zhi* 48 (0): E004.

Petrilli, C. M., S. A. Jones, J. Yang, H. Rajagopalan, L. F. Donnell, Y. Chernyak, K. Tobin, R. J. Cerfolio, F. Francois, and L. I. Horwitz. 2020. "Factors Associated with Hospitalization and Critical Illness among 4,103 Patients with COVID-19 Disease in New York City." *BMJ* 369: m1966.

Rasouli, N., and P. A. Kern. 2008. "Adipocytokines and the Metabolic Complications of Obesity." *Journal of Clinical Endocrinology and Metabolism* 93 (11 suppl 1): S64–73.

Reyes Gil, M., J. D. Gonzalez-Lugo, S. Rahman, M. Barouqa, J. Szymanski, K. Ikemura, Y. Lo, and H.H. Billett. 2020. "Correlation of Coagulation Parameters with Clinical Outcomes in Coronavirus-19 Affected Minorities in United States: Observational Cohort." *medRxiv* 2020: 2020.05.01.20087932. doi:10.1101/2020.05.01.20087932.

Richardson, S., J. S. Hirsch, M. Narasimhan, J. M. Crawford, T. McGinn, K. W. Davidson, and the Northwell COVID-19 Research Consortium. 2020. "Presenting Characteristics,

Comorbidities, and Outcomes among 5,700 Patients Hospitalized with COVID-19 in the New York City Area." *JAMA* 323 (20): 2052–59. doi:10.1001/jama.2020.6775.

Robinson, D. P., O. J. Hall, T. L. Nilles, J. H. Bream, and S. L. Klein. 2014. "17β-Estradiol Protects Females against Influenza by Recruiting Neutrophils and Increasing Virus-Specific CD8 T Cell Responses in the Lungs." *Journal of Virology* 88 (9): 4711–20.

Ruan, Q., K. Yang, W. Wang, L. Jiang, and J. Song. 2020. "Clinical Predictors of Mortality Due to COVID-19 Based on an Analysis of Data of 150 Patients from Wuhan, China." *Intensive Care Medicine* 46: 846–48. doi:10.1007/s00134-020-05991-x.

Ryan, P. M., and N. M. Caplice. 2020. "Is Adipose Tissue a Reservoir for Viral Spread, Immune Activation and Cytokine Amplification in COVID-19?" *Obesity* 28 (7): 1191–94. https://pubmed.ncbi.nlm.nih.gov/32314868/.

Sattar, N., I. B. McInnes, and J. J. V. McMurray. 2020. "Obesity a Risk Factor for Severe COVID-19 Infection: Multiple Potential Mechanisms." *Circulation* 142 (1): 4–6.

Saucillo, D. C., V. A. Gerriets, J. Sheng, J. C. Rathmell, and N. J. Maciver. 2014. "Leptin Metabolically Licenses T Cells for Activation to Link Nutrition and Immunity." *Journal of Immunology* 192 (1): 136–44.

Schneider, G., M. A. Kirschner, R. Berkowitz, and N. H. Ertel. 1979. "Increased Estrogen Production in Obese Men." *Journal of Clinical Endocrinology and Metabolism* 48 (4): 633–38.

Sheetz, M. J., and G. L. King. 2002. "Molecular Understanding of Hyperglycemia's Adverse Effects for Diabetic Complications." *JAMA* 288 (20): 2579–88.

Sheridan, P. A., H. A. Paich, J. Handy, E. A. Karlsson, M. G. Hudgens, A. B. Sammon, L. A. Holland, S. Weir, T. L. Noah, and M. A. Beck. 2012. "Obesity Is Associated with Impaired Immune Response to Influenza Vaccination in Humans." *International Journal of Obesity* 36 (8): 1072–77.

Simonnet, A., M. Chetboun, J. Poissy, V. Raverdy, J. Noulette, A. Duhamel, J. Labreuche, D. Mathieu, F. Pattou, M. Jourdain, T. L. I. C. COVID-19 and O. S. Group. 2020. "High Prevalence of Obesity in Severe Acute Respiratory Syndrome Coronavirus-2 (SARS-CoV-2) Requiring Invasive Mechanical Ventilation." *Obesity* 28 (7): 1195–99. doi:10.1002/oby.22831.

Singla, P., A. Bardoloi, and A. A. Parkash. 2010. "Metabolic Effects of Obesity: A Review." *World Journal of Diabetes* 1 (3): 76–88.

Stefan, N., A. L. Birkenfeld, M. B. Schulze, and D.S. Ludwig. 2020. "Obesity and Impaired Metabolic Health in Patients with COVID-19." *Nature Reviews Endocrinology* 16: 341–42. doi:10.1038/s41574-020-0364-6.

Tsai, S., X. Clemente-Casares, A. C. Zhou, H. Lei, J. J. Ahn, Y. T. Chan, O. Choi, H. Luck, M. Woo, S. E. Dunn, E. G. Engleman, T. H. Watts, S. Winer, and D. A. Winer. 2018. "Insulin Receptor-Mediated Stimulation Boosts T Cell Immunity during Inflammation and Infection." *Cell Metabolism* 28 (6): 922–34.e4.

Vabret, N., G. J. Britton, C. Gruber, S. Hegde, J. Kim, M. Kuksin, R. Levantovsky, L. Malle, A. Moreira, M. D. Park, L. Pia, E. Risson, M. Saffern, B. Salomé, M. E. Selvan, M. P. Spindler, J. Tan, V. van der Heide, J. K. Gregory, K. Alexandropoulos, N. Bhardwaj, B. D. Brown, B. Greenbaum, Z. H. Gümüş, D. Homann, A. Horowitz, A. O. Kamphorst, M. A. Curotto de Lafaille, S. Mehandru, M. Merad, R. M. Samstein, and the Sinai Immunology Review Project. 2020. "Immunology of COVID-19: Current State of the Science." *Immunity* 53 (6): 910–41.

Van der Weerd, K., W. A. Dik, B. Schrijver, D. H. Schweitzer, A. W. Langerak, H. A. Drexhage, R. M. Kiewiet, M. O. van Aken, A. van Huisstede, J. J. van Dongen, A. J. van der Lelij, F. J. Staal, and P. M. van Hagen. 2012. "Morbidly Obese Human Subjects Have Increased Peripheral Blood CD4+ T Cells with Skewing toward a Treg- and Th2-Dominated Phenotype." *Diabetes* 61 (2): 401–8.

WHO (World Health Organization). 2014. *Global Status Report on Noncommunicable Diseases 2014*. Geneva: World Health Organization.

Wollenstein-Betec, S., C. G. Cassandras, and I. C. Paschalidis. 2020. "Personalized Predictive Models for Symptomatic COVID-19 Patients Using Basic Preconditions: Hospitalizations, Mortality, and the Need for an ICU or Ventilator." *International Journal of Medical Informatics* 142: 104258. doi:10.1016/j.ijmedinf.2020.104258.

Wu, J., W. Li, X. Shi, Z. Chen, B. Jiang, J. Liu, D. Wang, C. Liu, Y. Meng, L. Cui, J. Yu, H. Cao, and L. Li. 2020. "Early Antiviral Treatment Contributes to Alleviate the Severity and Improve the Prognosis of Patients with Novel Coronavirus Disease (COVID-19)." *Journal of Internal Medicine* 288 (1): 128–38. doi:10.1111/joim.13063.

Xu, X., M. Han, T. Li, W. Sun, D. Wang, B. Fu, Y. Zhou, X. Zheng, Y. Yang, X. Li, X. Zhang, A. Pan, and H. Wei. 2020. "Effective Treatment of Severe COVID-19 Patients with Tocilizumab." *Proceedings of the National Academy of Sciences* 117 (20): 10970–75. doi:10.1073/pnas.2005615117.

Zhang, X., M. Zhang, Z. Zhao, Z. Huang, Q. Deng, Y. Li, A. Pan, C. Li, Z. Chen, M. Zhou, C. Yu, A. Stein, P. Jia, and L. Wang. 2020. "Geographic Variation in Prevalence of Adult Obesity in China: Results from the 2013–2014 National Chronic Disease and Risk Factor Surveillance." *Annals of Internal Medicine* 172 (4): 291–93.

Zheng, K. I., G. Feng, X. B. Wang, Q. F. Sun, K. H. Pan, T. Y. Wang, H. L. Ma, W. Y. Liu, J. George, and M. H. Zheng. 2020. "Obesity as a Risk Factor for Greater Severity of COVID-19 in Patients with Metabolic Associated Fatty Liver Disease." *Metabolism* 108: 154244. doi:10.1016/j.metabol.2020.154244.

Zhu, L., Z. G. She, X. Cheng, J. J. Qin, X. J. Zhang, J. Cai, F. Lei, H. Wang, J. Xie, W. Wang, H. Li, P. Zhang, X. Song, X. Chen, M. Xiang, C. Zhang, L. Bai, D. Xiang, M. M. Chen, Y. Liu, Y. Yan, M. Liu, W. Mao, J. Zou, L. Liu, G. Chen, P. Luo, B. Xiao, C. Zhang, Z. Zhang, Z. Lu, J. Wang, H. Lu, X. Xia, D. Wang, X. Liao, G. Peng, P. Ye, J. Yang, Y. Yuan, X. Huang, J. Guo, B. H. Zhang, and H. Li. 2020. "Association of Blood Glucose Control and Outcomes in Patients with COVID-19 and Pre-existing Type 2 Diabetes." *Cell Metabolism* 31 (6): 1068–77.e3.

# 7 Obesity-Prevention Strategies and Policies for Saudi Arabia

REEM F. ALSUKAIT, RASHA ALFAWAZ, ADWA ALAMRI, TAGHRED ALGHAITH,
MARIAM M. HAMZA, FAISAL BIN SUNAID, SAMEH EL-SAHARTY,
MAJID ALKHALAF, MOHAMMED ALLUHIDAN, AND CHRISTOPHER H. HERBST

## KEY MESSAGES

- Multisectoral and multicomponent policies are necessary to address the obesity epidemic.
- Saudi Arabia is at the regional forefront when it comes to innovative nutrition-related policies and has already implemented the largest global sugar-sweetened beverage tax (50 percent) and mandatory calorie menu labeling, among other actions.
- Despite these promising policies in Saudi Arabia, few effectiveness and impact evaluation studies exist, and it is unclear whether and to what extent they are successful.
- To inform effective policy design, evidence generation needs to be strengthened to ensure that the design of policies is optimized, based on local contexts, and is linked to studies or existing systems that monitor and evaluate effectiveness and impact.
- Such evidence can be based on a small-scale randomized trial, mixed-methods pilot studies, or secondary data evaluations such as purchasing or sales data.

## BACKGROUND

The health and economic burdens of overweight, obesity, and related noncommunicable diseases (NCDs) are large in Saudi Arabia and are likely to grow in the future as the population ages. Chapter 2 showed the current high prevalence of overweight and obesity in Saudi Arabia (58 percent of the total population) and the alarming increasing trend among children between 5 and 19 years of age, with a third of Saudi children having excess weight. Chapter 3 highlighted the multilevel determinants associated with weight gain in Saudi Arabia beyond individual-level control. Chapter 4 quantified the economic burden and found that it exceeds 12 percent of total annual health expenditures in Saudi Arabia and may reduce gross domestic product by 1.4 percent annually.

Chapters 5 and 6 showed that overweight and obesity are significant contributors to disease morbidity and mortality in Saudi Arabia and presented ways they exacerbate the risk of infectious diseases such as COVID-19.

Successful reductions of obesity require multicomponent policies and regulations to modify population-level dietary and physical activity habits. Complex systems, as well as environmental and individual behavioral challenges, are root causes of the increase in overweight and obesity prevalence. Dietary habits are determined by individual preferences and wider sociocultural factors including household lifestyle patterns, family and community pressures, and social norms. In addition, broader economic forces (for example, globalization and changes to the food system and agricultural practices) and commercial influences (for example, the marketing of unhealthy foods and the higher cost of healthy foods) play an oversized role in influencing consumer food habits.

Saudi Arabia has recently adopted many promising policies and interventions to promote healthier lifestyles and reduce overweight and obesity rates. These include excise taxes on sugary drinks, nutrition and calorie labeling, product reformulation efforts, nutrition standards in schools, and physical activity promotion campaigns. This chapter maps existing strategies to identify obesity-related national objectives, identifies relevant stakeholders, and provides a narrative review on the evidence of the effectiveness for existing policies and interventions in light of local and global experiences. It then considers key lessons learned and presents conclusions.

## OBESITY PREVENTION–RELATED STRATEGIES, OBJECTIVES, AND STAKEHOLDERS

This section summarizes national strategies' key objectives that explicitly mention obesity prevention, including those that focus on behavioral risk factors such as dietary risks and physical activity. A *strategy* can be defined as a general direction that is set for the sector and its various components to achieve a desired state in the future. *Inclusion criteria* are defined as having been published by a government entity within the past 10 years (2010–20). Table 7.1 provides a summary of strategies and plans reviewed in this section, and figure 7.1 highlights relevant stakeholder groups identified.

TABLE 7.1 **The eight obesity-related national strategies**

| NATIONAL STRATEGIES AND PLANS | AGENCY OWNERSHIP | IMPLEMENTATION PERIOD | SOURCE OR REFERENCE |
|---|---|---|---|
| Vision 2030 (quality of life program) | Vision Realization Office | 2016–30 | KSA 2016 |
| Obesity Control and Prevention Strategy | Public Health Authority | 2020–30 | SCDC 2019 |
| Obesity Control Program Strategy | Ministry of Health | 2014–25 | MOH 2014d |
| Healthy Food Strategy | Saudi Food and Drug Authority | 2018–30 | SFDA 2018a |
| Diet and Physical Activity Strategy | Ministry of Health | 2014–25 | MOH 2014a |
| Saudi Arabia National Strategy for Prevention of NCDs | Ministry of Health | 2014–25 | MOH 2014b |
| National Executive Plan for Diabetes Control | Ministry of Health | 2014–25 | MOH 2014c |
| National Strategy for Prevention of Cardiovascular Disease | Ministry of Health | 2010–20 | MOH 2010 |

*Source:* Original table for this publication.
*Note:* NCD = noncommunicable disease.

FIGURE 7.1

**Obesity prevention–related stakeholder groups**

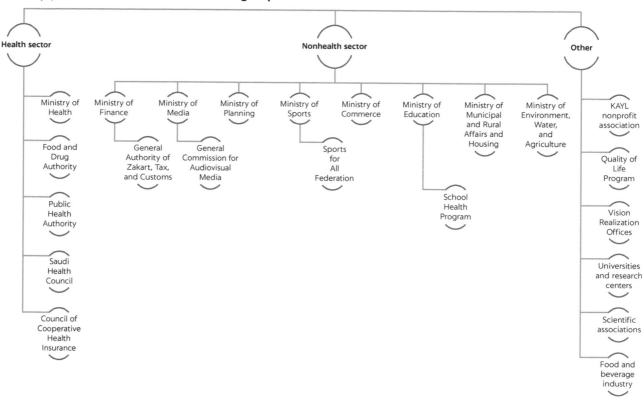

*Source:* Original figure for this publication.

## Overweight and obesity

The goal of stopping the annual increase in overweight and obesity rates is part of the National Strategy for Prevention of NCDs (MOH 2014b), the Obesity Control and Prevention Strategy (SCDC 2019), and the National Strategy for Prevention of Cardiovascular Disease (MOH 2010). The goal of the National Executive Plan for Diabetes Control (MOH 2014c) is to reduce the prevalence of overweight and obesity by 10 percent between 2014 and 2025. Similarly, the Diet and Physical Activity Strategy (MOH 2014a) aims to reduce overweight and obesity rates from 66 percent to 40 percent by 2025. Other obesity-related objectives include increasing public awareness around obesity and determining ways to prevent it by 50 percent, as mentioned in the Obesity Control and Prevention Strategy (SCDC 2019).

## Dietary risk factors

Multiple dietary risk factor objectives are mentioned in all the strategies in table 7.1 (except for the Quality of Life Program from Vision 2030). While the specific objectives and the degree of change desired vary, overall they can be summarized as (1) increasing the consumption of fruits and vegetables (three to five servings per day) by 20 percent; (2) reducing the consumption of salt, fat, and sugar; and (3) increasing public awareness about the importance of a healthy diet.

### Physical activity

Improving physical activity is a priority in Vision 2030 and is included in most of the strategies in table 7.1 (except the Healthy Food Strategy). There are three types of objectives: (1) to increase the prevalence rate of physical activity uptake once per week to 40 percent of the population or increase it by 20 percent from current levels, (2) lower the prevalence rate of physical inactivity to 20 percent of the population or by 10 percent, and (3) increase public awareness about the importance of physical activity.

## OBESITY-PREVENTION POLICIES AND THEIR EFFECTIVENESS EVIDENCE

This section summarizes the information on existing or proposed policies that are relevant to obesity prevention in Saudi Arabia and the evidence on their effectiveness. A *policy* can be defined as a deliberate system of principles to guide decisions and achieve rational outcomes. A policy is a statement of intent and is implemented as a procedure or protocol. Specifically, the section reviews the following policies: (1) fiscal policies (taxes and incentives); (2) nutrition-labeling policies (nutrition facts label, front-of-package labels, and calorie menu labels); (3) food and beverage product reformulations (mandatory and voluntary); (4) marketing restrictions of unhealthy foods and beverages; (5) school-based policies (for nutrition and physical activity); and (6) mass media campaigns (table 7.2).

### Fiscal policies

Fiscal policies to improve diet—particularly taxation and subsidies or incentives—are key population-based policy interventions to address overweight and obesity. There is strong evidence that increasing the price of taxed products and decreasing the price of subsidized products can change consumer purchasing behaviors. In a systematic review, researchers found that a 10 percent decrease in price (that is, a subsidy) increased the consumption of healthy foods by 12 percent (95 percent with CI = 10–15 percent) and a 10 percent increase in prices (that is, a tax) decreased the consumption of unhealthy foods by 6 percent (95 percent with CI = 4–8 percent) (Afshin et al. 2017). This section reviews sugar-sweetened beverage (SSB) taxation, the most popular tax to date, followed by unhealthy food and beverage taxation and healthy food subsidies and incentives.

#### Sugar-sweetened beverage taxation

SSB consumption is strongly linked to increased risk of type 2 diabetes, excess weight gain, and cardiovascular diseases (Hu 2013; Imamura et al. 2016; Malik 2017). SSBs have received intense attention from the public health community because, unlike other foods or beverages, they provide "empty" calories with little to no nutritional value; moreover, the potential mechanism of SSB-related weight gain is likely due to the drinks' higher energy content, reduced satiety compared with solid food, high glycemic load, and a reduced overall diet quality. They are also highly marketed to youth, further justifying their taxation (WHO 2017b).

**TABLE 7.2 Obesity-prevention policies in Saudi Arabia**

| TYPOLOGY | POLICY INSTRUMENT | IMPLEMENTED (YES/NO) | EVALUATION EVIDENCE |
|---|---|---|---|
| **Fiscal policies** | Sugar-sweetened beverage (SSB) taxation | Yes<br>• 2017—50 percent tax on carbonated drinks and 100 percent tax on energy drinks.<br>• 2019—50 percent tax expanded to include all SSBs. | Yes (partial)<br>• Increase in national prices.<br>• Reduction in national sales.<br>• No health impact evaluation studies. |
| | Unhealthy food and beverage taxation | No | No |
| | Healthy food subsidies and incentives | No | No |
| **Nutrition labeling** | Nutrition facts label | Yes<br>• 2020—policy updated to be more consumer friendly. | No |
| | Front of package labeling | Yes (voluntary)<br>• 2018—traffic-light label. | No |
| | Calorie labeling on menus | Yes<br>• 2019—all restaurants must display calorie information. | Yes (partial)<br>• Compliance rate is 70 percent in Riyadh and Qassim.<br>• One small-scale cross-sectional study found 87 percent of participants noticed the calorie information.<br>• Another small-scale cross-sectional study stated 62 percent of the participants said it will affect their food selection. |
| **Food and beverage product reformulations** | Multiple | Yes (mandatory and voluntary)<br>• 2018–20—multiple commitments. | No |
| **Marketing restrictions of unhealthy foods and beverages** | Restrictions to those targeting children under 15 years of age | Yes (voluntary)<br>• Unknown date | No |
| **School-based policies** | Rashaka Initiative for obesity | Yes<br>• 2017 | No |
| | Regulations for school canteens | Yes (mandatory)<br>• 2013 | Yes (partial)<br>• Compliance among boys' schools in Riyadh. |
| **Media campaigns** | Public awareness | Yes | No |

*Source:* Original table for this publication.

More than 46 countries, including five Arab Gulf ones, have implemented SSB taxes; evidence shows they work. A meta-analysis of real world SSB tax evaluations shows that that the average consumer will lower their SSB purchase by 10 percent if SSB prices rise 10 percent (implied price elasticity of demand of –1) (Teng et al. 2019). Because reductions in obesity levels will likely take years to emerge, researchers have used consumption changes to estimate longer-term health and economic implications. These modeling estimates broadly show meaningful reductions in both incidence and prevalence of NCDs, and thus health-care cost savings (Barrientos-Gutierrez et al. 2017; Briggs et al. 2017; Manyema et al. 2014; Sánchez-Romero et al. 2016).

Changes in the prices, purchases or sales, and consumption rates of SSBs vary greatly depending on the tax rate and design (Cawley et al. 2019; Salgado and Ng 2019). Findings to date show more responsiveness to excise taxes collected from manufacturers, distributors, or importers (rather than via sales taxes) (Cawley et al. 2019). Researchers estimated that a simple design change in the United States from a volume-based tax (1–2 cents per ounce) to the amount of sugar (0.5 cent per gram of sugar) would improve the SSB tax's health and economic gains by 30 percent (Grummon et al. 2019). Another study found that health and economic benefits were twice as large for tiered and sugar-content taxes as for volume-based taxes because of industry reformulation (Lee et al. 2020). However, taxing based on sugar content could result in nonnutritive sweetener substitutions whose long-term health implications are unclear at this time (de Koning et al. 2011, 2012). Table 7A.1 in annex 7A lays out selected examples of SSB or unhealthy food taxes and the evidence to date spanning measurements on changes in price, purchase or sales, and consumption, as well as revenue uses (when known). Table 7A.2 in annex 7A shows examples of different tax designs.

In 2017, Saudi Arabia implemented the largest tax rate in the world to date using an excise tax flat rate design imposed on energy drinks (100 percent) and carbonated drinks (50 percent); this was later expanded to include all SSBs in 2019 (GAZT n.d.-a, n.d.-b). Consumption of SSBs is high, as indicated in chapter 3. An evaluation study found that prices of carbonated drinks did increase in response to the tax, by 55 percent (Alsukait et al. 2020). Figure 7.2 shows the post-taxation decline of energy and carbonated drinks. Interestingly, sales of bottled water as a potential healthy substitute did not increase, unlike what was observed in Mexico (Alsukait et al. 2019).

In another more rigorous analysis using other Gulf Cooperation Council (GCC) countries as a comparison group, evidence shows sales of carbonated drinks declined by 35 percent in comparison to control (Alsukait et al. 2020) (figure 7.3).

### Unhealthy food and beverage taxation

A mounting body of evidence shows that increased consumption of ultraprocessed products (UPPs) in diets are linked to increased risk of obesity and many measures of cardiovascular disease, diabetes, hypertension, cancers, and total mortality (Lawrence and Baker 2019; Moubarac et al. 2013; Srour et al. 2019). UPPs are gaining popularity globally, forming a growing share of the diets of the

FIGURE 7.2

**Pre and post trends in volume sales per capita in comparison to other beverages in Saudi Arabia, 2010–18**

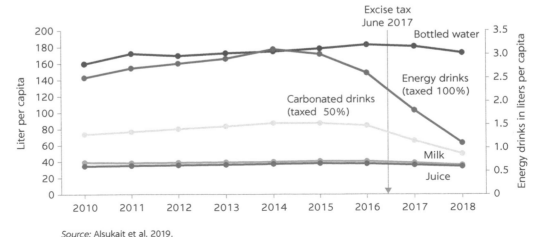

Source: Alsukait et al. 2019.

FIGURE 7.3

**Trends in carbonated drink volume per capita sales (liters), 2010–18**

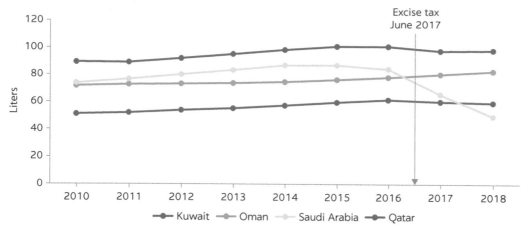

*Source:* Original figure for this publication, based on data from Alsukait et al. 2020.

very poor and now reaching infants and preschoolers (Baker et al. 2020; Monteiro et al. 2013; Pries, Filteau, and Ferguson 2019; Pries et al. 2019). Of 51 public health interventions, a modest 10 percent tax on junk food and drinks in just seven categories (biscuits, cakes, pastries, pies, snack foods, confectionary, and soft drinks) was highest ranked in terms of disability-adjusted life years saved—nearly five times as effective as a package of tobacco-control interventions that included a 10 percent tax increase on tobacco (van der Vliet et al. 2020).

A critical future direction to consider is to expand taxes to highly processed food (Carter et al. 2019; Srour et al. 2019). However, there is slower momentum around food taxes for two reasons. First, they are more difficult to justify since foods are more complex mixtures of nutrients while SSBs have no nutritional value. Second, there are concerns around such taxes creating a higher burden among the poor. When the economic burden of having these diseases is counted, however, the poor may benefit when taxes are imposed on unhealthy foods. Another important area for consideration is the degree of substitution effect, whereby consumers switch to lower-priced food products that may also be unhealthy. Taxing a broad tax base of highly processed foods will likely reduce the potential for such substitutions and likely be more effective. However, it could also be regressive and place a larger burden on the poor (Boysen et al. 2019).

Evidence for the two national unhealthy-food taxes in Hungary and Mexico shows significant effects despite their lower tax rates. Mexico's 2014 8 percent sales tax on unhealthy foods also resulted in a 5.8 percent decline in the purchase of taxed foods among households of medium socioeconomic status and a 10.2 percent decline among households of lower socioeconomic status (Batis et al. 2016; Taillie et al. 2017). Hungary's unhealthy-food taxes led to a decline in consumption of all processed foods by 3.4 percent, whereas unprocessed food consumption increased insignificantly by 1.1 percent (Bíró 2015).

### Healthy food subsidies and incentives

Moderate- to good-quality evidence supports the use of pricing incentives to increase consumption or purchases of fruits and vegetables (Batis et al. 2016). In a cost-effectiveness analysis of making fruits and vegetables more affordable through the Supplemental Nutrition Assistance Program in the United States, researchers found that it would reduce incidence of type 2 diabetes by 1.7 percent (95 percent confidence interval [CI] of 1.2, 2.2), myocardial infarction by 1.4 percent (95 percent CI of 0.9, 1.9), stroke by 1.2 percent (95 percent CI of 0.8, 1.6), and obesity by 0.2 percent (95 percent CI of 0.1, 0.3). Further, it would be cost saving from a societal perspective because of long-term reductions in type 2 diabetes and cardiovascular diseases (Choi, Seligman, and Basu 2017).

Incentives can come in the form of subsidies, rebates, discounts, or matches. Studies have shown, however, that efforts to lower costs of healthy foods (for example, agricultural subsidies or removal of past taxes on producers) are often only partially passed on as price reductions for the public (AEI 2017) and so are not necessarily an effective way for governments to be spending or lowering revenue if a key purpose is to change consumption behavior.

Another approach that more directly influences choices is to increase the ability of the population to afford healthier alternatives (Lee et al. 2019; Niebylski et al. 2015). This can be especially effective when targeted toward specific subpopulations that need to meet eligibility criteria (for example, income and asset ownership, age, and health condition). It can thus serve double duty by (1) addressing equity concerns (particularly when paired with tax policies to counter regressivity arguments) and (2) providing reinforcing messages about healthier versus unhealthy options. In a large-scale randomized trial, a 30 percent incentive on fruits and vegetables increased participants' consumption by 26 percent (Bartlett, Olsho, and Jacob 2014). However, most studies to date have occurred in the United States (19 studies) and other high-income countries (8 studies), with only one study each in Peru and South Africa (Healthy Food America n.d.).

Saudi Arabia could experiment with a fruit and vegetable subsidy or a 15 percent value added tax exemption on healthier products. The current fruit and vegetable consumption levels fall way below recommendations, as highlighted in chapter 3. While these programs might be popular, they can be expensive and must be carefully designed and implemented to improve obesity and NCD prevention value for money. Critical design decisions include identifying the target population, deciding how to determine eligibility or whether to make it conditional on certain behaviors (rather than making it too difficult to enroll and use), and deciding on the length of eligibility, the frequency/cycle of disbursement, the amount of incentive, and the foods covered, given their baseline levels of consumption and substitutes (Healthy Food America n.d.).

## Nutrition labeling

Nutrition labels are designed to help consumers make informed choices. When the information is noticeable and easily understood, it can propel consumers to make healthier food choices and discourage unhealthy food consumption. Nutrition labels can also encourage food and drink companies to improve the nutritional quality of their products. This subsection describes the different types of nutrition labels: nutrition facts labels, front-of-package labels, and calorie labels on menus.

### Nutrition facts label

The most common nutrition label is the nutrition facts label on the back or the side of packaged foods and beverages. This label typically includes information on energy (calories), fat, carbohydrates, protein, sugar, and sodium per serving size and their percentage of daily value based on a typical 2,000-calorie diet. However, evidence suggests it is difficult for people to understand these labels and there is little evidence that this strategy has positively influenced dietary outcomes (Helfer and Shultz 2014; Khandpur, Rimm, and Moran 2020; Variyam 2008). Proposed changes to improve the label include increasing the font size for calories, adding "added sugar" under total sugar, and changing the serving sizes to match what people typically consume in one setting (for example, for the full package of chips instead of per 1 ounce) (US FDA 2021). Studies suggest these new labels are likely more effective than the older version (Huang et al. 2019).

In Saudi Arabia, as part of the Healthy Food Strategy, the Saudi Food and Drug Authority (SFDA) issued a new nutrition facts label regulation (figure 7.4) that became effective in April 2021 (SFDA 2018a). This new label reflects serving sizes typically consumed in one setting, a larger font for calories and serving sizes, removal of calories from fat, and the addition of "added sugar" in grams under total sugar. The regulation is in the process of being adopted by other GCC countries (GSO 2018). Previous studies showed that only 38 percent of food products surveyed met the SFDA previous nutrition facts label requirements

**FIGURE 7.4**

**Example of the updated nutrition facts label**

| Nutrition Facts | |
|---|---|
| 8 servings per container | |
| **Serving size** | **2/3 cup (55g)** |
| **Amount per serving** | |
| **Calories** | **230** |
| | **% Daily Value\*** |
| **Total Fat** 8g | **10%** |
| Saturated Fat 1g | **5%** |
| *Trans* Fat 0g | |
| **Cholesterol** 0mg | **0%** |
| **Sodium** 160mg | **7%** |
| **Total Carbohydrate** 37g | **13%** |
| Dietary Fiber 4g | **14%** |
| Total Sugars 12g | |
| Includes 10g Added Sugars | **20%** |
| **Protein** 3g | |

\*The % Daily Value (DV) tells you how much a nutrient in a serving of food contributes to a daily diet, 2,000 calories a day is used for general nutrition advice

*Source:* SFDA 2018a.

(AlMughthem, Jradi, and Bawazir 2020). Evaluation studies on compliance with the new nutrition facts label and its impact on consumer behaviors in Saudi Arabia are urgently needed.

### Front-of-package labeling

Front-of-package labels are likely to be more effective than nutrition facts labels. Many countries are now mandating easier-to-understand front-of-package nutrition labels such as warning labels, Nutri-Score labels, traffic light labels, and positive labels (table 7.3). Nutri-Score is a label developed in France that assigns a single score to each product based on the product's overall healthfulness. In Ecuador, a mandatory multiple traffic light (MTL) front-of-package label for packaged, processed food products is implemented (World Cancer Research Fund International n.d.). Evidence thus far indicates that, despite most consumers' awareness and understanding of the label, it has not led to changes in purchasing behavior. Many of the studies—both randomized and nonrandomized—indicate that warning labels, traffic light labels, and Nutri-Score labels induce small improvements in the healthfulness of consumers' purchases (Finkelstein et al. 2019; Gorski Findling et al. 2018).

Among the front-of-package labels, simple, negative warning labels that clearly identify unhealthy products appear most effective (Corvalán et al. 2019). These labels help consumers quickly identify foods that are less healthy and encourage manufacturers to improve the nutritional qualities of their products to avoid carrying such negative front-of-package labels (Reyes et al. 2020; Shangguan et al. 2019; Vyth et al. 2010). Simulation and empirical studies suggest that such labels are more likely to be noticed, cause stronger emotional reactions, and lead consumers to choose healthier products (Kelly and Jewell 2018) while avoiding unhealthy ones compared to numeric nutrient information (Grummon and Hall 2020; Taillie, Hall, et al. 2020). In Chile, a real-world warning label policy evaluation showed that when mandating the use of warnings for products "high-in" sugar, saturated fats, sodium, or energy based on nutrient threshold values, purchases of beverages with "high-in" labels fell by 23.7 percent after implementation, with similar reductions across all income groups (Taillie, Reyes, et al. 2020).

In Saudi Arabia, as part of the Healthy Food Strategy, the SFDA issued a traffic light label voluntary standard (SFDA 2018a) (figure 7.5), which includes energy, fat, saturated fat, total sugar, and salt thresholds on a 100 grams per milliliter basis (Al-Jawaldeh et al. 2020). The design and standards followed the United Kingdom's guide to creating a front-of-package nutrition label (FoPNL) (Food Standards Scotland 2016). In 2020, the SFDA assessed the Saudi market uptake to the voluntary approach MTL scheme and found that 119 out of 4,335 food products applied FoPNL (1.8 percent), while 48 out of 119 food products applied MTL (40.34 percent) (Bin Sunaid et al. 2021). In addition, the SFDA found that the majority of food products for which the MTL scheme was implemented were green. Evaluation studies are urgently needed to measure the industry's compliance with the voluntary traffic light labels and their impact on consumer behaviors.

### Calorie labeling on menus

Globally, the evidence on the effectiveness of mandatory restaurant calorie labeling on consumer behaviors and restaurant menu offerings is limited. Except for a single systematic review in 2017 by Bleich and colleagues (2017), most of the

**TABLE 7.3 Front-of-package labels**

| TYPE OF LABEL | WHERE USED | EXAMPLES |
|---|---|---|
| Traffic lights | United Kingdom, the Republic of Korea, Ecuador, Sri Lanka | **PER 2/3 CUP**<br>MED **Fat** 2g<br>LOW **Saturated Fat** 0g<br>MED **Salt** 105mg<br>HIGH **Sugars** 6g<br>**Calories** 120 |
| Warning labels | Chile, Uruguay, Canada, Peru | ALTO EN AZÚCARES Ministerio de Salud · ALTO EN GRASAS SATURADAS Ministerio de Salud · ALTO EN SODIO Ministerio de Salud · ALTO EN CALORÍAS Ministerio de Salud |
| Nutri-Score | France, Belgium, Spain, Germany | **NUTRI-SCORE** A B C D E |
| Positive labels | Many countries, including Tunis and the United Arab Emirates |  HEALTHY FOODS — NATIONAL STRATEGY OF PREVENTION AND CONTROL OF THE OBESITY  وقاية weqaya |

*Source:* Al-Jawaldeh et al. 2020.

**FIGURE 7.5**

**Saudi Arabia's voluntary traffic light label, 2018**

*Sources:* (lower image) SFDA 2018b, https://sfda.gov.sa/sites/default/files/2019-11/ND2-min.jpg; (upper image) SFDA 2018c, https://sfda.gov.sa/sites/default/files/2019-11/ND6-min.jpg.

studies did not have the intended effect of decreasing calorie purchasing or consumption (Petimar et al. 2019; Swartz, Braxton, and Viera 2011). There are multiple potential explanations for the lack of strong effectiveness evidence for menu calorie labeling. One potential explanation suggests that it is effective in decreasing the number of calories ordered by health-oriented consumers, but consumers who value quantity and taste may increase the calories they order in response to menu calorie labeling. These two responses counterbalance each other, leading to its overall nonsignificant effect on calories ordered in restaurants (Berry et al. 2019). Another explanation for the lack of effectiveness is that consumers are not clear on what to do with calorie information, suggesting that front-of-package labels indicating which foods to consume or avoid may be more effective (Fernandes et al. 2016).

In Saudi Arabia, as part of the Healthy Food Strategy, the SFDA mandated all restaurants, cafés, ice cream shops, fresh juice shops, and bakeries in the country to display calorie content on their menus clearly next to each food item and each preparation method if varied (print and electronic), effective January 2019 (SFDA 2018a). Field visits to bakeries and patisseries in Riyadh and Qaseem by the SFDA suggest a 70 percent compliance rate (*Arab News* 2019). The most notable violations were miscalculating caloric content and not displaying it on all menus. However, the compliance rate nationally and at different food establishment types, including homes, is unclear.

Three studies to date have assessed the impact of the calorie labeling policy in Saudi Arabia. A study before and after policy implementation using transactional sales data for a large food restaurant chain in Riyadh found no significant impact from calorie labeling on total calorie intake but did find a slight decrease in total calories for those using online food ordering platforms (Alfawzan and Aljarallah 2020). Another cross-sectional study used an online survey of individuals and restaurant owners. It found that 62 percent of participants reported that the new labeling policy affected their food selections, prompting them to order different food items, eat less, change restaurants, or eat at restaurants less frequently. Sales of low- and high-energy meals increased and decreased in 44 percent and 39 percent of restaurants, respectively (Alkhaldy et al. 2020). Finally, another cross-sectional study asking participants directly about their experiences with calorie labeling in restaurants, fast food joints, and cafés in Riyadh found that a majority of respondents (87 percent) noticed calories were displayed on the menu but only half knew the recommended average daily caloric intake (Alassaf et al. 2020). Both studies had small sample sizes and were based on self-reported data. There is a strong need for more rigorous monitoring and evaluation of the calorie labeling policy.

## Food and beverage product reformulations

Product reformulation can help improve the quality of packaged food. Manufacturers typically reformulate their products either voluntarily, in response to changes in consumer preferences, or obligatorily, in response to government regulations. A study on the impact of different reformulation scenarios in France found the total impact of reformulation could amount to a 3.7–5.5 percent reduction in mortality (Leroy et al. 2016).

Mandatory product reformulation is more effective than voluntary commitments. A systematic review of the effectiveness of 26 policies (including voluntary limits and labeling) in real world settings to reduce trans fatty acids (TFAs) in food found that, overall, TFA content decreased with all types of policy interventions, with bans being most effective at eliminating TFA from the food supply (Downs, Thow, and Leeder 2013). Through multicomponent interventions, Denmark progressively reduced TFA consumption from 4.5 grams per day in 1976 to 1.5 grams per day in 1995, but TFAs were virtually eliminated after a law banning TFAs in manufactured food was implemented in 2004 (Hyseni et al. 2017). A study in Australia found that while current voluntary salt-reduction programs are cost-effective, population health benefits could be 20 times greater with government legislation on salt limits in processed foods (Cobiac, Vos, and Veerman 2010). Similarly, the UK SSB tax has been far more effective at decreasing sugar content than voluntary reduction in sugar content in prior years (Pell et al. 2021).

In Saudi Arabia, the SFDA issued a number of mandatory and voluntary product reformulation initiatives to encourage healthier changes in the food and beverage sector (SFDA 2018a; USDA FAS 2021). These are listed in table 7.4. The companies that signed these voluntary commitment initiatives are Nestlé Middle East, Mars Saudi Arabia & Gulf, Mondelez Arabia, Kellogg's Arabia, PepsiCo Global, Coca Cola, Unilever, General Mills Company, and Freezeland

**TABLE 7.4 Mandatory and voluntary regulations of food and beverage product reformulation in Saudi Arabia**

| MANDATORY | DATE OF IMPLEMENTATION | VOLUNTARY | DATE OF IMPLEMENTATION |
|---|---|---|---|
| Ban the use of *added sugar* or its sources (glucose syrup) and switch energy drinks to fresh juices and mixed juices in all food establishments in Saudi Arabia. | July 2020 | Replace *saturated fat* with unsaturated fat. | June 2018 |
| Set the maximum amount of *salt in* domestically produced bread at 1 gram (400 milligrams of sodium) per 100 grams of produced bread. | May 2019 | Reduce *portion sizes* for packaged food products. | June 2018 |
| Ban the use of *partially hydrogenated oils.* | January 2020 | Reduce the amount of *salt* in 21 food products other than bread. | January 2019 |

*Source:* Original table for this publication based on the Healthy Food Strategy (SFDA 2018a).

(Downs, Thow, and Leeder 2013). The companies are required to submit an annual report on the progress of their commitments to the SFDA (personal communication with SFDA). However, no evaluation studies exist yet.

## Marketing restrictions of unhealthy foods and beverages

Foods and drinks are promoted to children more than any other product type and in a far greater proportion than they are to adults (Singh et al. 2008). Children are exposed through television, at school and sports practice, in stores, at the movies, on mobile devices, and online (Institute of Medicine 2005). A 2019 study of television advertising in 22 countries around the world found, on average, four times more ads for unhealthy foods and drinks than for healthy ones during all television air time, and 35 percent more unhealthy food ads during children's peak viewing times (Kelly et al. 2019). While television has historically been the medium of choice to reach children, marketing via newer online, mobile, viral, and social media has increased considerably in recent years (Institute of Medicine 2005; Montgomery and Chester 2009).

Children are extremely vulnerable to food marketing, which can begin to affect them as early as preschool (Smith et al. 2019). Developmentally, they are highly impressionable, cannot yet recognize advertising intent, lack nutritional knowledge, and are motivated by immediate gratification rather than long-term consequences (Harris, Brownell, and Bargh 2009; Institute of Medicine 2005; PAHO 2011; Swinburn et al. 2011). These are reasons why the World Health Organization, the World Cancer Research Fund, and UNICEF, among others unequivocally recommend protecting children from exposure to unhealthy food marketing by restricting or banning the various forms of marketing targeting or viewed by children, by improving the nutritional profile of promoted products, or both (Institute of Medicine 2005; PAHO 2011).

Existing statutory regulations on unhealthy food marketing to children vary in what foods to include, how they define *children,* and which communication channels and marketing techniques are covered. However, the most common strategy is to restrict television advertising, primarily during children's programming (Taillie et al. 2019). Schools are also a common setting for restrictions. However, regulations on media such as cinema, mobile phone applications, print, packaging, and the internet are infrequent. Additionally, most policies focus on limiting child-directed marketing strategies such as licensed characters, with little attention paid to other marketing strategies such as health and nutrition claims (Taillie et al. 2019).

Emerging evaluation evidence from Chile's food labeling and marketing law is promising. Phase one of the law was applied only to children's broadcast media; it prohibited marketing to children under 14 years of age using themes or promotional strategies that appeal to children in any form of marketing, regardless of audience, media, or location (for example, interactive games, children's music, or apps). Evaluation from the first year shows that the percentage of television ads promoting unhealthy foods and drinks (that is, products that failed to meet the policies' nutrition criteria) decreased significantly—from 42 percent preregulation to 15 percent postregulation (Correa et al. 2020). Additionally, preschoolers' and adolescents' exposure to television advertising for regulated foods decreased significantly, by an average of 44 percent and 58 percent, respectively. Their exposure to regulated food advertising that featured child-directed appeals (for example, cartoon characters) also dropped by 35 percent and 52 percent, respectively (Carpentier et al. 2020).

In Saudi Arabia, the SFDA issued voluntary guidelines to restrict the marketing of unhealthy food and drink targeting children under 12 years of age. These guidelines target all media outlets (including social media). The criteria for unhealthy food are defined as all packaged food products or meals served in food establishments (restaurants, cafés, and other establishments) whose content exceeds either 30 percent of total energy from fat or 10 percent of total energy from saturated fat, or more than 400 milligrams of sodium per serving, or more than 10 percent of total energy from added sugar (SFDA n.d.).

## School-based policies

Schools are ideal vehicles for delivering overweight and obesity interventions to reach children. Children spend half of their waking hours and consume at least one-third of their daily calories in schools. Additionally, a recent systematic review of 50 trials found that school-based interventions are generally effective in reducing excessive weight gain of children, both as single component interventions (for example, physical activity only) and as multicomponent interventions (for example, physical activity and nutrition education). Specifically, physical activity interventions that had curricular sessions and emphasized participants' enjoyment were significantly more effective than interventions without these components, resulting in a drop in body mass index of 0.3 kilogram per square meter and 0.2 kilogram per square, respectively (Liu et al. 2019). Two systematic reviews found that school-based programs are likely effective in increasing the number of children engaged in in-school physical activity as well as the amount of time they spend engaged in these activities (Dobbins et al. 2013; Salmon et al. 2007).

Setting nutrition standards in schools can be effective in limiting unhealthy foods and promoting the consumption of healthier food options. A recent meta-analysis of 91 studies around the world found that setting nutrition standards increased fruit intake while reducing fat and sodium intake both within and outside of school settings (Micha et al. 2018). In 2012, Massachusetts implemented nutrition standards for foods sold in schools statewide; these standards have been associated with significant decreases in students' sugar consumption both during and after school hours (Cohen et al. 2018). In Brazil, an evaluation study seven years after implementation of the first municipal law regulating sales of unhealthy foods in schools found that nearly 70 percent of school vendors have stopped selling these items (Gabriel et al. 2009).

In Saudi Arabia, there are some school-based policies related to obesity prevention. In 2013, the country's Ministry of Education updated its Regulations of Health Conditions for School Canteens (MOE and MOH 2013), which contains a list of banned food items, namely, confectioneries, chocolates, chips, soda, sport drinks, sweetened beverages, all meat products, and fried food. Most boys' public high schools in Riyadh fully banned soda and sports drinks but offered highly processed energy-dense snacks for sale, including muffins, sweets, biscuits, cookies, and chips (Aldubayan and Murimi 2019). In 2017, the Ministry of Health and Ministry of Education launched the Rashaka Initiative program (box 7.1), which targets school-age students along with their parents and schoolteachers to increase their awareness about the importance of a healthy lifestyle. The initiative works toward improving the school environment by providing healthy food choices in school cafeterias (fruits, vegetables, whole-grain bread, and so on) and by inhibiting the sales of high-energy (high fat and sugar) snacks and drinks. It also promotes physical activity sessions (Al Eid et al. 2017). It is worth noting that, starting in 2017, girls' schools are able to hold physical activity classes as part of the King Abdullah Program for Education Development (*Tatweer*) initiative to increase physical activity in schools (Al-Hazzaa and AlMarzooqi 2018). However, to date there has been no evaluation evidence assessing the effectiveness or cost-effectiveness of this program.

## Media campaigns

Media campaigns are commonly used to affect various health behaviors in populations because of their ability to reach a wide audience at a relatively low cost (Wakefield, Loken, and Hornik 2010). A systematic review of overweight and obesity campaigns found that the evidence suggests that campaigns can have an impact on intermediate outcomes, such as knowledge and attitudes. However, evidence is still limited as to whether campaigns can influence behavior change (Kite et al. 2018). One study found that mass media campaigns (television, radio, cinema, online, and social media advertising, as well as stakeholder and community engagement) around the health harms of SSB consumption in Victoria resulted in a significant reduction in frequent SSB consumption compared to respondents from a different Australian state not exposed to the campaign (Morley et al. 2018).

As for physical activity promotion, a meta-analysis found that mass media campaigns boosted moderate intensity walking by 53 percent but neither reduced sedentary behavior nor led to achieving recommended levels of overall physical activity (Abioye, Hajifathalian, and Danasei 2013). Some interventions used posters and signs only to promote stair climbing and found that messages that are based on practical information, such as how many calories are lost by using the stairs (Eves et al. 2012), were more effective than motivational messages or signs (Avitsland, Solbraa, and Riiser 2017). Similar interventions were implemented in some workplaces in Saudi Arabia. However, evaluation studies are needed to explore the impact of these physical activity and healthy eating promotion campaigns and/or interventions in workplaces. One longitudinal study

**BOX 7.1**

## Rashaka initiative for obesity

The Rashaka Initiative screens for obesity and its complications considering the child's medical condition (including his or her body mass index, or BMI, measured by a trained nurse) and the family's medical history (see figure B7.1.1). Cases of obesity are identified and referred to primary health care professionals to receive medical care accordingly.

FIGURE B7.1.1

**Rashaka initiative flow chart**

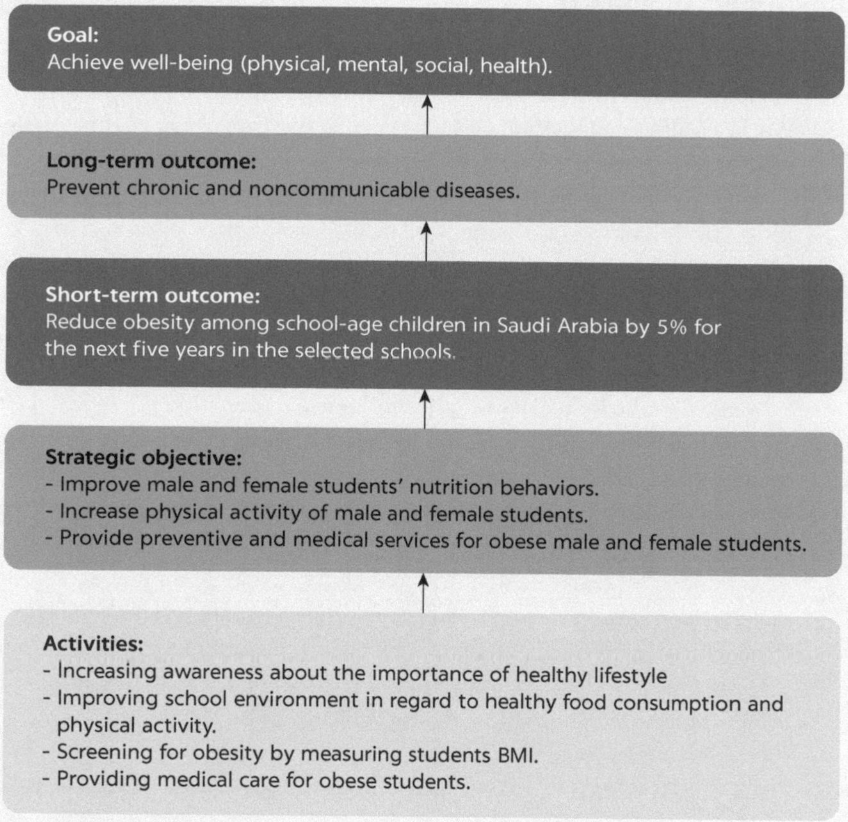

**Goal:**
Achieve well-being (physical, mental, social, health).

**Long-term outcome:**
Prevent chronic and noncommunicable diseases.

**Short-term outcome:**
Reduce obesity among school-age children in Saudi Arabia by 5% for the next five years in the selected schools.

**Strategic objective:**
- Improve male and female students' nutrition behaviors.
- Increase physical activity of male and female students.
- Provide preventive and medical services for obese male and female students.

**Activities:**
- Increasing awareness about the importance of healthy lifestyle
- Improving school environment in regard to healthy food consumption and physical activity.
- Screening for obesity by measuring students BMI.
- Providing medical care for obese students.

*Source:* Al Eid et al. 2017.

- The first phase of the program included 1,000 schools in six different regions: Aljouf, Jeddah (city), Makkah, Najran, Riyadh, and Eastern Region.
- Phase two of the program was to cover 6,000 schools by 2020 in all regions of Saudi Arabia, which is likely delayed because of the current COVID-19 situation (Al Eid et al. 2017).

actually examined the impact of a health promotion intervention in the workplace and found positive improvement (Altwaijri et al. 2019).

Increasing public awareness around obesity, healthy diet, and physical activity is emphasized in many of the national strategies in Saudi Arabia. A recent review of 10 physical activity–promoting initiatives in Saudi Arabia found that most of these initiatives were fragmented, short term, and not properly evaluated (Al-Hazzaa and AlMarzooqi 2018). Similar studies are needed to document and assess the impact of numerous public awareness campaigns related to obesity and healthy dietary patterns implemented in Saudi Arabia.

## KEY LESSONS LEARNED FROM GLOBAL EXPERIENCES

Building on global experience with obesity-related prevention policies, this section summarizes the four key lessons to consider for obesity-prevention efforts in Saudi Arabia to have a meaningful impact.

### Preventing and managing the food and beverage industry's conflict of interest

Involving industry in nutrition-related policy development, design, and implementation process early on can have negative consequences. In 2017, the World Health Organization (WHO) signaled its recognition of this problem of large corporations' potentially harmful roles in nutrition policy making in their draft Decision-Making Process and Tool (WHO 2017a). This tool is meant to assist governments in preventing and managing conflicts of interest in nutrition policy. While most WHO member states, nongovernmental organizations, and academic institutions strongly supported the tool, commercial sector organizations depicted it as inappropriate, unworkable, and incompatible with the Sustainable Development Goals (Lauber et al. 2020; Ralston et al. 2021).

Managing the industry's negative influence in nutrition policy will be challenging given the central role that food and beverage companies (particularly multi- or transnational companies) have in contemporary economies (Fooks and Godziewski 2020). However, with political will and commitment, this can be accomplished, and there are examples of mechanisms for doing so that have been adopted at regional, national, and global levels (Mialon et al. 2020). The main types of mechanisms include providing transparency; managing interactions with industry and conflicts of interest; identifying, monitoring, and educating about the practices of corporations and associated risks to public health; and prohibiting interactions with industry (Mialon et al. 2020).

### Using global and regional momentum to gather support

SSB taxes demonstrate the lead role that Saudi Arabia can play in influencing the health of not just Saudis but many GCC residents. This strong global momentum around SSB taxes, alongside other health taxes on tobacco and alcohol, may be aided by growing economic concerns due to COVID-19. However, the public's acceptance of new taxes (even if health related) may be low, and politicians may be reluctant to enact new or stricter consumption taxes at this time. One way to increase support for health taxes would be to link health taxes with financing new healthy food incentive and/or support programs for the neediest. The tax levels also need to be high enough to elicit responses from consumers (by lowering their demand for the products) and manufacturers (which will lower the sugar content if the tax is based on sugar density).

Front-of-package label policies, particularly mandatory warning labels, are also gaining strong momentum, especially since 2016, when Chile implemented the first phase of its food labeling and marketing law. In Latin America, Brazil, Chile, Mexico, Peru, and Uruguay have all passed or implemented mandatory warning forms of front-of-package labels. There is growing empirical evidence that these mandatory warning labels perform better than other mandated and voluntary front-of-package labels (Taillie, Hall, et al. 2020; Tallie, Reyes, et al. 2020); more research is under way as these policies become more widely implemented. Meanwhile, experimental studies show strong support for the promise they hold and the need for careful testing around the label design, size, color, placement, messaging used, and need to limit conflicting messages (Roberto et al. 2021).

Communication of the policies being considered and why there is a need for government action can also be bolstered through regional and global momentum, particularly given trading relationships. Common languages and media markets shared by countries within a region will also allow for potential crossover of mass media campaigns.

## Earmarking health tax revenues to support public health

To date, no country has explicitly earmarked revenues from national-level health taxes. However, local-level taxes have been a success, revenue-wise, via the creation of local commissions comprising community leaders and public health experts. Success can also be attributed to clear governance structures and grants administration systems to determine how the health tax revenue is spent. At the national level, something similar could be done via the creation of a national public health foundation, for example, which could receive an established share of the health tax revenues from tobacco, alcohol, sweetened beverages, and unhealthy ultraprocessed foods. Thailand's ThaiHealth provides an example of such an approach (Pongutta et al. 2019). The use of these health tax revenues can go toward the following:

- Mass media campaigns and public education of integrated policies
- Healthy food incentives toward the neediest (for example, cash transfer programs)
- Grants to small companies affected by the policies to help them adapt
- The marketing of healthy foods

## Developing a strict country-specific, nutrient-profiling model to undergird an integrated set of policies

To ensure that components of the diets that should be discouraged and those that should be encouraged are well targeted as well as consistently communicated to the public and industry, a series of well-integrated food and nutrition policies is needed. These policies will also provide a transparent and accountable way for industry to reformulate its products and innovate in ways that can be more supportive of health, so that they truly become partners with the government and health advocates. Accordingly, it is strongly recommended that a strict, evidence-based, country-specific nutrient profiling model be developed for the Saudi context (described in chapter 8).

## CONCLUSIONS

This chapter reviewed obesity prevention–related strategies, objectives, and policies and considered the evidence on their effectiveness and key lessons learned. These policies include ones that are implemented, proposed, or applicable to Saudi Arabia in light of local and global evidence and experiences.

While Saudi Arabia has made excellent strides toward implementing innovative policies that will likely have an impact on obesity prevention, a critical gap exists in implementation compliance as well as whether these policies are having their intended effect and how they can be built on and improved. Saudi Arabia has an opportunity to become a global innovation lab for overweight- and obesity-related policies and regulations if it invests in strong monitoring and evaluation frameworks and generates rigorous evidence, including small-scale randomized trials, mixed methods, secondary data analyses using scanner data or food-purchasing data, and large-scale evaluations.

## ANNEX 7A

TABLE 7A.1 **Selected examples of unhealthy beverage and food taxes (collected from distributors, manufacturers, or importers) and findings to date**

| EXAMPLES OF SITES WITH EXCISE TAXES | BRIEF DESCRIPTION OF TAX | PRICE CHANGE | VOLUME SALES OR PURCHASES CHANGE OF TAXED PRODUCTS | INTAKE CHANGE OF TAXED PRODUCTS | OTHER CHANGES | REVENUE USE | OTHER GAPS IN KNOWLEDGE |
|---|---|---|---|---|---|---|---|
| Berkeley, CA (since March 2015) | US$0.01 per ounce excise tax on SSBs. | ↑ | ↓ | ↔ ↓ | ↔ Unemployment to employment | Determined by committee or advisory board | Small geographical area (partially addressed by SSB taxes implemented in neighboring localities). |
| Oakland, CA (since July 2017) | US$0.01 per ounce excise tax on SSBs. | ↑↔ | ↔ | ↔ | ↓ Price promotions | Determined by committee or advisory board | Relatively low baseline levels of SSB consumption. |
| Philadelphia, PA (since Jan. 2017) | US$0.05 per ounce excise tax on both SSBs and artificially sweetened beverages. | ↑ | ↓ | ↓ or ↔ ↓ or ↔ | ↔ Employment | Office of Education (early-childhood education slots) and general budget | Some indication of cross-border shopping. |
| Mexico (since Jan 2014) | 1 peso per liter excise tax on SSBs. | ↑ | ↓ | ↓ | ↔ Unemployment to employment ↓ (Modeled) NCDs, mortality, and health care costs | General budget | Manufacturer response in terms of reformulations. |
| | 8 percent excise tax on nonessential foods with 275 kcals per 100 grams. | | ↓ | | ↔ Unemployment to employment | General budget | |
| United Kingdom (since April 2018) | 18 pence per liter for low sugar (5–8 grams; 24 pence per liter for high sugar (>8 grams sugar) among SSBs; excise tax. | ↑ | ↓ | TBD | ↓ Sugar ↓ Sugar content ↓ High sugar product availability ↓ Product size (Store brands) ↔ Stock market value | General budget | Impact of reformulations with artificially sweeteners unknown. |

*continued*

**TABLE 7A.1,** *continued*

| EXAMPLES OF SITES WITH EXCISE TAXES | BRIEF DESCRIPTION OF TAX | PRICE CHANGE | VOLUME SALES OR PURCHASES CHANGE OF TAXED PRODUCTS | INTAKE CHANGE OF TAXED PRODUCTS | OTHER CHANGES | REVENUE USE | OTHER GAPS IN KNOWLEDGE |
|---|---|---|---|---|---|---|---|
| South Africa (since April 2018) | 0.021 South African rand per gram of sugar in 100 milliliters of ready-to-drink SSBs above 4 g sugar excise tax. | ↑ | ↓ | ↓ | ↓ Sugar and calories | General budget (small percent given to Department of Health) | Impact of reformulations with artificially sweeteners unknown. |

*Source:* Original table for this publication.
*Note:* ↓ decrease; ↔ no effect; ↑ increase. NCDs = noncommunicable diseases; SSB = sugar-sweetened beverages; kcals = kilocalories; TBD = to be determined from ongoing research studies.

**TABLE 7A.2 Examples of different tax designs and evidence on their effectiveness**

| TYPE OF TAX | COUNTRY EXAMPLE | EVIDENCE | CONSIDERATIONS |
|---|---|---|---|
| Volume-based tax | Philadelphia, PA, United States implemented a US$0.02 per ounce tax on SSBs. | Lowered taxed beverage purchases by 38 percent with no negative impact on employment. | • Provides stable revenues, easier to administer<br>• Must be adjusted to inflation to avoid erosion over time<br>• Does not account for variations in sugar content<br>• Does not encourage industry reformulation |
| | Mexico implemented 1 peso per liter on all SSBs. | Overall, there was a 12 percent decrease in taxed beverage purchases posttax and a 4 percent increase in the purchases of unflavored bottled water compared to the counterfactual predicted beverage purchases without the tax. | |
| Sugar-content-based tax | South Africa announced charging about a tenth of a US$0.01 per gram of added sugar. | Not available yet. | • Easier for consumers to understand because it directly links amount of sugar to negative health outcomes<br>• Encourages industry reformulation<br>• Requires strong tax administration system |
| Tiered tax structure (different rates based on sugar content) | United Kingdom implemented a higher tax rate of 24 pence on drinks containing 8 grams of sugar per 100 milliliters and a lower tax of 18 pence on those with 5–8 grams of sugar per 100 milliliters. | The drinks over the lower tax sugar threshold had fallen by 33.8 percentage points.<br><br>Coca-Cola and Nestle have changed the formula for some soda products (Fanta has 24 percent less sugar). | • Encourages industry reformulation<br>• Requires strong tax administration system |
| Ad valorem tax (based on retail price) | GCC countries adopted a 50 percent tax on carbonated drinks and 100 percent tax on energy drinks. | Sales declined by 35 percent in Saudi Arabia compared to GCC countries without the tax. | • Easy to administer<br>• Accounts for inflation<br>• Potential for industry pricing manipulation<br>• No incentive for reformulation<br>• Not easy for consumers to understand |

*Source:* Original table for this publication.
*Note:* GCC = Gulf Cooperation Council; SSBs = sugar-sweetened beverages.

# REFERENCES

Abioye, A. I., K. Hajifathalian, and G. Danaei. 2013. "Do Mass Media Campaigns Improve Physical Activity? A Systematic Review and Meta-Analysis." *Archives of Public Health* 71 (1): 20. doi:10.1186/0778-7367-71-20.

Abu-Omar, K., A. Rutten, I. Burlacu, V. Schätzlein, S. Messing, and M. Suhrcke. 2017. "The Cost-Effectiveness of Physical Activity Interventions: A Systematic Review of Reviews." *Preventive Medicine Reports* 8: 72–78. doi:10.1016/j.pmedr.2017.08.006.

AEI (American Enterprise Institute). 2017. "Poverty, Hunger, and US Agricultural Policy: Do Farm Programs Affect the Nutrition of Poor Americans?" *AEI Post*, January 9. https://www.aei.org/research-products/report/poverty-hunger-and-us-agricultural-policy-do-farm-programs-affect-the-nutrition-of-poor-americans/.

Afshin, A., J. L. Peñalvo, L. Del Gobbo, J. Silva, M. Michaelson, M. O'Flaherty, S. Capewell, D. Spiegelman, G. Danaei, and D. Mozaffarian. 2017. "The Prospective Impact of Food Pricing on Improving Dietary Consumption: A Systematic Review and Meta-Analysis." *PLoS One* 12 (3): e0172277. doi:10.1371/journal.pone.0172277.

Alassaf, H. I., Y. A. Alaskar, B. F. Alqulaysh, M. A. Alshehri, M. Y. Alnosian, A. A. Alshamrani, and M. A. Al-Tannir. 2020. "Assessment of Knowledge, Attitudes and Practices of Saudi Adults about Calorie Labeling in Central Saudi Arabia." *Saudi Medical Journal* 41 (3): 296–303.

Aldubayan, K., and M. Murimi. 2019. "Compliance with School Nutrition Policy in Saudi Arabia: A Quantitative Study." *Eastern Mediterranean Health Journal* 25 (4): 230–38. doi:10.26719/emhj.18.034.

Al Eid, Ahmed J., Zahra A. Alahmed, Shaker A. Al-Omary, and Sabah M. Alharbi. 2017. "RASHAKA Program: A Collaborative Initiative between Ministry of Health and Ministry of Education to Control Childhood Obesity in Saudi Arabia." *Saudi Journal of Obesity* 5 (1): 22–27. http://www.saudijobesity.com/article.asp?issn=2347-2618;year=2017;volume=5;issue=1;spage=22;epage=27;aulast=Al#ref15.

Alfawzan, M., and A. Aljarallah. 2020. "The Impact of Calories Labeling Policy in Saudi Arabia: Comparing Physical and Online Channels." *PACIS 2020 Proceedings*, June. https://aisel.aisnet.org/pacis2020/151.

Al-Hazzaa, H. M., and M. A. AlMarzooqi. 2018. "Descriptive Analysis of Physical Activity Initiatives for Health Promotion in Saudi Arabia." *Frontiers in Public Health* 6: 329. doi:10.3389/fpubh.2018.00329.

Al-Jawaldeh, A., M. Rayner, C. Julia, I. Elmadfa, A. Hammerich, and K. McColl. 2020. "Improving Nutrition Information in the Eastern Mediterranean Region: Implementation of Front-of-Pack Nutrition Labelling." *Nutrients* 12 (2): 330. doi:10.3390/nu12020330.

Alkhaldy, A. A., D. S. Taha, S. E. Alsahafi, R. K. Naaman, and M. M. Alkhalaf. 2020. "Response of the Public and Restaurant Owners to the Mandatory Menu Energy-Labelling Implementation in Restaurants in Saudi Arabia." *Public Health Nutrition* May: 1–13. doi:10.1017/S1368980020000245.

AlMughthem, A., H. Jradi, and A. Bawazir. 2020. "Nutrition Food Labeling in the Saudi Market between Compliance and Relaxing Policy." *Asian Journal of Medicine and Health* June: 1–8. doi:10.9734/ajmah/2020/v18i530200.

Alsukait, R., P. Wilde, S. Bleich, G. Singh, and S. Folta. 2019. "Impact of Saudi Arabia's Sugary Drink Tax on Prices and Purchases (P10-066-19)." *Current Developments in Nutrition* 3 (nzz034.P10-066-19). doi:10.1093/cdn/nzz034.P10-066-19.

Alsukait, R., P. Wilde, S. N. Bleich, G. Singh, and S. C. Folta. 2020. "Evaluating Saudi Arabia's 50% Carbonated Drink Excise Tax: Changes in Prices and Volume Sales." *Economics and Human Biology* 38 (August): 100868. doi:10.1016/j.ehb.2020.100868.

Altwaijri, Y., S. Hyder, L. Bilal. M. T. Naseem, D. AlSaqabi, F. AlSuwailem, M. Aradati, and E. DeVol. 2019. "Evaluating the Impact of a Workplace Wellness Program in Saudi Arabia: An Intra-Department Study." *Journal of Occupational and Environmental Medicine* 61 (9): 760–66. doi:10.1097/JOM.0000000000001656. PMID: 31233008.

*Arab News*. 2019. "SFDA Finds 70 Per Cent Shops Labeling Food Correctly." June 7. https://www.arabnews.com/node/1507301/saudi-arabia.

Åvitsland, A., A. K. Solbraa, and A. Riiser. 2017. "Promoting Workplace Stair Climbing: Sometimes, Not Interfering Is the Best." *Archives of Public Health* 75 (2). doi:10.1186/s13690 -016-0170-8. PMID: 28078084; PMCID: PMC5220617.

Baker, P., P. Machado, T. Santos, K. Sievert, K. Backholer, M. Hadjikakou, C. Russell, O. Huse, C. Bell, G. Scrinis, A. Worsley, S. Friel, and M. Lawrence. 2020. "Ultra-Processed Foods and the Nutrition Transition: Global, Regional and National Trends, Food Systems Transformations and Political Economy Drivers." *Obesity Reviews* 12 (12): e13126. doi:10.1111/obr.13126.

Barrientos-Gutierrez, T., R. Zepeda-Tello, E. R. Rodrigues, A. Colchero-Aragonés, R. Rojas-Martínez, E. Lazcano-Ponce, M. Hernández-Ávila, J. Rivera-Dommarco, and R. Meza. 2017. "Expected Population Weight and Diabetes Impact of the 1-Peso-per-Litre Tax to Sugar Sweetened Beverages in Mexico." *PLoS One* 12 (5): e0176336. doi:10.1371/journal.pone.0176336.

Bartlett, S., L. Olsho, and K. Jacob. 2014. *Evaluation of the Healthy Incentives Pilot (HIP): Final Report*. Washington, DC: US Department of Agriculture, Food and Nutrition Service. http://www.fns.usda.gov/sites/default/files/HIP-Final.pdf.

Batis, C., J. A. Rivera, B. M. Popkin, and L. Smith Taillie. 2016. "First-Year Evaluation of Mexico's Tax on Nonessential Energy-Dense Foods: An Observational Study." *PLoS Medicine* 13 (7): e1002057. doi:10.1371/journal.pmed.1002057.

Berry, C., S. Burton, E. Howlett, and C. L. Newman. 2019. "Understanding the Calorie Labeling Paradox in Chain Restaurants: Why Menu Calorie Labeling Alone May Not Affect Average Calories Ordered." *Journal of Public Policy and Marketing* 38 (2): 192–213. doi:10.1177 /0743915619827013.

Bin Sunaid, Faisal F., Ayoub Al-Jawaldeh, Meshal W. Almutairi, Rawan A. Alobaid, Tagreed M. Alfuraih, Faisal N. Bensaidan, Atheer S. Alragea, Lulu A. Almutairi, Ali F. Duhaim, Talal A. Alsaloom, and Jana Jabbour. 2021. "Saudi Arabia's Healthy Food Strategy: Progress & Hurdles in the 2030 Road." *Nutrients* 13, (7): 2130. https://doi.org/10.3390/nu13072130.

Bíró, A. 2015. "Did the Junk Food Tax Make the Hungarians Eat Healthier?" *Food Policy* 54 (July): 107–15. doi:10.1016/j.foodpol.2015.05.003.

Bleich, S. N., C. D. Economos, M. L. Spiker, K. A. Vercammen, E. R. VanEpps, J. P. Block, B. Elbel, M. Story, and C. A. Roberto. 2017. "A Systematic Review of Calorie Labeling and Modified Calorie Labeling Interventions: Impact on Consumer and Restaurant Behavior." *Obesity* 25 (12): 2018–44. doi:10.1002/oby.21940.

Boysen, O., K. Boysen-Urban, H. Bradford, and J. Balié. 2019. "Taxing Highly Processed Foods: What Could Be the Impacts on Obesity and Underweight in Sub-Saharan Africa?" *World Development* 119: 55–67. doi:10.1016/j.worlddev.2019.03.006.

Briggs, A. D. M., O. T. Mytton, A. Kehlbacher, R. Tiffin, A. Elhussein, M. Rayner, S. A. Jebb, T. Blakely, and P. Scarborough. 2017. "Health Impact Assessment of the UK Soft Drinks Industry Levy: A Comparative Risk Assessment Modelling Study." *Lancet Public Health* 2 (1): e15–22. doi:10.1016/S2468-2667(16)30037-8.

Carpentier, F. R. Dillman, T. Correa, M. Reyes, and L. Smith Taillie. 2020. "Evaluating the Impact of Chile's Marketing Regulation of Unhealthy Foods and Beverages: Preschool and Adolescent Children's Changes in Exposure to Food Advertising on Television." *Public Health Nutrition* 23 (4): 747–55. doi:10.1017/S1368980019003355.

Carter, H. E., D. J. Schofield, R. Shrestha, and L. Veerman. 2019. "The Productivity Gains Associated with a Junk Food Tax and Their Impact on Cost-Effectiveness." *PLoS One* 14 (7): e0220209. doi:10.1371/journal.pone.0220209.

Cawley, J., A. M. Thow, K. Wen, and D. Frisvold. 2019. "The Economics of Taxes on Sugar-Sweetened Beverages: A Review of the Effects on Prices, Sales, Cross-Border Shopping, and Consumption." *Annual Review of Nutrition* 39 (1). doi:10.1146/annurev-nutr-082018-124603.

Choi, S. E., H. Seligman, and S. Basu. 2017. "Cost-Effectiveness of Subsidizing Fruit and Vegetable Purchases through the Supplemental Nutrition Assistance Program." *American Journal of Preventive Medicine* 52 (5): e147–55. doi:10.1016/j.amepre.2016.12.013.

Cobiac, L. J., T. Vos, and J. Lennert Veerman. 2010. "Cost-Effectiveness of Interventions to Reduce Dietary Salt Intake." *Heart* 96 (23): 1920–25. doi:10.1136/hrt.2010.199240.

Cohen, J. F. W., M. T. Gorski Finding, L. Rosenfeld, L. Smith, E. B. Rimm, and J. A. Hoffman. 2018. "The Impact of One Year of Healthier School Food Policies on Students' Diets During and Outside of the School Day." *Journal of the Academy of Nutrition and Dietetics* 18 (12): 2296 –2301. https://www.jandonline.org/article/S2212-2672(18)31348-0/fulltext.

Correa, T., M. Reyes, L. Smith Taillie, C. Corvalán, and F. R. Dillman Carpentier. 2020. "Food Advertising on Television Before and After a National Unhealthy Food Marketing Regulation in Chile, 2016–2017." *American Journal of Public Health* 110 (7): 1054–59. doi:10.2105 /AJPH.2020.305658.

Corvalán, C., M. Reyes, M. L. Garmendia, and R. Uauy. 2019. "Structural Responses to the Obesity and Non-Communicable Diseases Epidemic: Update on the Chilean Law of Food Labelling and Advertising." *Obesity Reviews: An Official Journal of the International Association for the Study of Obesity* 20 (3): 367–74. doi:10.1111/obr.12802.

de Koning, L., V. S. Malik, M. D. Kellogg, E. B. Rimm, W. C. Willett, and F. B. Hu. 2012. "Sweetened Beverage Consumption, Incident Coronary Heart Disease, and Biomarkers of Risk in Men." *Circulation* 125 (14): 1735–41, S1. doi:10.1161/CIRCULATIONAHA.111.067017.

de Koning, L., V. S. Malik, E. B. Rimm, W. C. Willett, and F. B. Hu. 2011. "Sugar-Sweetened and Artificially Sweetened Beverage Consumption and Risk of Type 2 Diabetes in Men." *American Journal of Clinical Nutrition* 93 (6): 1321–27. doi:10.3945/ajcn.110.007922.

Dobbins, M., H. Husson, K. DeCorby, and R. L. LaRocca. 2013. "School-Based Physical Activity Programs for Promoting Physical Activity and Fitness in Children and Adolescents Aged 6 to 18." *Cochrane Database of Systemic Reviews* (2): CD007651. doi:10.1002/14651858 .CD007651.pub2.

Downs, S. M., A. M. Thow, and S. R. Leeder. 2013. "The Effectiveness of Policies for Reducing Dietary Trans Fat: A Systematic Review of the Evidence." *Bulletin of the World Health Organization* 91 (April): 262–69. doi:10.2471/BLT.12.111468.

Evenson, K. R., A. H. Herring, and S.L. Huston. 2005. "Evaluating Change in Physical Activity with the Building of a Multi-Use Trail." *American Journal of Preventive Medicine* 28 (2 suppl 2): 177–85.

Eves, F. F., O. J. Webb, C. Griffin, and J, Chambers. 2010. "A Multi-Component Stair Climbing Promotional Campaign Targeting Calorific Expenditure for Worksites: A Quasi-Experimental Study Testing Effects on Behaviour, Attitude and Intention." *BMC Public Health* 12 (423). doi:10.1186/1471-2458-12-423.

Fernandes, A. C., R. C. Oliveira, R. P. C. Proença, C. C. Curioni, V. M. Rodrigues, and G. M. R. Fiates. 2016. "Influence of Menu Labeling on Food Choices in Real-Life Settings: A Systematic Review." *Nutrition Reviews* 74 (8): 534–48. doi:10.1093/nutrit/nuw013.

Finkelstein, E. A., F. J. L. Ang, B. Doble, W. H. M. Wong, and R. M. van Dam. 2019. "A Randomized Controlled Trial Evaluating the Relative Effectiveness of the Multiple Traffic Light and Nutri-Score Front of Package Nutrition Labels." *Nutrients* 11 (9): 2236. doi:10.3390/nu11092236.

Food Standards Scotland. 2016. *Guide to Creating a Front of Pack Nutrition Label for Pre-Packed Products Sold through Retail Outlets.* Aberdeen: Food Standards Scotland. https://www .foodstandards.gov.scot/publications-and-research/publications/guide-to-creating -a-front-of-pack-nutrition-label-for-pre-packed-products-s.

Fooks, G. J., and C. Godziewski. 2020. "The World Health Organization, Corporate Power, and the Prevention and Management of Conflicts of Interest in Nutrition Policy: Comment on 'Towards Preventing and Managing Conflict of Interest in Nutrition Policy? An Analysis of Submissions to a Consultation on a Draft WHO Tool.'" *International Journal of Health Policy and Management.* https://plu.mx/plum/a/?doi=10.34172/ijhpm.2020.156.

Gabriel, C. G., and C. Vasconcelos, D. F. Andrade, and BeA. Schmitz. 2009. "First Law Regulating School Canteens in Brazil: Evaluation after Seven Years of Implementation." *Archives of Latin America Nutrition* 59 (2): 128–38. https://www.alanrevista.org/ediciones/2009/2/art-3/.

GAZT (General Authority of Zakat and Tax). n.d.-a. "Excise Tax." E-Services Portal, accessed September 29, 2018. http://www.gazt.gov.sa/en.

GAZT (General Authority of Zakat and Tax). n.d.-b. "User Manual and Guidelines." Help Center Portal, accessed October 19, 2020. http://www.gazt.gov.sa/en.

Gorski Findling, M. T., P. M. Werth, A. A. Musicus, M. A. Bragg, D. J. Graham, B. Elbel, and C. A. Roberto. 2018. "Comparing Five Front-of-Pack Nutrition Labels' Influence on Consumers' Perceptions and Purchase Intentions." *Preventive Medicine* 106: 114–21. doi:10.1016/j.ypmed.2017.10.022.

Grummon, A. H., and M. G. Hall. 2020. "Sugary Drink Warnings: A Meta-Analysis of Experimental Studies." *PLoS Medicine* 17 (5): e1003120. doi:10.1371/journal.pmed.1003120.

Grummon, A. H., B. B. Lockwood, D. Taubinsky, and H. Allcott. 2019. "Designing Better Sugary Drink Taxes." *Science* 365 (6457): 989–90. doi:10.1126/science.aav5199.

GSO (GCC Standardization Organization). 2018. *Final Draft of Standard FDS, Prepared by GSO Technical Committee No. TC05, GSO 05/FDS 2233, Requirements of Nutritional Labelling.* Riyadh: Gulf Cooperation Council. https://members.wto.org/crnattachments/2018/TBT /SAU/18_5864_00_e.pdf.

Harris, J. L., K. D. Brownell, and J. A. Bargh. 2009. "The Food Marketing Defense Model: Integrating Psychological Research to Protect Youth and Inform Public Policy." *Social Issues and Policy Review* 3 (1): 211–71. doi:10.1111/j.1751-2409.2009.01015.x.

Healthy Food America. n.d. *Main Report: Healthy Food Pricing Incentives—Designing Successful Programs.* Seattle: Healthy Food America. https://www.healthyfoodamerica .org/healthy_food_pricing_incentives.

Helfer, P., and T. R. Shultz. 2014. "The Effects of Nutrition Labeling on Consumer Food Choice: A Psychological Experiment and Computational Model." *Annals of the New York Academy of Sciences* 1331: 174–85.

Hu, F. B. 2013. "Resolved: There Is Sufficient Scientific Evidence That Decreasing Sugar-Sweetened Beverage Consumption Will Reduce the Prevalence of Obesity and Obesity-Related Diseases." *Obesity Reviews* 14 (8): 606–19. doi:10.1111/obr.12040.

Huang, Y., C. Kypridemos, J. Liu, Y. Lee, J. Pearson-Stuttard, B. Collins, P. Bandosz, S. Capewell, L. Whitsel, P. Wilde, D. Mozaffarian, M. O'Flaherty, R. Micha, and Food-PRICE Project. 2019. "Cost-Effectiveness of the US Food and Drug Administration Added Sugar Labeling Policy for Improving Diet and Health." *Circulation* 139 (23): 2613–24. doi:10.1161 /CIRCULATIONAHA.118.036751.

Hyseni, L., H. Bromley, C. Kypridemos, M. O'Flaherty, F. Lloyd-Williams, M. Guzman-Castillo, J. Pearson-Stuttard, and S. Capewell. 2017. "Systematic Review of Dietary Trans-Fat Reduction Interventions." *Bulletin of the World Health Organization* 95 (12): 821–30G. doi:10.2471/BLT.16.189795.

Imamura, F., L. O'Connor, Z. Ye, J. Mursu, Y. Hayashino, S. N. Bhupathiraju, and N. G. Forouhi. 2016. "Consumption of Sugar-Sweetened Beverages, Artificially Sweetened Beverages, and Fruit Juice and Incidence of Type 2 Diabetes: Systematic Review, Meta-Analysis, and Estimation of Population Attributable Fraction." *British Medical Journal* 351: h3576. doi:10.1136/bjsports-2016-h3576rep.

Institute of Medicine. 2005. *Food Marketing to Children and Youth: Threat or Opportunity?* Washington, DC: National Academies Press. doi:10.17226/11514.

Kelly, B., and J. Jewell. 2018. *What Is the Evidence on the Policy Specifications, Development Processes and Effectiveness of Existing Front-of-Pack Food Labelling Policies in the WHO European Region?* Copenhagen: WHO Regional Office for Europe. https://www.euro.who .int/en/publications/abstracts/what-is-the-evidence-on-the-policy-specifications ,-development-processes-and-effectiveness-of-existing-front-of-pack-food-labelling-policies -in-the-who-european-region-2018.

Kelly, B., S. Vandevijvere, S. H. Ng, J. Adams, L. Allemandi, L. Bahena-Espina, S. Barquera, E. Boyland, P. Calleja, I. C. Carmona-Garcés, L. Castronuovo, D. Cauchi, T. Correa, C. Corvalán, E. L. Cosenza-Quintana, C. Fernández-Escobar, L. I. González-Zapata, J. Halford, N. Jaichuen, M. L. Jensen, T. Karupaiah, A. Kaur, M. F. Kroker-Lobos, Z. Mchiza, K. Miklavec, W. Parker, M. Potvin Kent, I. Pravst, M. Ramírez-Zea, S. Reiff, M. Reyes, M. Á. Royo-Bordonada, P. Rueangsom, P. Scarborough, M. V. Tiscornia, L. Tolentino-Mayo, J. Wate, M. White, I. Zamora-Corrales, L. Zeng, and B. Swinburn. 2019. "Global Benchmarking of Children's Exposure to Television Advertising of Unhealthy Foods and Beverages across 22 Countries." *Obesity Reviews: An Official Journal of the International Association for the Study of Obesity* 20 Suppl 2 (November): 116–28. doi:10.1111/obr.12840.

Khandpur, N., E. B. Rimm, and A. J. Moran. 2020. "The Influence of the New US Nutrition Facts Label on Consumer Perceptions and Understanding of Added Sugars: A Randomized Controlled Experiment." *Journal of the Academy of Nutrition and Dietetics* 120 (2): 197–209. doi:10.1016/j.jand.2019.10.008.

Kite, J., A. Grunseit, E. Bohn-Goldbaum, B. Bellew, T. Carroll, and A. Bauman. 2018. "A Systematic Search and Review of Adult-Targeted Overweight and Obesity Prevention Mass Media Campaigns and Their Evaluation: 2000–2017." *Journal of Health Communication* 23 (2): 207–32. doi:10.1080/10810730.2018.1423651.

KSA (Kingdom of Saudi Arabia). 2016. *Health Sector Transformation Program: Vision 2030*. Ryadh: KSA. https://www.vision2030.gov.sa/v2030/vrps/hstp/.

Lauber, K., R. Ralston, M. Mialon, A. Carriedo, and A. B. Gilmore. 2020. "Non-Communicable Disease Governance in the Era of the Sustainable Development Goals: A Qualitative Analysis of Food Industry Framing in WHO Consultations." *Globalization and Health* 16: 76. doi:10.1186/s12992-020-00611-1.

Lawrence, M. A., and P. I. Baker. 2019. "Ultra-Processed Food and Adverse Health Outcomes." *British Medical Journal* 365 (May): l2289. doi:10.1136/bmj.l2289.

Lee, Y., D. Mozaffarian, S. Sy, Y. Huang, J. Liu, P. E. Wilde, S. Abrahams-Gessel, T. de Souza Veiga Jardim, T. A. Gaziano, and R. Micha. 2019. "Cost-Effectiveness of Financial Incentives for Improving Diet and Health through Medicare and Medicaid: A Microsimulation Study." *PLoS Medicine* 16 (3): e1002761. doi:10.1371/journal.pmed.1002761.

Lee, Y., D. Mozaffarian, S. Sy, J. Liu, P. E. Wilde, M. Marklund, S. Abrahams-Gessel, T. A. Gaziano, and R. Micha. 2020. "Health Impact and Cost-Effectiveness of Volume, Tiered, and Absolute Sugar Content Sugar-Sweetened Beverage Tax Policies in the United States." *Circulation* 142 (6): 523–34. doi:10.1161/CIRCULATIONAHA.119.042956.

Leroy, P., V. Réquillart, L.-G. Soler, and G. Enderli. 2016. "An Assessment of the Potential Health Impacts of Food Reformulation." *European Journal of Clinical Nutrition* 70 (6): 694–99. doi:10.1038/ejcn.2015.201.

Liu, Z., H.-M. Zu, L.-M. Wen, Y.-Z. Peng, S. Zhou, W.-H. Li, and H.-H. Wang. 2019. "A Systematic Review and Meta-Analysis of the Overall Effects of School-Based Obesity Prevention Interventions and Effect Differences by Intervention Components." *International Journal of Behavioral Nutrition and Physical Activity* 16: 95. doi:10.1186/s12966-019-0848-8.

Malik, V. S. 2017. "Sugar-Sweetened Beverages and Cardiometabolic Health." *Current Opinion in Cardiology* 32 (5): 572–79. doi:10.1097/HCO.0000000000000439.

Manyema, M., L. J. Veerman, L. Chola, A. Tugendhaft, B. Sartorius, D. Labadarios, and K. J. Hofman. 2014. "The Potential Impact of a 20% Tax on Sugar-Sweetened Beverages on Obesity in South African Adults: A Mathematical Model." *PLoS One* 9 (8): e105287. doi:10.1371/journal.pone.0105287.

Mialon, M., S. Vandevijvere, A. Carriedo-Lutzenkirchen, L. Bero, F. Gomes, and M. Petticrew. 2020. "Mechanisms for Addressing and Managing the Influence of Corporations on Public Health Policy, Research and Practice: A Scoping Review." *British Medical Journal Open* 10 (7): e034082. doi:10.1136/bmjopen-2019-034082.

Micha, R., D. Karageorgou, I. Bakogianni, E. Trichia, L. P. Whitsel, M. Stolry, J. L. Peñalvo, and D. Mozaffarian. 2018. "Effectiveness of School Food Environment Policies on Children's Dietary Behaviors: A Systematic Review and Meta-Analysis." *PLoS One* 13 (3): e0194555.

MOE and MOH (Ministry of Education and Ministry of Health). 2013. *Health Requirements for School Canteens*. Riyadh: MOE (in Arabic). https://departments.moe.gov.sa/schoolaffairsagency/RelatedDepartments/SchoolHealth/Documents/--%D8%A7%D9%84%D8%A7%D8%B4%D8%AA%D8%B1%D8%A7%D8%B7%D8%A7%D8%AA%20%D8%A7%D9%84%D8%B5%D8%AD%D9%8A%D8%A9%20%D8%A7%D9%84%D9%85%D8%B1%D9%81%D9%82%D8%A9%20%D8%A8%D8%A7%D9%84%D8%AA%D8%B9%D9%85%D9%8A%D9%85-.pdf.

MOH (Ministry of Health). 2010. *National Strategy for Prevention of Cardiovascular Disease*. Riyadh: MOH. https://extranet.who.int/ncdccs/Data/SAU_B4_الخطة الوطنية لمكافحة الأمراض القلبية والوعائية.doc.

MOH (Ministry of Health). 2014a. *Diet and Physical Activity Strategy (DAPS)*. Riyadh: MOH. https://extranet.who.int/ncdccs/Data/SAU_B11_KSA NATIONAL STRATEGY FOR DIET AND PHYSICAL ACTIVITY.pdf.

MOH (Ministry of Health). 2014b. *KSA National Strategy for Prevention of NCDs*. Riyadh: MOH. https://extranet.who.int/ncdccs/Data/SAU_B3_الخطة الوطنية لمكافحة الأمراض غير السارية المعدلة.doc.

MOH (Ministry of Health). 2014c. *National Executive Plan for Diabetes Control.* Riyadh: MOH. https://extranet.who.int/ncdccs/Data/SAU_B6_الخطة الوطنية للسكري.doc.

MOH (Ministry of Health). 2014d. *Obesity Control Program Strategy 2014–2025.* Riyadh: MOH. https://extranet.who.int/ncdccs/Data/SAU_B10_استراتيجة برنامج مكافحة السمنة.docx.

Monteiro, C. A., J.-C. Moubarac, G. Cannon, S. W. Ng, and B. Popkin. 2013. "Ultra-Processed Products Are Becoming Dominant in the Global Food System." *Obesity Reviews* 14 (November): 21–28. doi:10.1111/obr.12107.

Montgomery, K. C., and J. Chester. 2009. "Interactive Food and Beverage Marketing: Targeting Adolescents in the Digital Age." *Journal of Adolescent Health* 45 (3) (Supplement): S18–29. doi:10.1016/j.jadohealth.2009.04.006.

Morley, B. C., P. H. Niven, H. G. Dixon, M. G. Swanson, A. B. McAleese, and M. A. Wakefield. 2018. "Controlled Cohort Evaluation of the LiveLighter Mass Media Campaign's Impact on Adults' Reported Consumption of Sugar-Sweetened Beverages." *British Medical Journal Open* 8 (4): e019574. doi:10.1136/bmjopen-2017-019574.

Moubarac, J.-C., A. P. B. Martins, R. M. Claro, R. B. Levy, G. Cannon, and C. A. Monteiro. 2013. "Consumption of Ultra-Processed Foods and Likely Impact on Human Health. Evidence from Canada." *Public Health Nutrition* 16 (12): 2240–48. doi:10.1017/S1368980012005009.

Niebylski, M. L., K. A. Redburn, T. Duhaney, and N. R. Campbell. 2015. "Healthy Food Subsidies and Unhealthy Food Taxation: A Systematic Review of the Evidence." *Nutrition* 31 (6): 787–95. doi:10.1016/j.nut.2014.12.010.

PAHO (Pan American Health Organization). 2011. *Recommendations from a Pan American Health Organization Expert Consultation on the Marketing of Food and Non-Alcoholic Beverages to Children in the Americas.* Washington, DC: Pan American Health Organization. https://iris.paho.org/handle/10665.2/3594.

Pell, D., O. Mytton, T. L. Penney, A. Briggs, S. Cummins, C. Penn-Jones, M. Rayner, et al. 2021. "Changes in Soft Drinks Purchased by British Households Associated with the UK Soft Drinks Industry Levy: Controlled Interrupted Time Series Analysis." *BMJ* 372. https://www.bmj.com/content/372/bmj.n254.

Petimar, J., F. Zhang, L. P. Cleveland, D. Simon, S. L. Gortmaker, M. Polacsek, S. N. Bleich, E. B. Rimm, C. A. Roberto, and J. P. Block. 2019. "Estimating the Effect of Calorie Menu Labeling on Calories Purchased in a Large Restaurant Franchise in the Southern United States: Quasi-Experimental Study." *British Medical Journal* 367 (October): l5837. doi:10.1136/bmj.l5837.

Pongutta, S., R. Suphanchaimat, W. Patcharanarumol, and V. Tangcharoensathien. 2019. "Lessons from the Thai Health Promotion Foundation." *Bulletin of the World Health Organization* 97 (3): 213–20. doi:10.2471/BLT.18.220277.

Pries, A. M., S. Filteau, and E. L. Ferguson. 2019. "Snack Food and Beverage Consumption and Young Child Nutrition in Low- and Middle-Income Countries: A Systematic Review." *Maternal and Child Nutrition* 15 Suppl 4 (June): e12729. doi:10.1111/mcn.12729.

Pries, A. M., A. M. Rehman, S. Filteau, N. Sharma, A. Upadhyay, and E. L. Ferguson. 2019. "Unhealthy Snack Food and Beverage Consumption Is Associated with Lower Dietary Adequacy and Length-for-Age z-Scores among 12-23-Month-Olds in Kathmandu Valley, Nepal." *Journal of Nutrition* 149 (10): 1843–51. doi:10.1093/jn/nxz140.

Ralston, R., S. E. Hil, F. Silva Gomes, and J. Collin. 2021. "Towards Preventing and Managing Conflict of Interest in Nutrition Policy? An Analysis of Submissions to a Consultation on a Draft WHO Tool." *International Journal of Health Policy and Management* 10 (5): 255–65. doi:10.34172/ijhpm.2020.52.

Reyes, M., L. Smith Taillie, B. Popkin, R. Kanter, S. Vandevijvere, and C. Corvalán. 2020. "Changes in the Amount of Nutrient of Packaged Foods and Beverages after the Initial Implementation of the Chilean Law of Food Labelling and Advertising: A Nonexperimental Prospective Study." *PLoS Medicine* 17 (7): e1003220. doi:10.1371/journal.pmed.1003220.

Rissel, C., S. Greaves, L. M. Wen, M. Crane, and C. Standen. 2015. "Use of and Short-Term Impacts of New Cycling Infrastructure in Inner-Sydney, Australia: A Quasi-Experimental Design." *International Journal of Behavioral Nutrition and Physical Activity* 12: 129.

Roberto, C. A., S. W. Ng, D. Hammond, S. Barquera, A. Jauregui, L. Smith Taillie. 2021. "The Influence of Front-of-Package Nutrition Labeling on Consumer Behavior and Product Reformulation." *Annual Review of Nutrition* 41 (October): 529–50. doi: 10.1146/annurev-nutr-111120-094932.

Salgado, J. C., and S. W. Ng. 2019. "Understanding Heterogeneity in Price Changes and Firm Responses to a National Unhealthy Food Tax in Mexico." *Food Policy* 89 (December): 101783. doi:10.1016/j.foodpol.2019.101783.

Salmon, J., M. L. Booth, P. Phongsavan, N. Murphy, and A. Timperio. 2007. "Promoting Physical Activity Participation among Children and Adolescents." *Epidemiologic Reviews* 29 (1): 144–59.

Sánchez-Romero, L. M., J. Penko, P. G. Coxson, A. Fernández, A. Mason, A. E. Moran, L. Ávila-Burgos, M. Odden, S. Barquera, and K. Bibbins-Domingo. 2016. "Projected Impact of Mexico's Sugar-Sweetened Beverage Tax Policy on Diabetes and Cardiovascular Disease: A Modeling Study." *PLoS Medicine* 13 (11): e1002158. doi:10.1371/journal.pmed.1002158.

SCDC (Saudi Center for Disease Prevention and Control). 2019. *Obesity Control and Prevention Strategy 2020–2030.* Unpublished SCDC document.

SFDA (Saudi Food and Drug Authority). 2018a. *Healthy Food Strategy* (استراتيجية الغذاء الصحي). Riyadh: SFDA. https://old.sfda.gov.sa/ar/awareness/Documents/SFDA-HealthyFoodStrategy.pdf.

SFDA (Saudi Food and Drug Administration). 2018b. *Traffic Light Label Example.* Riyadh: SFDA. https://sfda.gov.sa/sites/default/files/2019-11/ND2-min.jpg.

SFDA (Saudi Food and Drug Administration). 2018c. *Traffic Light Label Example.* Riyadh: SFDA https://sfda.gov.sa/sites/default/files/2019-11/ND6-min.jpg.

SFDA (Saudi Food and Drug Administration). n.d. "Guidelines for Marketing Requirements of Food Directed to Children," vers. 1. Riyadh: SFDA. https://istitlaa.ncc.gov.sa/ar/health/sfda/kidsfood/Documents/%D9%85%D8%B3%D9%88%D8%AF%D8%A9%20%D8%AF%D9%84%D9%8A%D9%84%20%D8%B6%D9%88%D8%A7%D8%A8%D8%B7%20%D9%88%D8%A7%D8%B4%D8%AA%D8%B1%D8%A7%D8%B7%D8%A7%D8%AA%20%D8%A7%D9%84%D8%A7%D8%B9%D9%84%D8%A7%D9%86%20%D8%B9%D9%86%20%D8%A7%D9%84%D8%A3%D8%BA%D8%B0%D9%8A%D8%A9%20%D8%A7%D9%84%D9%85%D9%88%D8%AC%D9%87%D8%A9%20%D9%84%D9%84%D8%A3%D8%B7%D9%81%D8%A7%D9%84.pdf.

Shangguan, S., A. Afshin, M. Shulkin, W. Ma, D. Marsden, J. Smith, M. Saheb-Kashaf, P. Shi, R. Micha, F. Imamura, and D. Mozaffarian. 2019. "A Meta-Analysis of Food Labeling Effects on Consumer Diet Behaviors and Industry Practices." *American Journal of Preventive Medicine* 56 (2): 300–14. doi:10.1016/j.amepre.2018.09.024.

Shephard, R. J. 2008. "Is Active Commuting the Answer to Population Health?" *Sports Medicine* 38 (9): 751–8.

Shu, S., D. C. Quiros, R. Wang, and Y. Zhu. 2014. "Changes of Street Use and On-Road Air Quality before and after Complete Street Retrofit: An Exploratory Case Study in Santa Monica, California." *Transportation Research Part D: Transport and Environment* 32: 387–96.

Singh, A. S., C. Mulder, J. W. R. Twisk, W. van Mechelen, and M. J. M. Chinapaw. 2008. "Tracking of Childhood Overweight into Adulthood: A Systematic Review of the Literature." *Obesity Reviews: An Official Journal of the International Association for the Study of Obesity* 9 (5): 474–88. doi:10.1111/j.1467-789X.2008.00475.x.

Smith, R., B. Kelly, H. Yeatman, and E. Boyland. 2019. "Food Marketing Influences Children's Attitudes, Preferences and Consumption: A Systematic Critical Review." *Nutrients* 11 (4). doi:10.3390/nu11040875.

Srour, B., L. K. Fezeu, E. Kesse-Guyot, B. Allès, C. Méjean, R. M. Andrianasolo, E. Chazelas, M. Deschasaux, S. Hercberg, P. Galan, C. A. Monteiro, C. Julia, and M. Touvier. 2019. "Ultra-Processed Food Intake and Risk of Cardiovascular Disease: Prospective Cohort Study (NutriNet-Santé)." *British Medical Journal* 365 (May): l1451. doi:10.1136/bmj.l1451.

Stokes, R. J., J. MacDonald, and G. Ridgeway. 2008. "Estimating the Effects of Light Rail Transit on Health Care Costs." *Health and Place* 14: 45–58.

Swartz, J. J., D. Braxton, and A. J. Viera. 2011. "Calorie Menu Labeling on Quick-Service Restaurant Menus: An Updated Systematic Review of the Literature." *International Journal of Behavioral Nutrition and Physical Activity* 8: 135.

Swinburn, B. A., G. Sacks, K. D. Hall, K. McPherson, D. T. Finegood, M. L. Moodie, and S. L. Gortmaker. 2011. "The Global Obesity Pandemic: Shaped by Global Drivers and Local Environments." *Lancet* 378 (9793): 804–14. doi:10.1016/S0140-6736(11)60813-1.

Taillie, L. S., E. Busey, F. Mediano Stoltze, and F. R. Dillman Carpentier. 2019. "Governmental Policies to Reduce Unhealthy Food Marketing to Children." *Nutrition Reviews* 77 (11): 787–816. doi:10.1093/nutrit/nuz021.

Taillie, L. S., M. G. Hall, B. M. Popkin, S. W. Ng, and N. Murukutla. 2020. "Experimental Studies of Front-of-Package Nutrient Warning Labels on Sugar-Sweetened Beverages and Ultra-Processed Foods: A Scoping Review." *Nutrients* 12 (2): 569. https://www.mdpi .com/2072-6643/12/2/569.

Taillie, L. S., M. Reyes, M. Arantxa Colchero, B. Popkin, and C. Corvalán. 2020. "An Evaluation of Chile's Law of Food Labeling and Advertising on Sugar-Sweetened Beverage Purchases from 2015 to 2017: A Before-and-After Study." *PLoS Medicine* 17 (2): e1003015. doi:10.1371 /journal.pmed.1003015.

Taillie, L. S., J. A. Rivera, B. M. Popkin, and C. Batis. 2017. "Do High vs. Low Purchasers Respond Differently to a Nonessential Energy-Dense Food Tax? Two-Year Evaluation of Mexico's 8% Nonessential Food Tax." *Preventive Medicine* 105S (December): S37–42. doi:10.1016/j .ypmed.2017.07.009.

Teng, A. M., A. C. Jones, A. Mizdrak, L. Signal, M. Genç, and N. Wilson. 2019. "Impact of Sugar-Sweetened Beverage Taxes on Purchases and Dietary Intake: Systematic Review and Meta-Analysis." *Obesity Reviews: An Official Journal of the International Association for the Study of Obesity* 20 (9): 1187–204. doi:10.1111/obr.12868.

US FDA (US Food and Drug Administration). 2021. *Changes to the Nutrition Facts Label*. Washington, DC: US Food and Drug Administration. https://www.fda.gov/food/food-labeling -nutrition/changes-nutrition-facts-label.

USDA FAS (United States Department of Agriculture, Foreign Agricultural Service). 2021. *Food and Agricultural Import Regulations and Standards Country Report: Saudi Arabi*. Report no. SA2020-0023. Riyadh: United States Department of Agriculture. https://apps.fas.usda.gov /newgainapi/api/Report/DownloadReportByFileName?fileName=Food%20and%20 Agricultural%20Import%20Regulations%20and%20Standards%20Country%20Report _Riyadh_Saudi%20Arabia_12-31-2020.

van der Vliet, N., A. W. M. Suijkerbuijk, A. T. de Blaeij, G. A. de Wit, P. F. van Gils, B. A. M. Staatsen, R. Maas, and J. J. Polder. 2020. "Ranking Preventive Interventions from Different Policy Domains: What Are the Most Cost-Effective Ways to Improve Public Health?" *International Journal of Environmental Research and Public Health* 17 (6): 2160. doi:10.3390 /ijerph17062160.

Variyam, J. N. 2008. "Do Nutrition Labels Improve Dietary Outcomes?" *Health Economics* 17 (6): 695–708.

Vyth, E. L., I. H. M. Steenhuis, A. J. C. Roodenburg, J. Brug, and J. C. Seidell. 2010. "Front-of-Pack Nutrition Label Stimulates Healthier Product Development: A Quantitative Analysis." *International Journal of Behavioral Nutrition and Physical Activity* 7 (September): 65. doi:10.1186/1479-5868-7-65.

Wakefield, M. A., B. Loken, and R. C. Hornik. 2010. "Use of Mass Media Campaigns to Change Health Behaviour." *Lancet* 376 (9748): 1261–71. doi:10.1016/S0140-6736(10)60809-4.

WHO (World Health Organization). 2017a. *Decision-Making Process and Tool: Draft Approach for the Prevention and Management of Conflicts of Interest in the Policy Development and Implementation of Nutrition Programmes at Country Level*. Geneva: World Health Organization. https://www.who.int/nutrition/consultation-doi/nutrition-tool.pdf?ua=1.

WHO (World Health Organization). 2017b. *Taxes on Sugary Drinks: Why Do It? Together Let's Beat NCDs*. Geneva: WHO. http://apps.who.int/iris/bitstream/10665/250303/1/WHO -NMH-PND-16.5-eng.pdf.

World Cancer Research Fund International. n.d. NOURISHING Database, "Nutrition Label Standards and Regulations on the Use of Claims and Implied Claims on Food 2020," accessed August 7, 2020. https://policydatabase.wcrf.org/level_one?page=nourishing-level -one#step2=0#step3=309.

# 8 Food Systems Approach to Nutrition Policies in Saudi Arabia

SHU WEN NG, REEM F. ALSUKAIT, MOHAMMED ALLUHIDAN,
ADWA ALAMRI, RASHA ALFAWAZ, OMAR ALHUMAIDAN,
TAGHRED ALGHAITH, MAJID ALKHALAF, AND CHRISTOPHER H. HERBST

## KEY MESSAGES

- The food systems around the world are not sustainable and do not support healthy diets for the population.
- It is possible to transform food systems to provide a triple win—for people, for the economy, and for the planet.
- Several countries—such as Mexico, Chile, and the United Kingdom—have incorporated systems-based strategies to address their food systems and make them work better for their populations and environments.
- In developing a Saudi-specific nutrient-profiling model (NPM), it is necessary to consider key sources of nutrients, decide whether to develop an entirely new model or adapt one that already exists and determine what that means for Saudi Arabia, and decide what to include and determine how it applies across the country's food supply, among other issues.
- Unintended consequences also must be addressed, which would entail developing ways to monitor for consequences and to mitigate them.
- Applying an NPM to Saudi Arabia for transforming its food system should include both developing policies that reduce the intake of unhealthy foods and those that increase the intake of healthy foods.
- Polices should be sequenced to both provide momentum and increase impact over time.

## WHY WE NEED A TRANSFORMATION OF THE FOOD SYSTEM

Most food systems around the world today are not sustainable and are operating well beyond planetary boundaries (GLOPAN 2020).[1] Poor diets delivered by these food systems not only cause significant damage to public health but also contribute to environmental degradation. Food systems produce a quarter of greenhouse gas emissions (Rose et al. 2017). A shift toward a healthier diet with fewer animal products and less food waste can help achieve both health and environmental goals (Rose, Heller, and Roberto 2019). Therefore, system-level solutions that address both challenges are necessary to achieve many of the United Nations' Sustainable Development Goals (SDGs): for example, SDGs 1, 2, 12, 14, and 15)(Thow and Nisbett 2019).

In Saudi Arabia, transforming the food system into a system that is healthier and more sustainable is critical. As shown in previous chapters, with more than 70 percent of the population being overweight and diet-related noncommunicable diseases (NCDs) such as hypertension and diabetes escalating, a shift toward healthier diets could reduce the burden on health care systems and result in potential savings of direct and indirect costs. Furthermore, with the growing population size and an urbanization rate of over 86 percent, food and water security represent a significant challenge in the country, with 80 percent of food being imported in Saudi Arabia (Lovelle 2015). Despite these concerns, a recent comprehensive study by the Saudi Grains Organization found that 33 percent of food is wasted in Saudi Arabia (SAGO 2018); this represents 184 kilograms of food loss or waste per capita per year—the equivalent of 12,980 million riyals annually (SAGO 2018). A call to estimate the real cost of the country's food was highlighted during the G20 task force work on sustainable energy, water, and food systems in Saudi Arabia (Laborde, Parent, and Piñeiro 2020).

Wins for people, the planet, and prosperity do not need to be mutually exclusive—triple wins can be achieved. The second *Foresight Report* from the Global Panel on Agriculture and Food Systems for Nutrition lays out the necessary steps to transform the food system (GLOPAN 2020). The four objectives of this transformation are to (1) ensure the availability of nutrient-rich foods sustainably produced; (2) make sustainable, healthy diets accessible to all; (3) make sustainable, healthy diets affordable to all; and (4) influence demand by making sustainable, healthy diets desirable to all (figure 8.1).

**FIGURE 8.1**

**Priority policy actions to transition food systems toward sustainable, healthy diets**

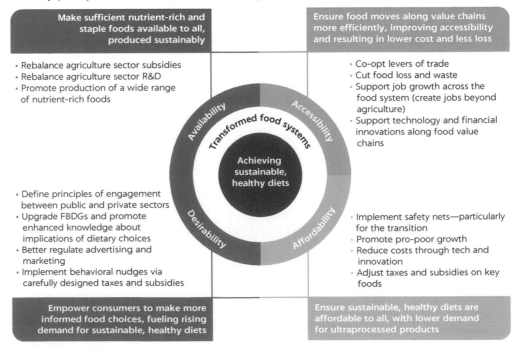

*Source:* GLOPAN 2020.
*Note:* R&D = research and development; FBDGs = food-based dietary guidelines.

Three case studies highlight the experiences of countries with integrated and systems-based strategies (Mexico, Chile, and the United Kingdom) and the sequencing of various initiatives (annex 8A). Overall, the case studies show that engaging with industry too early in the process can be counterproductive and greatly delay efforts to make impactful change in the public's understanding and actualization of behavior change. Additionally, when a more complete policy package is staged in its implementation or becomes fully implemented, much larger transformations of the food system can be realized. That said, integrated and vertical sequencing (using regulations that build on each other) or horizontal sequencing (with regulations that get stricter over time) of policies also make evaluations of each of the policies that make up the overall package extremely difficult to assess, so teasing out the contribution of each of the various components becomes more challenging.

Similar to the countries in the three case studies, Saudi Arabia has the capacity and resources to catalyze the collective action to transform its and its region's food system. Given the stage of the nutrition transition in Saudi Arabia and existing dietary trends, it would be best to begin with policies and actions aimed at discouraging diets that are detrimental to the country's people and environment. Using the four priority policies actions of the *Foresight Report* (GLOPAN 2020), a nutrient profiling model (NPM) can be used to develop a thoughtful sequencing of policies and their implementation to reduce the availability, accessibility, affordability, and desirability of unhealthful products. This can be achieved by creating sequenced actions along two dimensions. The first is *vertical sequencing*, which occurs when new policies build on existing policies. The second dimension is *horizontal sequencing*, which allows a reasonable period of time for industry to adapt in a stepwise manner to improve its offerings, as the regulations also get stricter over time. A next stage once meaningful progress has been made on discouraging poor diets would be to encourage diets that benefit people and the environment and again can be tackled along vertical and horizontal sequenced policies using food-based dietary guidelines (FBDGs) that do not contradict the NPM as the basis (WHO EMRO 2017).

The following sections first describe trends in key sources of nutrients of concern in Saudi Arabia ("Trends in Key Sources of Nutrients of Concern: Ultraprocessed Products"), then lay out considerations in developing a Saudi Arabia–specific NPM aimed at addressing these trends ("Considerations for Developing a Saudi-Specific NPM to Discourage Ultraprocessed Foods and Beverages") and how to apply the NPM for integrated policies ("Applying a Saudi-Specific NPM for Transforming the Food System"). The chapter ends with conclusions.

## TRENDS IN KEY SOURCES OF NUTRIENTS OF CONCERN: ULTRAPROCESSED PRODUCTS

Saudis are consuming more processed packaged foods over time; 65–70 percent of food and beverages sold in Saudi Arabia are either processed or ultraprocessed, as shown using aggregate data from Euromonitor (figures 8.2 through 8.5). Specifically, the share of the ultraprocessed foods' contribution to total calories sold rose steadily between 2010 (8.7 percent) and 2019 (10.4 percent). There has been a corresponding decrease in the share of fresh foods over this period. The slight reduction in total calories appear to be at least

FIGURE 8.2

**Calories sold from food and beverage categories in Saudi Arabia (kilocalories per capita per day), 2010–19**

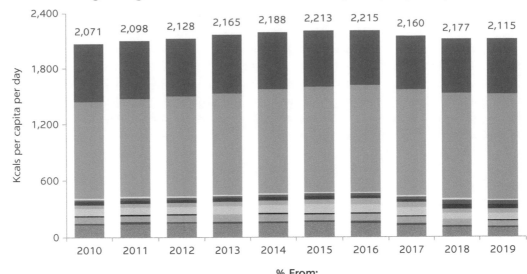

| % From: | 2010 | 2011 | 2012 | 2013 | 2014 | 2015 | 2016 | 2017 | 2018 | 2019 |
|---|---|---|---|---|---|---|---|---|---|---|
| Beverages | 11.1% | 11.2% | 11.3% | 11.4% | 11.6% | 11.5% | 11.3% | 10.1% | 8.9% | 8.4% |
| Ultraprocessed foods | 8.7% | 9.0% | 9.1% | 9.4% | 9.6% | 9.9% | 10.2% | 10.3% | 10.4% | 10.4% |
| Other processed, packaged foods | 50.0% | 50.1% | 50.4% | 50.6% | 50.9% | 51.4% | 51.6% | 52.2% | 52.8% | 53.2% |
| Fresh foods | 30.1% | 29.7% | 29.2% | 28.7% | 27.9% | 27.2% | 26.9% | 27.4% | 27.9% | 28.0% |

- Fresh foods
- Ice cream and frozen and chilled desserts
- Savory snacks
- Cakes and pastries
- Other (nonsugary) drinks
- SSBs
- Other processed, packaged foods
- Sweet biscuits and snack bars
- Confectionary and sweet spreads
- Alcohol
- Other sugary drinks

*Source:* Original figure for this publication based on data from Euromonitor International, http://www.portal .euromonitor.com, accessed December 2020.
*Note:* SSB = sugar-sweetened beverages; kcals = kilocalories. *Fresh foods* refers only to fresh uncooked and unprocessed foods (packaged and unpackaged).

partly due to a reduction in calories from sugar-sweetened beverages (SSBs) since 2017, but it is important to note that these data reflect sales, not actual intake. Thus, it is unclear whether the slight caloric reduction reflects a reduction in caloric intake and/or reductions in food waste among consumers, or something else. We also see that these ultraprocessed foods and sugary drinks (collectively termed *ultraprocessed products,* or UPP) contribute between 330 and 400 kilocalories (kcals) per capita per day in Saudi Arabia, or around 17–20 percent of calories in Saudi Arabia. These are conservative estimates, as there are likely other processed packaged foods that also contribute to excess intakes of nutrients that can be harmful to health such as sodium, sugar, and saturated fats.

Beyond the population health implications of high intakes of these nutrients of concern in Saudi Arabia, there are also environmental implications. Production of ultraprocessed foods and SSBs contributes significantly to water use and carbon emissions from the farm through to the fork (Fardet and Rock 2020; Harris et al. 2020). While we are still at an early stage in fully understanding and documenting the environmental impacts of ultraprocessed diets, it is clear that

FIGURE 8.3

**Sugar sold from nonalcoholic beverages and foods (packaged and fresh) in Saudi Arabia, 2010–19**

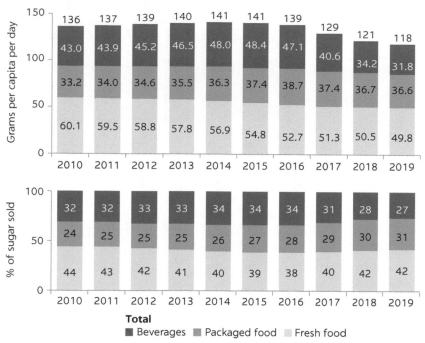

*Source:* Original figure for this publication based on data from Euromonitor International, http://www.portal.euromonitor.com, accessed December 2020.
*Note:* For a 2,000 kcal diet, WHO recommended that sugar intakes be limited to <50 g. WHO = World Health Organization; kcal = kilocalorie; g = grams.

policies are needed to shift toward diets that better support population and planetary health (Springmann et al. 2020; Willett et al. 2019).

## CONSIDERATIONS FOR DEVELOPING A SAUDI-SPECIFIC NPM TO DISCOURAGE ULTRAPROCESSED FOODS AND BEVERAGES

Nutrient profiling provides a means of differentiating between foods and nonalcoholic beverages (henceforth "foods") that are more likely to be part of a healthy diet from those that are less likely. Nutrient profiling has been recognized by WHO as a useful tool for a variety of applications. As there is no standardized method to identify foods as "healthy" or "unhealthy," it is difficult to implement policies that require regulations regarding the health status of foods. Nutrient profiling can serve as a solution, as it is an accepted scientific method to identify and categorize food based on the level of health according to its nutritional composition (Rayner, Scarborough, and Kaur 2013).

Nutrient profiling is a tool used to categorize foods, not diets, but it can also be used through policy to improve the overall nutritional quality of diets. NPMs can be used to underpin policies and regulations on front-of-package labeling (FOPL), restrictions of marketing to children, school food guidelines, health and nutrition claims on foodstuffs, food taxation and subsidies, food

FIGURE 8.4

**Saturated fat sold from nonalcoholic beverages and foods (packaged and fresh) in Saudi Arabia, 2010–19**

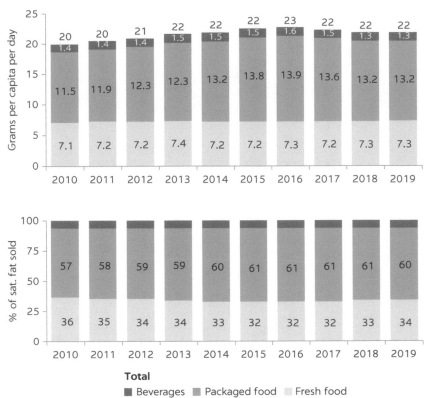

*Source:* Original figure for this publication based on data from Euromonitor International, http://www.portal.euromonitor.com, accessed December 2020.
*Note:* For a 2,000 kcal diet, WHO recommends that saturated fats intakes be limited to <22.5 g. kcal = kilocalorie; WHO = World Health Organization; g = grams.

fortification, and food procurement regulations (such as informing foods in group or congregate settings such as hospitals, prisons, old age homes, and so on) and to inform welfare support schemes (Labonté et al. 2018). NPMs can also be applied to foods served at quick-serve restaurants (for example, fast food or chain restaurants). As noted in earlier sections, several countries have effectively introduced mandatory food polices that make use of NPMs. A single, well-designed NPM to define unhealthy foods can help provide consistency across policies, minimize confusion, reduce administrative burden (Sacks et al. 2011), and address international trade concerns—which is an argument frequently raised by opponents to such policies (Snowdon and Thow 2013; Thow et al. 2017).

There are a variety of different NPMs worldwide. To select a suitable, context-specific NPM to be used for food policy, context-specific data should be used and a stepwise approach needs to be followed. The subsection "Integrated Policies to Reduce the Intake of Unhealthy Foods in Saudi Arabia" will present data on trends in sources of top contributors of calories, saturated fats, trans fats, sugar, and sodium for Saudi Arabia. The subsection "Integrated Policies to Increase the Intake of Healthy Foods in Saudi Arabia" will follow the NPM section in the WHO draft guidelines on FOPL to discuss key considerations for developing a Saudi-specific NPM. The subsection "The Importance of Coordinating and Sequencing Policies" will lay out other potential consequences and ways to mitigate.

FIGURE 8.5

**Salt sold from nonalcoholic beverages and foods (packaged and fresh) in Saudi Arabia, 2010–19**

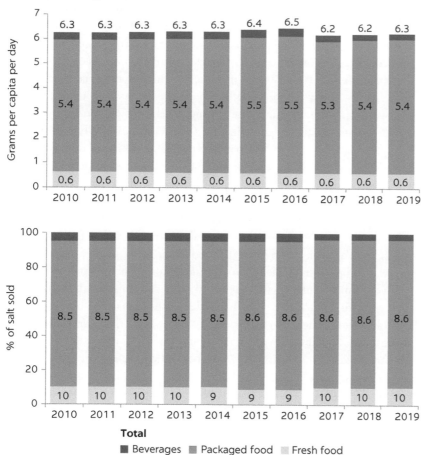

WHO recommends that salt intake be limited to <5g per day

*Source:* Original figure for this publication based on data from Euromonitor International, http://www.portal.euromonitor.com, accessed December 2020.
*Note:* WHO recommends that salt intakes be limited to <5 g per day. WHO = World Health Organization; g = grams.

## How to develop or adapt an NPM for Saudi Arabia

Identifying UPPs and processed foods high in nutrients that are harmful to health is a key goal of a Saudi-specific NPM given the diets in Saudi Arabia. The NPM section in the WHO guidelines on FOPL recommends six steps in the development or adaptation of an NPM (WHO 2019). It is important to note that, although this is presented as steps, in practice the steps are interrelated and interdependent, and decisions made in one step affect the decisions made in other steps (Verhagen and Berg 2008).

The six steps are as follows:

1. Determine whether to develop a new model or adapt an existing one.
2. Determine which nutrients to incorporate into the NPM.
3. Determine which food groups to include.
4. Determine the applicability of the NPM.
5. Validate the NPM through testing.
6. Consider other issues related to implementing NPMs.

### Developing a new NPM versus adapting an existing one

The WHO Eastern Mediterranean Regional Office (EMRO) NPM for the marketing of unhealthy food and nonalcoholic beverages to children was published in 2017 (WHO EMRO 2017). The model was first tested before 2014 in Bahrain, the Islamic Republic of Iran, Kuwait, Lebanon, Morocco, Oman, and Tunisia. These countries applied it to a nationally generated list of between 100 and 200 foods that are either (1) frequently marketed to children or (2) commonly consumed (ideally, a combination of both). Some adjustments were made following a 2014 consultation to confirm that the model categorized foods in line with national food-based dietary guidelines (WHO EMRO 2017). While this EMRO NPM was designed to be applied to marketing, in theory, it can apply to a series of policies. For example, for each of the 18 food categories in the EMRO NPM, the regional guidance lists the accompanying international customs tariff codes for member countries to consider using for policies where applicable (for example, fiscal policies). This NPM could be adapted for Saudi Arabia across a set of regulated policies, but a key challenge is that having 18 food categories with different and selected nutrient thresholds for each category may prove too complex to properly implement, monitor, and enforce a mandatory policy.

The current voluntary Saudi Food and Drug Administration (SFDA) FOP multiple traffic light (MTL) labeling system uses across-the-board nutrient threshold values rather than food category–specific nutrient threshold values. The nutrients included cover total fat, saturated fat, total sugar,[2] and salt with thresholds to determine green, amber/yellow, or red for each of these nutrient labels; this is based on the UK values (for the United Kingdom's voluntary MTL labels) in terms of amounts of these nutrients per 100 grams (g) or milliliters (ml) (Al-Jawaldeh et al. 2020). Along with the SFDA MTL, other NPMs have been adopted in Saudi Arabia by the Saudi National Nutrition Committee (NNC). Another example for a nutrient profile model that uses across-the-board nutrient threshold values is the UK Ofcom NPM, which has recently been adopted by the Saudi NNC. This model provides a single score for any given food product according to its nutrient composition in terms of 100 g or ml. This is carried out by calculating the number of points of "nutrients to limit" subtracted by points of "nutrients to encourage." The process to score the nutritional quality is based on the Swedish Keyhole labeling scheme and US manufacturers' Smart Choices program (Rayner, Scarborough, and Lobstein 2009). Given that this model is already in place, this is a logical NPM to work from. There are potential adaptations around the threshold values or nutrients included to enable one to apply it to mandatory policies like FOP labels, marketing restrictions, or taxes. To provide some reference for comparison, annex 8B lays out several key dimensions of the WHO EMRO NPM for marketing restrictions; the NPMs for the SFDA voluntary MTL; the mandatory Chile and Mexico FOP warning labels; and the Food Standards Australia/New Zealand NPM that has been used for both voluntary and mandatory measures. To provide more detailed comparisons, table 8.1 shows the nutrients included and thresholds set for NPMs used in Saudi Arabia and Chile for specific policies to date.

There is a strong consensus, including from the WHO guidelines (WHO 2019), that the base or reference is by volume or weight of products as reflected in the EMRO marketing NPM, the SFDA's voluntary MTL, the Saudi NNC NPM, and regulations in Chile and the United Kingdom. Moreover, current mandatory nutritional information in Saudi Arabia is per 100 g for foods and per 100 ml

TABLE 8.1 **Nutrients of concern and threshold values for nutrient-profiling models in use in Saudi Arabia and Chile**

| NUTRIENTS OF CONCERN AND THRESHOLDS CURRENTLY USED | FOR VOLUNTARY MTL FOP LABELS IN SAUDI ARABIA | | | FOR MANDATORY FOP & MARKETING RESTRICTIONS IN CHILE (3RD/FINAL PHASE) |
|---|---|---|---|---|
| | Low | Medium | High | Warning |
| **100 g of food** | | | | |
| Total fat | ≤ 3.0 g | >3.0 g to ≤ 17.5 g | >17.5 g | |
| Saturated fat | ≤ 1.5 g | >1.5 g to ≤ 5.0 g | >5.0 g | >4.0 g |
| Total sugars | ≤ 5.5 g | >5.0 g to ≤ 22.5 g | >22.5 g | >10.0 g |
| Salt | ≤ 0.3 g | >0.3 g to ≤ 1.5 g | >1.5 g | >1 g<br>Sodium: >400 mg |
| **Calories** | | | | 275 kcals |
| **100 ml of beverage** | | | | |
| Total fat | ≤ 1.5 g | >1.5 g to ≤ 8.75 g | >8.75 g | |
| Saturated fat | ≤ 0.75 g | >0.75 g to ≤ 2.5 g | >2.5 g | >3.0 g |
| Total sugars | ≤ 2.5 g | >5.0 g to ≤ 11.25 g | >11.25 g | >5.0 g |
| Salt | ≤ 0.3 g | >0.3 g to ≤ 0.75 g | >0.75 g | >0.25 g<br>Sodium: >100 mg |
| Calories | | | | 70 kcals |

*Sources:* Data for Chile from Corvalán et al. 2019; data for Saudi Arabia from SFDA 2020.
*Note:* FOP = front of package; g = grams; kcal = kilocalorie; mg = milligram; ml = milliliter; MTL = multiple traffic light.

format for liquids. Thus, using this approach is also practical. There are two possible approaches for the proposed NPM: a threshold (cutoff point) approach and a continuous (score-based) approach.

*Threshold- or cutoff-based NPMs* identify predetermined cutoff points that will classify foods in a binary manner. Different cutoff points can be used for different nutrients within one food (for example, a different cutoff point each for sugar, sodium, and saturated fat). No calculations or comparisons need to be made before classifying a food, as it either meets the cutoff point or it does not, which makes the approach easy to use. This has been used for mandatory policies in Chile and Mexico, as well as the voluntary MTL FOPL approach in Saudi Arabia.

*Continuous, score-based NPMs* award points based on various criteria for various nutrients, and a summative healthfulness score is calculated from this score, depending on the NPM's criteria. To date, this has been used only on voluntary approaches such as Australia's Health Star Rating and France's Nutri-Score labels. The rationale is that foods are composed of many nutrients and a single cutoff would result in the loss of valuable information. However, this argument holds true only when both positive and negative nutrients are considered or when the NPM is being used to underpin a positive logo that focuses only on whole, minimally processed foods.

For Saudi Arabia's NPM to be able to underpin policies that aim to change unhealthy consumption patterns, a cutoff-point model will be most appropriate. It needs to be straightforward and make it easy to identify which products are less healthy and need to be regulated by policy. Continuous models require making a number of different calculations; these models can be human resource heavy and, ultimately, when used together with labels or claims, a cutoff point is still used to determine whether a product complies or not, or is red, yellow, or green. In this sense, a scoring approach is always used in conjunction with a threshold approach.

## Deciding which nutrients and food components to incorporate into the NPM

A key goal of NPMs, given the diets in Saudi Arabia, would be to identify foods high in nutrients or food components that are harmful to health. According to a review of NPMs used in government-led nutrition policies, all 78 NPMs included nutrients that need to be limited. The most common nutrients of concern were salt (sodium), saturated fat, and total sugar (Labonté et al. 2018).

There is a strong basis for the inclusion of salt (sodium), saturated fat, and total sugar based on current evidence and for consistency in including them in all government-led NPMs, but the inclusion of total fat is not necessary. In both the SFDA NPM for MTL and the Saudi NNC NPM, the nutrients included are total fat, saturated fats, salt (sodium), and total sugar. WHO recommends an intake of between 15 percent and 30 percent of total calories from all forms of fat. However, fat, per se, is not harmful to health, but rather the type of fat is what matters. Indeed, certain components, such as mono- and polyunsaturated fatty acids, are beneficial to health and are protective against certain NCDs such as cardiovascular disease. Recently, the US dietary guidelines have removed total fat as a nutrient of concern to focus instead on unhealthy saturated fats, including trans fats (Dietary Guidelines Advisory Committee 2020). Since January 2020, the SFDA has implemented its regulation number SFDA.FD 2483, issued in 2018, banning the use of partially hydrogenated oils (trans fats) in all food products (SFDA 2018). Assuming this trans-fat ban is well enforced, the inclusion of trans fat as a criterion may not be necessary. If the trans-fat ban is not well enforced, however, then its inclusion as a criterion should be strongly considered. Given the obesity and NCD trends in Saudi Arabia, excessive caloric intake appears to be a concern in the country, so it may be wise to also include calories and caloric density as a criterion in the NPM, in place of total fats. This switch would also more appropriately educate the public about the nutrients of concern.

Nonsugar sweeteners (NSS) are a food component that has been getting more attention in recent years, yet there is no global consensus on the longer-term health implications of prolonged and/or larger doses of NSS intake. With growing recognition of the need to lower sugar density in products, manufacturers are turning to NSS (often also referred to as *nonnutritive sweeteners* or *artificial sweeteners*) for maintaining sweet taste with far fewer or no calories (Bandy et al. 2020; Dunford et al. 2018; Piernas, Ng, and Popkin 2013; Popkin and Hawkes 2016; Scarborough et al. 2020). One fear around the increase in NSS in foods and beverages is the impact on sweetness preference and habituation among children. Among adults, we see different outcomes in widely conflicting human studies looking at gut health, brain response, and heart health (de Koning et al. 2011, 2012; Duffey et al. 2012; Lutsey, Steffen, and Stevens 2008).

NSS also have a negative environmental impact, which is an important consideration under the current context of climate change. Their development requires the use of scarce water resources and generates solid waste (Borges et al. 2017). They do not degrade but remain present as trace pollutants in water after wastewater treatments (Lange, Scheurer, and Brauch 2012). The dearth of information on their use (both types and amounts) in the Saudi and global food supply means that it is challenging to study these questions. As part of regulation SFDA.FD 2233:2018, Saudi Arabia requires the listing of NSS and their amounts (milligrams per liter or milligrams per kilogram of the product) (GSO 2018). This will create a useful start for monitoring the presence and amount of NSS in Saudi food purchases and diets. Careful assessment of whether manufacturers or distributors are indeed complying with this regulation is greatly needed.

## Deciding which food groups to include in the NPM

The criteria underpinning an NPM can be applied indiscriminately, using the same criteria, across all major foods; alternatively, they can differentiate between food categories, using a different set of criteria for different individual food groups. This allows for either comparison across different food categories or comparison within food categories (WHO 2019). As noted, the WHO EMRO NPM for restricting marketing to children has 18 food categories with different nutrients and threshold criteria, while the NPMs for the SFDA voluntary MTL and Saudi NNC NPM simply categorize products or foods versus beverages and apply the same set of nutrient thresholds. Similarly, other locations with NPMs applied for mandatory policies have used across-category criteria for solids/foods or liquids/beverages based on reconstituted values (typically only with water, which adds weight or volume but no other nutrients). If the SFDA approach of an across-category criteria is applied to mandatory policies, then implementation, monitoring, and enforcement will be much less complicated for the food and beverage industry to implement and regulatory agencies to monitor and enforce. See table 8.2 for a summary of pros and cons of these different approaches.

TABLE 8.2 **Pros and cons of the category-specific and across-category approaches**

| CRITERIA | PROS | CONS |
|---|---|---|
| **Category-specific criteria** | • Criteria can be informed by the nutritional content of existing foods in the category. | • Provides leeway for the food industry to manipulate within category (e.g., cutoff may be higher for inherently high-sodium foods—although the sodium still poses a health risk). <br> • Numerous categories with different thresholds make it difficult for regulators to implement. |
| **Across-category criteria** | • Establish consistent criteria (e.g., for all foods and beverages) <br> • Simple to implement, not resource intensive <br> • Limits the risk of misinterpretation or incorrect classification | • Reformulation may be muted within a category if changes are needed for most of the foods in that category. <br> • All foods are treated in the same way, regardless of their inherent nutrient composition. |

*Source:* Original table for this publication.

## Determining applicability across the food supply

From an implementation perspective, since nutrition information panels are readily available on packaged but not on fresh foods or prepared foods, it will be challenging to apply the NPM beyond packaged foods and beverages at this time. The current ability to apply the NPM only to packaged foods and beverages is in line with recommendations to limit the intake of ultraprocessed foods, which are predominately packaged. Nonetheless, this current limited scope should not prevent future efforts to consider expanding the application of NPMs to food service—for example, if reporting the relevant nutrient information becomes required. An NPM should be able to be applied to most food and beverage categories within the marketplace. The more broadly it is applied, the more public awareness is increased and the greater the success of the food policy it is underpinning (WHO 2019). Conversely, it is not advised to use the NPM for the following:

- *Infant formula*. Breastmilk is the gold standard for infant feeding. There are strict criteria that infant formula has to meet (WHO 2019).
- *Food for special medical purposes*. Food for medical purposes has strict criteria and serves a special medical purpose; these foods are not appropriate to include in the NPM.
- *Foods that meet specific Codex Alimentarius guidelines*. Foods with a package surface area of less than 10 square centimeters are exempt from mandatory food labels. As these foods do not contain nutrition information panels, which is necessary for the application of the NPM, they can be excluded from the NPM criteria.

## Choosing the values and validation of proposed NPMs

As discussed in previous sections, the most appropriate and relevant nutrient cutoffs must take into consideration that the purpose of the NPM is to underpin mandatory food policy regulation in Saudi Arabia. Thus, the NPM will use a negative approach: to discourage the consumption of foods containing high concentrations of nutrients or food components that are harmful to health. A cutoff-based, across-category model—using a "per 100 g" or "per 100 ml" base starting with packaged foods and beverages—is most appropriate for Saudi Arabia given existing labeling requirements. Nutrients or food components of concern that have been identified for inclusion in the NPM include saturated fat, trans fat, sodium, total sugar, and NSS (with calories as an option to consider including). Finally, a suitable NPM can be adapted rather than developing a new NPM.

Based on the considerations presented, there are two options for the Saudi context. The first option is to build a score-based NPM such as the one used in the United Kingdom for its marketing regulations, given that Saudi Arabia also already adapted the United Kingdom's approach for MTL on its package fronts. As noted, the focus should be on nutrients to be discouraged. The United Kingdom's NPM for marketing regulations include saturated fats, total sugar, sodium, and calories, with points associated with each nutrient based on its value as shown in table 8.3. Each product is thus scored to obtain a total "A" points. Food scoring four or more points, and drinks scoring one or more points, are classified as "less healthy" and are subject to the UK's Office of Communication's controls of advertising of "less healthy" foods to children on

TABLE 8.3 **Calculating "A" points using the UK's score-based nutrient profiling model for regulating marketing to children**

| POINTS | SATURATED FAT (G) | TOTAL SUGAR (G) | SODIUM (MG) | CALORIES IN KCALS (KJ) |
|---|---|---|---|---|
| 0 | ≤ 1 | ≤ 4.5 | ≤ 90 | ≤ 80 kcals (335 kJ) |
| 1 | > 1 | > 4.5 | > 90 | > 80 kcals (335 kJ) |
| 2 | > 2 | > 9 | > 180 | > 160 kcals (670 kJ) |
| 3 | > 3 | > 13.5 | > 270 | > 240 kcals (1,005 kJ) |
| 4 | > 4 | > 18 | > 360 | > 320 kcals (1,340 kJ) |
| 5 | > 5 | > 22.5 | > 450 | > 400 kcals (1,675 kJ) |
| 6 | > 6 | > 27 | > 540 | > 480 kcals (2,010 kJ) |
| 7 | > 7 | > 31 | > 630 | > 560 kcals (2,345 kJ) |
| 8 | > 8 | > 36 | > 720 | > 640 kcals (2,680 kJ) |
| 9 | > 9 | > 40 | > 810 | > 720 kcals (3,015 kJ) |
| 10 | > 10 | > 45 | > 900 | > 800 kcals (3,350 kJ) |

*Source:* DOH 2011.

*Note:* g = gram; kcal = kilocalorie; kJ = kilojoule; mg = milligram.

television. For example, a cookie product has an NIP that says that per 100 g of this cookie contains 2.5 g saturated fat, 12 g sugar, 120 g sodium, and 200 kilocalories (or 840 kilojoules). The total "A" points for this cookie product would be: 2 + 2 + 1 + 1 = 6. Therefore, this cookie product will exceed the score-based thresholds based on this NPM.

The UK NPM for marketing regulations also allows up to 5 "C" points if a product does not have 11 or more "A" points. The "C" point scoring (not presented here) is based on the percentage of the product's content that comprises fruit, vegetables, nuts, and legumes (FVNL), amount of fiber (g), and amount of protein (g) and is used in the UK to balance out (deduct from) the "A" points. It is not recommended that "C" points be used for Saudi Arabia for obesity and NCD prevention because simply having more protein, for example, does not take away from the health-related concerns of having excessive levels of saturated fat, sugar, sodium, or calories. Moreover, operationalizing the "C" point components in a transparent and enforceable way would not be possible in Saudi Arabia given that products' FVNL content is not required to be reported

The second option is to adapt the Chile NPM for the Saudi context. The Chile NPM has shown some promising results in the food policies it is underpinning there, and other countries (Peru, for example) have adopted this NPM in their regulations. In Chile, fresh, whole foods were considered the gold standard. The nutritional composition of nutrients of concern in these foods informed decision-making. Fresh, whole foods that had not been altered in any way—by ingredient addition, dehydration, grinding, or any other kind of processing—were included. The nutritional composition of whole cow's milk informed the cutoffs for beverages. The selected foods, as well as their nutritional content, were based on the US Department of Agriculture nutrient database (Corvalán et al. 2019). Twelve food categories were included: beef products; cereal grains and pasta; dairy and egg products; finfish and shellfish products; fruits and fruit juices; lamb, veal, and game products; legumes and legume products; nut and seed products; pork products; poultry products; spices and herbs; and vegetables and vegetable products. Juices, concentrates, skins, and carcasses were excluded, and each item was included only once (in instances where there was more than one variant of the same food). In total, 358 products were included, and cutoff points were selected between the 90th and 99th percentiles for the included nutrients of concern (Corvalán et al. 2019).

Replicating this process for Saudi Arabia, which would require data on fresh, whole foods commonly consumed, is possible. Given the fact that these are based on fresh, whole foods that tend to be similar in nutrient composition across countries, it is expected that similar values will hold for Saudi Arabia. Table 8.4 proposes potential cutoff points to consider given values used in Chile. Once these Saudi cutoff points are derived, it would then be necessary to validate the NPM. Using the example of the cookie product noted earlier, the cookie would exceed the cutoff points for sugar.

Conceptually, the differences between these two options lie in the fact that the UK-based approach provides an option for manufacturers to balance across multiple nutrients of concern based on scores, while the Chile approach is more definitive. Consequently, the Chile approach is also less confusing and difficult to apply to a large market with a diverse mixture of products. Additionally, the UK approach may open doors for industry to advocate for allowing "C" points (for FVNL, fiber, and protein) to help neutralize the "A" points (from nutrients of concern). Thus, it may be wise to avoid having such an option available.

In terms of practical differences between these two options, NPMs are difficult to validate because there is no gold standard for classifying the healthfulness of foods. However, running comparisons across different NPMs, such as between the two options listed above, will allow policy makers to determine the potential pros and cons of the various NPM designs and better adapt and adjust a Saudi-specific policy so that it will more likely achieve its intended purpose. Thus, the goal of validity testing is to ensure that error is reduced. One can test construct validity by assessing how well an NPM accurately identifies unhealthy foods. Criterion-related validity is considered more

TABLE 8.4 **Proposed Saudi Arabia nutrient-profiling model cutoff points based on Chile's Cutoff points**

| NUTRIENT | CUTOFF VALUE TO DENOTE EXCESSIVE AMOUNTS |
|---|---|
| **100 g of food** | |
| Saturated fat | >4.0 g[a] |
| Total sugars | >10.0 g[a] |
| Salt | >1 g[a] |
| | Sodium >400 mg |
| **Energy or calories** | >275 kcals[a] |
| **100 ml of beverage** | |
| Saturated fat | >2.5 g[b] |
| Total sugars | >5.0 g[a] |
| Salt | >0.75 g[b] |
| | Sodium >300 mg |
| Energy or calories | >70 kcals[a] |

*Sources:* Data for Chile from Corvalán et al. 2019; data for Saudi Arabia from SFDA 2020.
*Note:* g = gram; kcal = kilocalorie; mg = milligram; ml = milliliter.
a. Same as Chile's final phase.
b. Current maximum for voluntary multiple traffic light front-of-package labeling in Saudi Arabia.

robust, but it is also time consuming, expensive, and logistically challenging—and consequently very few NPMs are tested this way. An alternative would be to test any proposed NPM alongside various other existing NPMs used for similar objectives against the packaged food supply in Saudi Arabia. This would require collecting and using data about the nutritional composition of the products and foods available in Saudi Arabia and applying the various NPMs to this same set of data. Each item can then be classified as either compliant or noncompliant, depending on the nutritional criteria of the NPM being evaluated. Differences between models regarding the proportion of foods identified as compliant can be described using tests of proportions. It would also be possible to calculate the mean and median content of nutrients of concern among noncompliant products compared across NPMs. The level of agreement between various NPMs can be evaluated using pairwise rank correlation coefficients overall and by category.

## Consider other issues related to implementing NPMs

Practical considerations need to be made regarding the nutrients of concern to be included in an NPM, to ensure that implementation is feasible. Without clear, easily available nutritional information about the nutrients included, the application and evaluation of the NPM will be difficult:

- To apply any NPM, the nutritional composition of nutrients of concern must be displayed on food packages. This is most practically displayed in the nutrition information panels (NIPs) on the back or side of the package; and this information should be mandatory on food packaging for nutrients included in the NPM.
- If manufacturers do not comply with displayinan an NIP on their food packaging, it is recommended that the regulatory agency (SFDA) assume that nutrients of concern not listed on the NIP are either high or excessive. This will incentivize manufacturers to include the necessary information.
- The NPM should be applied to foods and beverages in the as-consumed form. Thus, food labels should include the nutritional composition per 100 g "as-consumed" alongside the "as-packaged" composition if reconstitution through home preparation is required (for example, concentrated fruit drinks). It is advisable to include in regulations that, should the "as-consumed" information be missing, the NPM criteria will be applied to the "as-packaged" information.
- Should an NPM used in regulation contain a positive point—such as UK NPM for marketing regulations' use of FVNL points—it should be mandatory to include the percentage of FVNL (either in the NIP or in the ingredients list) to allow accurate monitoring of the NPM implementation.
- It is recommended that the weight of each NSS be included as a mandatory and enforced requirement to ensure that changes in the food supply can be accurately monitored.

## Potential unintended consequences and ways to mitigate them

Any new regulations targeting current attributes of concern will meet with subsequent introductions of new ingredients and products by industry to avoid or minimize the effect of such regulations on their profitability. Policies that the chosen NPM undergirds may intensify the push toward reformulations and the use of new ingredients. This was the case with NNS and will likely occur with the use of potassium salts and unsaturated fats as sodium and saturated fat substitutes, respectively. This means that the scientific community's understanding of how the various combinations and doses of foods, ingredients, and chemicals we are exposed to affect our health over time is still evolving and growing. Researchers and regulatory agencies must be vigilant and thoughtful in establishing mechanisms with which to periodically assess and improve these regulations to ensure that they evolve with the food landscape to best protect people's health.

## APPLYING A SAUDI-SPECIFIC NPM FOR TRANSFORMING THE FOOD SYSTEM

When a more complete policy package is implemented, much larger transformations to the food system can be realized. The subsection "Integrated Policies to Reduce the Intake of Unhealthy Foods in Saudi Arabia" discusses policies to reduce the intake of unhealthy foods in Saudi Arabia, followed by policies to increase the intake of healthy foods in "Integrated Policies to Increase the Intake of Healthy Foods in Saudi Arabia." The subsection "The Importance of Coordinating and Sequencing Policies" provides an example of sequencing policies across the stages.

### Integrated policies to reduce the intake of unhealthy foods in Saudi Arabia

Given the current high prevalence of obesity and NCDs in Saudi Arabia, the first stage should use a Saudi-specific NPM as the basis for defining "unhealthy" foods and beverages to discourage (figure 8.6). Several policies and activities can then be operationalized using this NPM. Together these can work effectively to reduce the desirability, availability, and accessibility of unhealthy foods.

Given that Saudi Arabia already taxes SSBs, it would be logical to implement an FOP warning label system to inform consumers when products exceed NPM thresholds. The design of the FOP label should be based on consumer focus group testing, followed by experimental approaches, such as randomized controlled trials or cross-over designs, to ensure that the labels are visible and salient as well as simple and easy to understand across a wide spectrum of people in Saudi Arabia. Ideally, the label or labels should leverage automatic associations through symbols or icons, shapes, and colors to help consumers interpret nutrition information quickly and accurately; they should also integrate informational and emotional messaging so that consumers will be discouraged from purchasing and consuming unhealthy products (Clarke et al. 2020; Hammond 2011).

The formation of an independent expert committee, such as the Saudi National Nutrition Committee, with no commercial interests that can guide and advise on the process and assess findings will ensure the integrity of the work. The FOPL can also serve as a visual guide for advertising agencies, distributors, retailers, and institutions to help them comply with several policies around marketing restrictions, tax liability, food vending and procurement, and sponsorships. Additionally, a warning-type FOPL will induce manufacturers to lower

**FIGURE 8.6**

**Stage 1: Reduce the intake of unhealthy foods in Saudi Arabia**

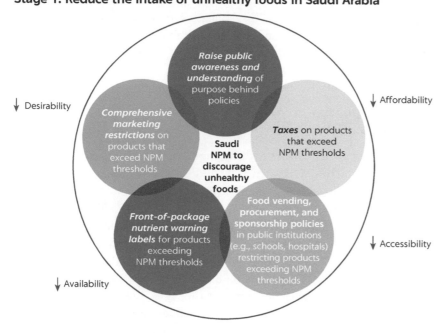

*Source:* Original figure for this publication.
*Note:* NPM = nutrient profiling model.

the nutrients of concern to avoid the label, marketing, tax, and sale or vending restrictions (Roberto et al. 2021). It may also induce manufacturers and retailers to find alternative ways to distract from these warning labels via competing positive claims about the product (for example, "high in vitamin C") or positioning products in a particular way to hide the labels. Therefore, the regulatory language and guidance documents provided to industry need to cover and prevent these issues as well.

All these policies will need to be supported by a public awareness campaign leading up to the expected implementation to ensure that there is understanding around the purpose and interpretation of the labels. Together these actions will provide a clear and consistent message to all about the health-related harms of products carrying the warning labels. Such vertical sequencing also applies within policies. The scope of the policies can also be expanded over time. For example, for marketing restrictions, the policy may start with TV, print, radio, and outdoor advertisements such as billboards and storefront signs but can expand to cover all digital media over time. The more comprehensive these regulations can be in the earlier phases, the better—but some flexibility to accommodate implementation within a feasible timeframe should also be allowed to ensure buy-in from all agencies tasked with enforcing these policies. Meanwhile, horizontal sequencing allows time for industry to adapt in a stepwise manner to improve its offerings.

Depending on the gap between the current food supply and the NPM criteria and thresholds, it may be better to break the thresholds into two phases, with each phase getting meaningfully stricter over time. However, it is not recommended that the implementation of the final phase be more than three years from the start of the first phase. Otherwise, the overall impact of the policies on diets and health will likely continue to be slow or stagnant. Besides the evidence base needed to justify each policy design and its implementation, it will also be important to ensure that the legal and regulatory framework allows each of these policies to be implemented and to withstand industry challenges, including trade-related challenges, particularly given the large share of foods in Saudi Arabia that are imported.

## Integrated policies to increase the intake of healthy foods in Saudi Arabia

After a series of strict policies to discourage unhealthy foods is implemented, it would be useful to address increasing the desirability, availability, accessibility, and affordability of healthy foods in Saudi Arabia's food system. The basis for these policies should be updated, Saudi-specific Food Based Dietary Guidance (FBDG) that explicitly recommends reducing the intake of unhealthy foods subject to stage 1 policies while recommending increasing the intake of healthy foods supported by stage 2 policies (figure 8.7). Care should also go into ensuring that the updated Saudi FBDG emphasizes whole and minimally processed foods and does not contradict the NPM. Brazil provides a strong example for how to solicit stakeholder input, and thus to develop and design FBDGs that incorporate not just food-based recommendations but also behaviors like cooking, eating with others, meal planning, and learning to be aware of food advertising and marketing.

Moving to stage 2 should not occur until there is meaningful progress in stage 1 in order to minimize the risks of efforts turning to self-regulatory

FIGURE 8.7

**Stage 2: Increase the intake of healthy foods in Saudi Arabia**

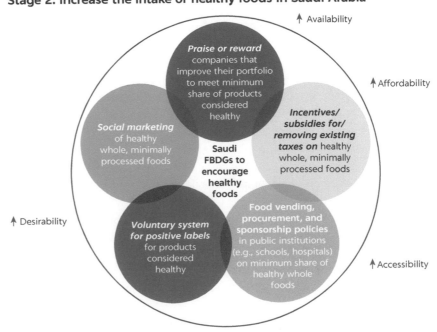

*Source:* Original figure for this publication.
*Note:* FBDGs = food-based dietary guidelines.

approaches often proposed by industry (see annex 8A for examples from Mexico, Chile, and the United Kingdom). There needs to be a clear distinction between foods to encourage the use of those that are whole and minimally processed, and this needs to be based on strict criteria for what are deemed healthy. This will help ensure that there is no room for industry manipulation and use of "health halos" (when consumers overestimate healthfulness) on their products or portfolio.

Once a warning-type FOP is well implemented in Saudi Arabia, a voluntary system for positive labels based on the Saudi FBDGs already noted should be considered to help Saudis further distinguish truly healthy options from "not unhealthy" ones. Again, these labels can serve as useful visuals and a monitoring device for implementing food vending, procurement, and sponsorship policies in public institutions such as schools and hospitals. New policies in stage 2 requiring a minimum share of healthy whole foods could then be considered working hand in hand with the restrictions of unhealthy foods already implemented via warning labels in stage 1. It could also be possible to engage manufacturers and retailers to voluntarily pledge to meet minimum targets around improving their market share and sales portfolio that qualify for positive labels. Recognizing entities that meet these healthy benchmarks can be a way for companies to compete to do better together. It will also likely encourage them to more actively market and promote their healthier products.

To counter concerns around the income regressivity of unhealthy food tax policies from stage 1, it would be wise to consider directing some of those tax revenues toward households in need through the country's existing Citizens Account program (managed by the Saudi Ministry of Labor and Social Development), particularly given heightened need related to longer-term economic impacts from the COVID-19 pandemic. To specifically support healthier diets, it is also possible to consider targeted incentives to these households to select whole and minimally processed foods. Other ways to direct tax revenues from stage 1 include developing and launching mass media campaigns to make healthy foods appealing (fun, cool, interesting, tasty, and so forth) or by creating a grant mechanism that small food and beverage companies can access to help them adapt their portfolio and it make it less unhealthy.

## The importance of coordinating and sequencing policies

It is well understood that any single policy alone will be insufficient to make meaningful change in diets and health (of people and the planet). The impact of coordinated policies, if well designed, may be larger than their parts. As Chile's example shows, it is possible and ideal to have a set of well-coordinated policies working in tandem. If it is politically and administratively feasible to implement them together in Saudi Arabia, that would be ideal. However, if that is not possible (for example, due to resource constraints), then considering how to sequence the policies is an alternative approach to ensuring that the policies build on each other and can become meaningfully restrictive or expanded over time. Sequencing policies may also help provide momentum and some earlier quick wins to allow for continued improvements over time.

The first dimension is *vertical sequencing*, which occurs when policies build on existing policies. For example, an FOP warning label used to indicate that a product does not conform to the NPM criteria and thresholds may be an early policy. Subsequent policies may then use the FOP warning labels to operationalize what products are (or are not) allowed to be advertised on TV, radio, or digitally; what products are (or are not) allowed to be available, sold, or marketed in schools and hospitals; and/or what products are (or are not) subject to a health tax. The public will thus be given a consistent message around what products are unhealthy. Likewise, industry will be encouraged to reformulate their products to meet the NPM criteria or thresholds to avoid the warning label, advertise their product, sell their product in all venues, and/or avoid a tax. The timing of these vertical sequence elements will be a function of what is feasible politically and administratively; it could be the case (as it was in Chile) that it is possible to apply several of these concurrently. Cross-ministry and cross-department (for example, health, education, and media finance ministries or departments) and cross-agency (for example, the food and drug authority, communications and information technology commission, and tax authority) coordination would be essential to ensure consistent interpretation and operationalization of regulations.

The second dimension is *horizontal sequencing,* which allows a reasonable period of time for industry to adapt in a stepwise manner to improve its offerings. Depending on the gap between the current food supply and the NPM criteria and thresholds, it is possible to break up the thresholds into two or three phases, with each phase getting meaningfully stricter over time. For example, as seen in table 8.5, it might be that for stage 1, the NPM be first applied to FOP warning labels based on a slightly higher threshold for nutrients of concern, package marketing restrictions, and restrictions on TV, print, radio, and outdoor advertisement in the first phase. In the second phase, the final thresholds for nutrients of concern may be applied for marketing restrictions not covered in the first phase, including digital marketing. It is not recommended that the implementation of the final phase take place more than three years from the start of the first phase. Otherwise, the overall impact of the policies on diets and health will likely continue to be slow or stagnant. Again, Chile provides a good example for this in its phased approach.

Throughout, the relevant Saudi stakeholder groups will need to coordinate and collaborate to ensure that the regulations are implementable and enforceable (table 8.5). Mechanisms for monitoring, reporting, and penalizing will need to be developed and tracked as transparently as possible. The formation of a cross-ministerial group those composition is vetted in a transparent manner would be ideal. The UK government's cross-department regulatory approach in tackling other action items from its Childhood Obesity: A Plan for Action report (GOV.UK 2016a) and its Tackling Obesity Government Strategy provides a useful template. Careful management of ways that the food and beverage industry may try to interfere with the policies are also needed throughout the process using the WHO Decision-Making Process and Tool (WHO 2017) with clear policies around declarations on perceived and real conflicts of interests (Fooks and Godziewski 2020; Lauber et al. 2020; Mialon 2020; Ralston et al. 2021). Additionally, an independent implementation process and outcome/impact evaluations of these policies should be planned and carried out to learn lessons around the potential barriers and types of opposition strategies by industry as well as additional opportunities to strengthen or improve the policies.

TABLE 8.5 **Sequencing of stages for policy integration**

| ACTORS | YEAR 0 | YEAR 1 | YEAR 2 | YEAR 3 |
|---|---|---|---|---|
| Cross-ministry and cross-agency collaboration and coordination | **Stage 1 integrated policies** | | | |
| | o Validate Saudi Arabia's NPM<br>o Test FOP designs (focus groups and RCT)<br>o Draft regulations, reporting, and enforcement mechanisms based on the NPM<br>o Manage engagement with stakeholders | o Announce integrated policies over two phases of NPM<br>o Manage engagement with stakeholders | o Implement phase 1 of the NPM for:<br>• FOP warning label<br>• Package marketing restrictions<br>• TV, print, radio, outdoor advertisement restrictions | o Implement phase 2 of the NPM for:<br>• FOP warning label<br>• Package marketing restrictions<br>• TV, print, radio, outdoor advertisement restrictions<br>• All digital marketing restrictions |
| | | | o Announce taxes and food vending and procurement policies based on the NPM<br>o Determine the use of tax revenues<br>o Manage engagement with stakeholders | o Implement tax and food vending and procurement policies based on phase 2 of the NPM<br>o Manage engagement with stakeholders |
| | | | Public awareness campaign | |
| | **Stage 2 integrated policies** | | | |
| | | o Update the Saudi Arabia FBDGs<br>o Test voluntary positive FOP design with high standards relative to Saudi Arabia's FBDGs<br>o Draft regulations and benchmarks for recognition ensuring that they do not contradict stage 1 policies<br>o Develop mechanism for receipt of subsidies, incentives, and grants<br>o Manage engagement with stakeholders | | o Implement subsidies and incentives/grants to qualifying households and entities<br>o Manage engagement with stakeholders<br>o Implement social marketing of healthy foods<br>o Recognize entities that meet healthy benchmarks |
| Regulators and researchers | Baseline data collection | Data collection | Stage 1 phase 1 data collection | Stage 1 phase 2 plus stage 2 data collection |

*Source:* Original table for this publication.
*Note:* FBDGs = food-based dietary guidelines; FOP = front of package; NPM = nutrient-profiling model; RCT = randomized controlled trial.

## CONCLUSIONS

There is an urgent need for significant, strong, and effective policies aimed at improving the food environment and food system to address the existing health crisis and resultant economic toll in Saudi Arabia, and to prevent these crises from worsening. A thoughtful series of policies that first address the need to reduce the intake of unhealthy foods, followed by policies to increase the intake of healthy foods, is possible with political commitment and mechanisms to prevent corporate interests from limiting or watering down the intent of the policies (Fooks and Godziewski 2020; Lauber et al.2020; Mialon et al. 2020; Ralston et al. 2021).

For continued improvements in the foods and beverages that are available, accessible, desirable, and affordable to the people of Saudi Arabia, further regulations will be needed. There is already an abundance of global evidence around the type and design of policies that are likely to work well if industry interference is well managed. To date, efforts in Saudi Arabia have involved consultation with industry and voluntary approaches, which have resulted in little movement.

Only the tax regulation on carbonated drinks and energy drinks imposed since 2017 in Saudi Arabia has been shown to produce meaningful change (Alsukait et al. 2020). The expansion of this tax to all SSBs in 2019 has yet to be evaluated. The conditions that will allow for achieving improved dietary preference and intake, and thus resultant health and economic well-being in the longer term, can be classified as being necessary (that is, whenever success is achieved, the condition is present) or sufficient (that is, the condition leads to success but is not the only condition that does so):

- Necessary conditions:
  o Mechanisms or processes to minimize industry interference
  o Political commitment met with cross-ministerial and cross-agency coordination and collaboration
  o Well-designed regulations and policies with a strong evidence base and legal basis that meet regional and global agreements
- Sufficient conditions:
  o Integrated policies
  o Engagement with civil society (for example, health advocates and health researchers)
  o Public support
  o Regional or global momentum
  o Engagement with selected industry members who show commitment to be part of the solution

Efforts to establish the necessary conditions need to be put in place and activated to ensure success in addressing the health and economic crises facing Saudi Arabia. The probability, degree, and speed of success can be further amplified if some of the sufficient conditions are also met.

## ANNEX 8A: CASE STUDIES OF COUNTRIES WITH INTEGRATED AND SYSTEMS-BASED STRATEGIES

### Mexico

The National Agreement for Healthy Nutrition (ANSA) was a multisectoral guideline that took many years of concerted effort to be finally agreed upon in 2010 (Barquera, Campos, and Rivera 2013). Mexico's National Institute of Public Health (Instituto Nacional de Salud Pública), along with other key stakeholders, started formulating its obesity and noncummicable disease (NCD) prevention strategy in the early 2000s. ANSA was nonbinding, but it committed the signatories—comprising seven national ministries and CONMEXICO (an umbrella trade association representing 43 leading food and beverage companies)—to work toward 10 strategic goals in the battle against obesity, including increasing breast-feeding, nutrition literacy, access to potable water, and decreasing the intake of high-caloric foods and beverages. Several published papers have documented the process for its development and challenges along the way (Barquera, Campos, and Rivera 2013).

Concurrently—because of the country's high prevalence of diabetes, obesity, and related NCDs—there were pushes for specifically addressing the high consumption of sugar-sweetened beverages (SSBs) in Mexico. These pushes included the creation of Beverage Guidelines for Mexico in 2008 (Rivera et al.

2008) and efforts around an SSB tax, which failed between 2008 and 2012 (James, Lajous, and Reich 2020). In 2013, the policy paper "Obesity in Mexico: Recommendations for a State Policy," along with other key academic studies, illustrated the population's high consumption of SSBs and related health implications (Rivera-Dommarco et al. 2012).

Alongside the scientific evidence, public health and civil society advocacy groups launched a strong mass media campaign and lobbying effort in 2013, arguing for an SSB tax—not only to prevent diseases but also to fund the availability of potable water in schools across Mexico (see photo 8A.1 for an example). This garnered tremendous public support, despite significant pushback and counter-lobbying by the beverage industry, which had ties to many politicians.

The world's first national-level SSB excise tax was implemented in Mexico in January 2014. The tax was 1 peso per liter excise tax on SSBs and a separate 8 percent ad valorem tax on nonessential food. The food tax was a surprise addition (which advocates did not push for) that was intended to address concerns that the SSB tax would unfairly target a subset of the industry. Outcome evaluation studies have found that increases in prices acted largely as intended (Colchero et al. 2015), resulting in a significant reduction in SSB purchases of 6 percent in the first year (Colchero et al. 2016). This reduction, which grew to 10 percent by the second year (Colchero et al. 2017), increased bottled water purchases (Colchero et al. 2016) and saw no change in total employment (Guerrero-López, Molina, and Colchero 2017). Additionally, Mexico's tax reduced SSB consumption most significantly among lower-income and high-volume consumers, the two groups facing the greatest health risk (Ng et al. 2018).

Impact-evaluation studies show promising positive health outcomes. A 10 percent reduction in sugary drink consumption among Mexican adults from 2013 to 2022 would result in an estimated 189,300 fewer cases of type 2

**PHOTO 8A.1**

**Example of campaign material by advocates for the sugar-sweetened beverages tax to fund drinking fountains in schools**

*Source:* © Alianza por la Salud Alimentaria. Used with the permission of Alianza por la Salud Alimentaria. Further permission required for reuse.

diabetes, 20,400 fewer strokes and heart attacks, 18,900 fewer deaths, and US$983 million saved in Mexico (Sánchez-Romero et al. 2016). Based on the first-year reduction in sugary drink consumption in Mexico, it is estimated that 10 years after implementation, Mexico's sugary drink tax will result in an average 2.5 percent reduction in obesity prevalence (with the largest reductions for lowest-income groups) (Barrientos-Gutierrez et al. 2017).

Following the success of Mexico's taxes, front-of-package labeling (FOPL) was viewed as a critical initiative to address obesity and NCDs in Mexico (Barrientos-Gutierrez et al. 2017). Building on regulatory designs from Chile (described in a following case study), studies conducted in Mexico laid the groundwork for establishing the need for easy-to-understand FOPL using "black seals" that could inform consumers across all economic and educational levels about products that contain excessive amounts of nutrients of concern, as well as whether they contain caffeine or artificial sweeteners, which are not recommended for children in Mexico (figure 8A.2).

Mass media campaigns and lobbying (on both sides of the issue) followed, resulting in the nearly unanimous passage of the new FOPL law (Crosbie, Carriedo, and Schmidt 2020; NOM-051-SCFI/SSA1-2010 2010) in October 2019 (photo 8A.3). Industry countered by threatening legal suits citing international laws and guidelines, including the World Trade Organization, Codex Alimentarius, and the North American Free Trade Agreement and its successor the United States–Mexico–Canada Agreement, despite past failures to do so in Chile. The new FOPL law has been in effect since October 2020 and will be evaluatd.

Continued educational campaigns to inform consumers on how to use these black seals are ongoing. Some new messages encourage consumers to choose healthier alternatives without black seals that better support or strengthen immunity, particularly in light of the COVID-19 pandemic. Also in 2020, two states in Mexico (Tabasco and Oaxaca) passed and implemented bans on the distribution, donation, gift, sale, and supply of sugary beverages and high-calorie packaged foods in stores and schools to children and adolescents (*Mexico News*

**FIGURE 8A.2**

**Complete set of black seal labels that might be applied on front-of-package labeling for Mexico based on product characteristics**

*Source:* White and Barquera 2020.
*Note:* Column headings in English, left to right: excess calories, excess sugars, excess sodium, excess saturated fats, excess trans fats, and contains artificial sweeteners; avoid for children.

PHOTO 8A.3

**Example of campaign among public health advocates in support of Mexico's front-of-package labeling regulation**

*Source:* © Alianza por la Salud Almentaria, https://alianzasalud.org.mx/wp-content/uploads/2020/11/bn-2011-campania-corta-por-lo-sano-ok.jpg. Used with the permission of Alianza por la Salud Alimentaria. Further permission required for reuse.

*Daily* 2020). Several other states are also proposing such regulations and are discussing the use of the new black seal FOP warning labels to identify banned items.

## Chile

Chile passed a landmark Food Labeling and Marketing Law in 2012 that aimed to address the obesity epidemic, particularly in children. Following a protracted process, the implementation details were published in 2015 (Dintrans et al. 2020), and the law was implemented starting June 2016. Regulated foods were defined based on a specially developed nutrient profile using minimally processed foods as the benchmark. For liquids, amounts of calories, sugars, saturated fats, and sodium in 100 milliliters (ml) of cow's milk were used as cutoffs. For solid foods, values within the 90th–99th percentile range for calories and critical nutrients were selected as the cutoff within a list of minimally or nonprocessed foods (Corvalán et al. 2019). A staggered implementation of the regulation with nutrient cutoffs becoming increasingly strict over a three-year period (phase 2 by June 2018, and the final phase by June 2019) was chosen to allow manufacturers to adapt to these regulations. Several multinational food companies mounted legal challenges against aspects of this law, but none of these lawsuits have been successful to date (Boza Martínez, Polanco, and Espinoza 2019).

Regulated foods were forbidden to be sold or offered for free at kiosks, cafeterias, and feeding programs at schools and nurseries. A stop sign, black seal stating "High in [nutrient]" was chosen as the mandatory warning label for packaged regulated foods. Products with at least one black seal were not allowed to be marketed to children under 14 years in any media (including digital) or in schools. Products with any seal were also no longer allowed to use packaging or marketing specifically appealing to children on their packaging or marketing materials (for example, cartoons, free toys, and so on) (photo 8A.4).

A series of studies to date have found that, since the first phase of the Chilean law, consumers' use and understanding of the seals is high and there have been improvements in consumers' knowledge and attitudes around nutrition and health (Correa et al. 2019); consumers, regardless of educational level, are purchasing fewer regulated products (Taillie et al. 2020); and the formulation of products available in the Chilean market and in schools has changed to reduce the nutrients of concern (Massri et al. 2019; Reyes et al. 2020). Additionally, the advertising restrictions have translated to less children's TV exposure to unhealthy food advertising (Correa et al. 2020; Jensen et al. 2020).

To complement the food labeling and marketing effort, the government changed its beverage tax in 2014 to a tiered tax structure. The tax went from a 13 percent ad valorem tax to a tiered tax structure with no taxes on plain water and plain dairy-based drinks; 10 percent on all nonalcoholic beverages with sweeteners and less than 6.25 grams (g) sugar; and 18 percent on all nonalcoholic beverages with sweeteners equal to or over 6.25 g sugar. Because of the relatively small increase (plus 5 percentage points) and decrease in prices (minus 3 percentage points), evaluations of this tax restructuring have shown that the price changes were muted (that is, they were partially absorbed by suppliers) and changes in purchases were consequently small (Caro et al. 2018).

PHOTO 8A.4

**Example of cereal before (left) and after (right) Chile's food labeling and marketing law**

This finding, in contrast to Mexico's experience, highlights the need for sufficiently large price changes to result in measurable responses.

There is ongoing discussion around furthering policy integration efforts by linking the tax designs in Chile with its Food Labeling and Marketing Law. Simulations of expanding the tax to include unhealthy processed foods in Chile show that with such a tax, in line with food labeling and marketing regulations, household purchases of these items would fall dramatically (Caro et al. 2017; Colchero, Paraje, and Popkin 2020). In addition, there would be reductions in nutrients of concern in Chile (sugar, sodium, saturated fats, and calories) linked with the most common NCDs (Caro et al. 2017).

## The United Kingdom

The United Kingdom began with a more voluntary approach involving public-private partnerships. In more recent years, however, it has shifted toward more regulatory approaches because of a lack of progress or improvement from approaches that are based on such partnerships, combined with greater urgency regarding the dangers of obesity and NCDs in its population, particularly in the context of the COVID-19 pandemic.

In 2011 the UK Department of Health launched the Public Health Responsibility Deal, which sought to use a systems approach to work collectively with businesses and the voluntary sector to deliver public health improvements through their influence on food, alcohol, physical activity, behaviors, and health in the workplace (Knai et al. 2018). Each of the five network participants (food, alcohol, physical activity, health at work, and behavior change) agreed to an initial set of collective pledges (DOH n.d.). Alcohol and food pledges have a strong focus on actions that manufacturers, retailers, and the out-of-home dining and catering sector as well as bars and pubs can deliver (DOH n.d.). Part of this pledge also included manufacturers voluntarily applying a multiple traffic light (MTL) logo, to show whether a product is high (red), medium (amber), or low (green) in fat, saturated fat, salt, and sugars, including the total calories (kilocalories and kilojoules) it provides (figure 8A.5).

Independent evaluations of the Responsibility Deal suggest that companies' progress reports were of poor quality and difficult to harmonize across companies

FIGURE 8A.5

**Example of UK multiple traffic light front-of-package labeling**

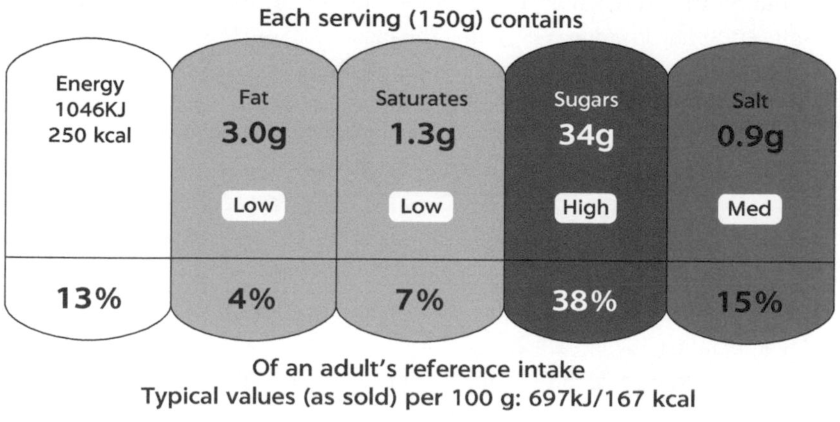

Each serving (150g) contains

| Energy 1046KJ 250 kcal | Fat 3.0g Low | Saturates 1.3g Low | Sugars 34g High | Salt 0.9g Med |
| 13% | 4% | 7% | 38% | 15% |

Of an adult's reference intake
Typical values (as sold) per 100 g: 697kJ/167 kcal

*Source:* Food Standards Agency 2020.
*Note:* g = grams; kcal = kilocalories; kJ = kilojoules.

(there was a lack of common metrics), and the food pledges did not reflect the most effective strategies to improve diet (Knai et al. 2015). Additionally, companies appeared to have committed to interventions that probably were already under way (the added value of pledges was minimal), allowing companies the opportunity to present themselves favorably while legitimizing industry's involvement in public health policies (Douglas et al. 2018). Moreover, the lack of enforcement or penalty limited the ability of the Responsibility Deal to encourage companies to go beyond business as usual (Knai et al. 2015), and therefore will not produce meaningful health improvements (Laverty et al. 2019).

In 2018, the UK government implemented the Soft Drink Industry Levy (SDIL), which was explicitly designed to encourage producers of added-sugar soft drinks to reformulate their products (GOV.UK 2016b). The SDIL applies to the production and importation of soft drinks (and alcoholic drinks with up to 1.2 percent alcohol by volume) containing added sugar. It has a lower rate for added-sugar drinks with a total sugar content of 5 g or more per 100 milliliters (ml) and a higher rate for drinks with 8 g or more per 100 ml. The objectives of the SDIL were to reduce the sugar content in products, reduce portion sizes for added-sugar drinks, and induce importers to import reformulated drinks with low added sugar to encourage consumers of soft drinks to move to healthier choices.

Evaluations of whether and to what extent the reformulation and reduction pledges and the SDIL have contributed to reformulations have occurred and are continuing. To date, findings from the voluntary targets have been mixed across various outcomes on salt (Public Health England 2020a), sugar (GOV.UK 2018, 2019; Public Health England 2020b), and calorie reduction. Meanwhile, sugar reduction from the UK SDIL (SSB tax) is much greater than that seen for the food categories included in the voluntary sugar reduction program. Additionally, independent evaluations of the SDIL (White et al. n.d.) suggest that reformulations, changes in product offerings, and overall reductions in purchases of high-sugar beverages have occurred (Bandy et al. 2020; Scarborough et al. 2020).

Since 2019, the UK government has been taking a cross-department regulatory approach in tackling other action items from its *Childhood Obesity: A Plan for Action* report (GOV.UK 2016a). This approach was further bolstered by the Tackling Obesity Government Strategy, introduced in July 2020 in recognition that people living with overweight or obesity are at greater risk of being seriously ill and dying from COVID-19. As part of all these efforts, the UK government has been seeking public comments on several regulatory actions:

- January 2019: Restricting promotions of food and drink high in fat, sugar, and salt (HFSS) by location (restricting the placement of HFSS food and drink at main selling locations in stores, such as checkouts, aisle ends, and store entrances) and by price (restricting volume-based price promotions of HFSS food and drink that encourage people to buy more than they need—for example, "buy one, get one free" and free refills of sugary soft drinks).
- February 2019: Banning direct advertising of HFSS foods and beverages on the entire Transport for London network as part of the larger London Food Strategy.
- March 2019: Further advertising restrictions in place until after 9 pm for HFSS products to reduce children's exposure to HFSS product advertising on TV and online.
- July 2020: Revisiting the existing voluntary FOPL MTL system in the United Kingdom, in terms of what nutrients to include and whether there should be changes to the existing FOPL.

- November 2020: Introducing a total online HFSS advertising restriction (as an extension of the 2019 TV and online 9 pm cutoff restriction) to further and more effectively reduce the amount of HFSS advertising that children are exposed to, given the growth in children's online viewing and targeted advertising via online media.

## ANNEX 8B: EXAMPLES OF APPLIED OR RECOMMENDED NUTRIENT PROFILING MODELS

TABLE 8B.1. **Summary of selected applied or recommended nutrient profiling models**

| | WHO EMRO NPM (2017) | SAUDI TRAFFIC LIGHT FOPL (2018) | SAUDI NATIONAL NUTRITION COMMITTEE NPM (2020) | CHILE (2016) | MEXICO (2020) | FSANZ NPSC (UPDATED 2016) |
|---|---|---|---|---|---|---|
| **Name of the NPM** | WHO East Mediterranean Regional Office (EMRO) NPM for marketing food and nonalcoholic beverages to children | SFDA Multiple Traffic Light FOPL | Nutrient Profiling Score based on UK Ofcom NPM | Chilean Warning Seals 2016, 2018, and 2019 | Mexico Warning Seals 2020 | Food Standards Australia New Zealand (FSANZ) Nutrient Profiling Score Criteria (NPSC) |
| **Country** | EMRO countries | Saudi Arabia | Saudi Arabia | Chile | Mexico | Australia New Zealand South Africa |
| **Mandatory or voluntary** | Voluntary, can be made mandatory by member countries | Voluntary | Voluntary; can be made mandatory by relevant authorities | Mandatory | Mandatory | Australia and New Zealand = voluntary South Africa = mandatory if making claims |
| **Original aim** | Restriction of marketing of unhealthy foods to children | FOP informational multiple traffic light label | · Developing or adopting a scientific tool for food categorization in Saudi Arabia | · Restriction of marketing to children under 14 years · FOP warning label | FOP warning label | · Australia and New Zealand = reformulation of products · South Africa = regulation of health claims |
| **Rationale or basis** | Based on WHO Population Nutrient Intake Goals | Guiding consumers to the selection of foods | Guiding consumers to the selection of foods | Implement the thresholds progressively, with most permissive (June 2016) to more restrictive (June 2018) to final criteria (June 2019) | PAHO NPM used as a basis; law and final regulations passed March 27, 2020 | Guiding consumers to the selection of foods consistent with the Australian and New Zealand dietary guidelines and developed with the collaboration of food industry Based on guideline daily amounts of 2,000 kilocalories for women |

*continued*

**TABLE 8B.1,** *continued*

|  | WHO EMRO NPM (2017) | SAUDI TRAFFIC LIGHT FOPL (2018) | SAUDI NATIONAL NUTRITION COMMITTEE NPM (2020) | CHILE (2016) | MEXICO (2020) | FSANZ NPSC (UPDATED 2016) |
|---|---|---|---|---|---|---|
| **Foods included by NPM** | Across the board: all packaged foods and food service items are included | Across the board: applies to all national and imported packaged foods and beverages | Across the board: applies to all national and imported packaged foods and beverages with added free sugars, sodium, or saturated fat | Across the board: applies to all national and imported packaged foods and beverages with added sugars, sodium, or saturated fat | Across the board: applies to all national and imported packaged foods and beverages with added free sugars, sodium, or saturated fat | Across the board: all foods included; three food groups—beverages, cheese and fats, all other foods |
| **Foods excluded by NPM (i.e., no cutoffs)** | • Special foods and supplements recommended for people with specific disease conditions<br>• Alcoholic drinks<br>• Breastmilk substitutes, including follow-up formula and growing-up milk | None | • Unpackaged foods<br>• Foods for medicinal purposes<br>• Dietary supplements<br>• Infant formula and follow-up milk | • Unpackaged foods<br>• Packaged foods with no added sugar, sodium, or saturated fats<br>• Dietary supplements<br>• Infant formula | • Unpackaged foods<br>• Foods for medicinal purposes<br>• Dietary supplements<br>• Infant formula and follow-up milk | None |
| **Approach used in calculation and cutoff used** | Category based (18 categories) thresholds for select nutrients | Threshold per nutrient | Threshold per nutrient | Threshold per nutrient | Threshold per nutrient | Scoring: final score determines number of stars for Australia health-star rating, or whether a food is eligible to make a health claim in South Africa. |
| **Reference amount** | 100 g (solids) or 100 ml (liquids) | 100 g (solids) or 100 ml (liquids) | 100 g (solids) or 100 ml (liquids) | 100 g (solids) or 100 ml (liquids) | Calories (kcal) and caloric density | 100 g (solids) or 100 ml (liquids) |
| **Negative nutrient selection** | Calories<br>Total fat<br>Saturated fat<br>Total sugar<br>Added sugar<br>Salt (g sodium = 2.5 g salt) | Trans fat<br>Saturated fat<br>Total sugar<br>Salt (1 g sodium = 2.5 g salt) | Energy<br>Saturated fats<br>Sugars<br>Sodium | Calories<br>Saturated fat<br>Total sugar<br>Sodium | Calories<br>Trans fat<br>Saturated fat<br>Free sugar<br>Sodium | Baseline points:<br>Calories<br>Saturated fats<br>Sugars<br>Sodium |

*continued*

**TABLE 8B.1,** *continued*

| | WHO EMRO NPM (2017) | SAUDI TRAFFIC LIGHT FOPL (2018) | SAUDI NATIONAL NUTRITION COMMITTEE NPM (2020) | CHILE (2016) | MEXICO (2020) | FSANZ NPSC (UPDATED 2016) |
|---|---|---|---|---|---|---|
| **Positive nutrient selection** | No positive nutrients included | No positive nutrients included | • Percent fruits, vegetables, nuts, and legumes<br>• Protein<br>• Dietary fiber Final score = baseline points – modifying points | No positive nutrients included | No positive nutrients included | Modifying points:<br>• Percent of fruits, vegetables, nuts, and legumes<br>• Protein<br>• Dietary fiber Final score = baseline points – modifying points<br><br>South Africa: Can carry claim if score ≤ 4 (food); ≤ 1 (beverage) and ≤ 28 (cheese and fats) |

*Note:* FOPL = front-of-package labeling; g = grams; kcal = kilocalories; ml = milliliter; NPM = nutrient profiling model; PAHO = Pan American Health Organization; SFDA = Saudi Food and Drug Authority.

## NOTES

1. Food systems include the related resources, inputs, production, transport, processing and manufacturing industries, retailing, and consumption of food as well as their impacts on environment, health, and society (UN 2020).
2. Total sugars comprise all mono- and disaccharides, regardless of source, whereas both added and free sugars exclude the sugars that naturally occur in dairy products and intact fruit and vegetables.

## REFERENCES

Al-Jawaldeh, A., M. Rayner, C. Julia, I. Elmadfa, A. Hammerich, and K. McColl. 2020. "Improving Nutrition Information in the Eastern Mediterranean Region: Implementation of Front-of-Pack Nutrition Labelling." *Nutrients* 12 (2): 330. doi:10.3390/nu12020330.

Alsukait, R., P. Wilde, S. N. Bleich, G. Singh, and S. C. Folta. 2020. "Evaluating Saudi Arabia's 50% Carbonated Drink Excise Tax: Changes in Prices and Volume Sales." *Economics and Human Biology* 38: 100868. doi:10.1016/j.ehb.2020.100868.

Bandy, L., P. Scarborough, R. Harrington, M. Rayner, and S. Jebb. 2020. "Reductions in Sugar Sales from Soft Drinks in the UK from 2015 to 2018." *BMC Medicine* 18 (20). doi:10.1186/s12916-019-1477-4.

Barquera, S., I. Campos, and J. A. Rivera. 2013. "Mexico Attempts to Tackle Obesity: The Process, Results, Push Backs and Future Challenges." *Obesity Reviews* 14 (S2): 69–78. doi:10.1111/obr.12096.

Barrientos-Gutierrez, T., R. Zepeda-Tello, E. R. Rodrigues, A. Colchero-Aragonés, R. Rojas-Martínez, E. Lazcano-Ponce, M. Hernández-Ávila, J. Rivera-Dommarco, and R. Meza. 2017. "Expected Population Weight and Diabetes Impact of the 1-Peso-per-Litre Tax to Sugar Sweetened Beverages in Mexico." *PLoS One* 12 (5): e0176336. doi:10.1371/journal.pone.0176336.

Borges, M. C., M. L. Louzada, T. H. de Sá, A. A. Laverty, D. C. Parra, and J. M. Garzillo. 2017. "Artificially Sweetened Beverages and the Response to the Global Obesity Crisis." *PLoS Med* 14 (1): e1002195. doi:10.1371/journal.pmed.1002195.

Boza Martínez, S., R. Polanco, and M. Espinoza. 2019. "Nutritional Regulation and International Trade in APEC Economies: The New Chilean Food Labeling Law." *Asian Journal of WTO and International Health Law and Policy* 14 (1): 73–113. doi:10.2139/ssrn.3362184.

Caro, J. C., C. Corvalán, M. Reyes, A. Silva, B. Popkin, and L. S. Taillie. 2018. "Chile's 2014 Sugar-Sweetened Beverage Tax and Changes in Prices and Purchases of Sugar-Sweetened Beverages: An Observational Study in an Urban Environment." *PLOS Medicine*. https://journals.plos.org/plosmedicine/article?id=10.1371/journal.pmed.1002597.

Caro, J. C., S. W. Ng, L. S. Taillie, and B. M. Popkin. 2017. "Designing a Tax to Discourage Unhealthy Food and Beverage Purchases: The Case of Chile." *Food Policy* 71: 86–100. doi:10.1016/j.foodpol.2017.08.001.

Clarke, N., E. Pechey, D. Kosīte, L. M. König, E. Mantzari, and A. K. M. Blackwell. 2020. "Impact of Health Warning Labels on Selection and Consumption of Food and Alcohol Products: Systematic Review with Meta-Analysis." *Health Psychology Review* 2020: 1–24. doi:10.1080/17437199.2020.1780147.

Colchero, M. A., G. Paraje, and B. M. Popkin. 2020. "The Impacts on Food Purchases and Tax Revenues of a Tax Based on Chile's Nutrient Profiling Model." Global Food Research Program Working Paper, under review, University of North Carolina at Chapel Hill.

Colchero, M. Arantxa, B. M. Popkin, J. A. Rivera, and S. W. Ng. 2016. "Beverage Purchases from Stores in Mexico under the Excise Tax on Sugar Sweetened Beverages: Observational Study." *BMJ* 352: h6704. https://www.bmj.com/content/352/bmj.h6704.

Colchero, M. A., J. A. Rivera-Dommarco, B. M. Popkin, and S. W. Ng. 2017. "In Mexico, Evidence of Sustained Consumer Response Two Years After Implementing a Sugar-Sweetened Beverage Tax." *Health Affairs* 36 (3): 564–71. doi:10.1377/hlthaff.2016.1231.

Colchero, M. Arantxa, J. C. Salgado, M. Unar-Munguía, M. Molina, S. Ng, and J. A. Rivera-Dommarco. 2015. "Changes in Prices after an Excise Tax to Sweetened Sugar Beverages Was Implemented in Mexico: Evidence from Urban Areas." *PLoS One* 10 (12): e0144408. doi:10.1371/journal.pone.0144408.

Correa, T., C. Fierro, M. Reyes, F. R. Dillman Carpentier, L. S. Taillie, and C. Corvalan. 2019. "Responses to the Chilean Law of Food Labeling and Advertising: Exploring Knowledge, Perceptions and Behaviors of Mothers of Young Children." *International Journal of Behavioral Nutrition and Physical Activity* 16 (1): 21. doi:10.1186/s12966-019-0781-x.

Correa, T., M. Reyes, L. S. Taillie, C. Corvalán, and F. R. Dillman Carpentier. 2020. "Food Advertising on Television before and after a National Unhealthy Food Marketing Regulation in Chile, 2016–2017." *American Journal of Public Health* 110 (7): 1054–59. doi:10.2105/AJPH.2020.305658.

Corvalán, C., M. Reyes, M. L. Garmendia, and R. Uauy. 2019. "Structural Responses to the Obesity and Non-Communicable Diseases Epidemic: Update on the Chilean Law of Food Labelling and Advertising." *Obesity Reviews: An Official Journal of the International Association for the Study of Obesity* 20 (3): 367–74. doi:10.1111/obr.12802.

Crosbie, E., A. Carriedo, and L. Schmidt. 2020. "Hollow Threats: Transnational Food and Beverage Companies' Use of International Agreements to Fight Front-of-Pack Nutrition Labeling in Mexico and Beyond." *International Journal of Health Policy and Management* (August 10). doi:10.34172/ijhpm.2020.146.

De Koning, L., V. S. Malik, M. D. Kellogg, E. B. Rimm, W. C. Willett, and F. B. Hu. 2012. "Sweetened Beverage Consumption, Incident Coronary Heart Disease, and Biomarkers of Risk in Men." *Circulation* 125 (14): 1735–41. doi:10.1161/circulationaha.111.067017.

De Koning, L., V. S. Malik, E. B. Rimm, W. C., Willett, and F. B. Hu. 2011. "Sugar-Sweetened and Artificially Sweetened Beverage Consumption and Risk of Type 2 Diabetes in Men." *American Journal of Clinical Nutrition* 93 (6): 1321–27. doi:10.3945/ajcn.110.007922.

Dietary Guidelines Advisory Committee. 2020. *Scientific Report of the 2020 Dietary Guidelines Advisory Committee: Advisory Report to the Secretary of Agriculture and the Secretary of Health and Human Services*. Washington, DC: US Department of Agriculture, Agricultural Research Service. https://www.dietaryguidelines.gov/sites/default/files/2020-07/ScientificReport_of_the_2020DietaryGuidelinesAdvisoryCommittee_first-print.pdf.

Dintrans, P. V., L. Rodriguez, J. Clingham-David, and T. Pizarro. 2020. "Implementing a Food Labeling and Marketing Law in Chile." *Health Systems and Reform* 6 (1): e1753159. doi:10.1080/23288604.2020.1753159.

DOH (Department of Health, United Kingdom). 2011. *Nutrient Profiling Technical Guidance*. London: Department of Health. https://assets.publishing.service.gov.uk/government /uploads/system/uploads/attachment_data/file/216094/dh_123492.pdf.

DOH (Department of Health, United Kingdom). n.d. *Public Health Responsibility Deal, National Archives*. London: Department of Health. https://webarchive.nationalarchives.gov .uk/20180201175857/https://responsibilitydeal.dh.gov.uk/pledges/.

Douglas, N., C. Knai, M. Petticrew, E. Eastmure, M. A. Durand, and N. Mays. 2018. "How the Food, Beverage and Alcohol Industries Presented the Public Health Responsibility Deal in UK Print and Online Media Reports." *Critical Public Health* 28 (4): 377–87. doi:10.1080/095 81596.2018.1467001.

Duffey, K. J., L. Steffen, L. Van Horn, D. Jacobs Jr, and B. Popkin. 2012. "Dietary Patterns Matter: Diet Beverages and Cardiometabolic Risks in the Longitudinal Coronary Artery Risk Development in Young Adults (CARDIA) Study." *American Journal of Clinical Nutrition* 95 (4): 909–15. doi:10.3945/ajcn.111.026682.

Dunford, E. K., L. S. Taillie, D. R. Miles, H. Eyles, L. Tolentino-Mayo, and S. W. Ng. 2018. "Non-Nutritive Sweeteners in the Packaged Food Supply—An Assessment across 4 Countries." *Nutrients* 10 (2): 257. doi:10.3390/nu10020257.

Fardet, A., and E. Rock. 2020. "Ultra-Processed Foods and Food System Sustainability: What Are the Links?" *Sustainability* 12 (15): 6280.

Food Standards Agency. 2020. "Check the Label: How to Use Nutritional Labels on Pre-Packed Foods to Find Calorie, Fat, Saturates, Sugars and Salt Content Information." London: Food Standards Agency, updated January 23. https://www.food.gov.uk/safety-hygiene /check-the-label.

Fooks, G. J., and C. Godziewski. 2020. "The World Health Organization, Corporate Power, and the Prevention and Management of Conflicts of Interest in Nutrition Policy; Comment on 'Towards Preventing and Managing Conflict of Interest in Nutrition Policy? An Analysis of Submissions to a Consultation on a Draft WHO Tool.'" *International Journal of Health Policy and Management*. doi:10.34172/IJHPM.2020.156.

GLOPAN (Global Panel on Agriculture and Food Systems for Nutrition). 2020. *Foresight 2.0 Report: Future Food Systems—For People, Our Planet, and Prosperity*. London: GLOPAN. https://www.glopan.org/foresight2/.

GOV.UK. 2016a. *Childhood Obesity: A Plan for Action*. London: Department of Health and Social Care. https://assets.publishing.service.gov.uk/government/uploads/system/uploads /attachment_data/file/546588/Childhood_obesity_2016__2__acc.pdf.

GOV.UK. 2016b. "Soft Drinks Industry Levy." Policy Paper, HM Revenue and Customs, London. https://www.gov.uk/government/publications/soft-drinks-industry-levy /soft-drinks-industry-levy.

GOV.UK. 2018. *Sugar Reduction: Report on First Year Progress*. London: Public Health England. https://www.gov.uk/government/publications/sugar-reduction-report -on-first-year-progress.

GOV.UK. 2019. *Sugar Reduction: Progress between 2015 and 2018*. London: Public Health England. https://www.gov.uk/government/publications/sugar-reduction-progress -between-2015-and-2018.

GSO (GCC Standardization Organization). 2018. *Final Draft of Standard FDS, Prepared by GSO Technical Committee No. TC05, GSO 05/FDS 2233, Requirements of Nutritional Labelling*. Riyadh: Gulf Cooperation Council. https://members.wto.org/crnattachments/2018/TBT /SAU/18_5864_00_e.pdf.

Guerrero-López, C. M., M. Molina, and M. Arantxa Colchero. 2017. "Employment Changes Associated with the Introduction of Taxes on Sugar-Sweetened Beverages and Nonessential Energy-Dense Food in Mexico." *Preventive Medicine* 105S: S43–9. doi:10.1016/j.ypmed .2017.09.001.

Hammond, D. 2011. "Health Warning Messages on Tobacco Products: A Review." *Tobacco Control* 20 (5): 327–37. doi:10.1136/tc.2010.037630.

Harris, F., C. Moss, E. J. M. Joy, R. Quinn, P. F. D. Scheelbeek, A. D. Dangour, and R. Green. 2019. "The Water Footprint of Diets: A Global Systematic Review and Meta-analysis." *Advances in Nutrition* 11 (2): 375–86. doi:10.1093/advances/nmz091.

James, E., M. Lajous, and M. R. Reich. 2020. "The Politics of Taxes for Health: An Analysis of the Passage of the Sugar-Sweetened Beverage Tax in Mexico." *Health Systems and Reform* 6 (1): e1669122. doi:10.1080/23288604.2019.1669122.

Jensen, M. L., F. Dillman Carpentier, L. Adair, C. Corvalán, B. M. Popkin, and L. S. Taillie. 2020. "Examining Chile's Unique Food Marketing Policy: TV Advertising and Dietary Intake in Preschool Children, a Pre- and Post-Policy Study." *Pediatric Obesity* 16 (4): e12735. doi:10.1111/ijpo.12735.

Knai, C., M. Petticrew, N. Douglas, M. A. Durand, E. Eastmure, and E. Nolte. 2018. "The Public Health Responsibility Deal: Using a Systems-Level Analysis to Understand the Lack of Impact on Alcohol, Food, Physical Activity, and Workplace Health Sub-Systems." *International Journal of Environmental Research and Public Health* 15 (12): 2985. doi:10.3390/ijerph15122895.

Knai, C., M. Petticrew, M. A. Durand, E. Eastmure, L. James, A. Mehrotra, C. Scott, and N. Mays. 2015. "Has a Public–Private Partnership Resulted in Action on Healthier Diets in England? An Analysis of the Public Health Responsibility Deal Food Pledges." *Food Policy* 54: 1–10. doi:10.1016/j.foodpol.2015.04.002.

Labonté, M. -È, T. Poon, B. Gladanac, M. Ahmed, B. Franco-Arellano, M. Rayner, and M. R. L'Abbé. 2018. "Nutrient Profile Models with Applications in Government-Led Nutrition Policies Aimed at Health Promotion and Noncommunicable Disease Prevention: A Systematic Review." *Advances in Nutrition* 9 (6): 741–88. doi:10.1093/advances/nmy045.

Laborde, D., M. Parent, and V. Piñeiro. 2020. *The True Cost of Food*. G20 Insights. https://www.g20-insights.org/?s=the+true+cost+of+food.

Lange, F. T., M. Scheurer, and H. J. Brauch. 2012. "Artificial Sweeteners—A Recently Recognized Class of Emerging Environmental Contaminants: A Review." *Analytical and Bioanalytical Chemistry* 403 (9): 2503–18. doi:10.1007/s00216-012-5892-z.

Lauber, K., R. Ralston, M. Mialon, A. Carriedo, and A. B. Gilmore. 2020. "Non-Communicable Disease Governance in the Era of the Sustainable Development Goals: A Qualitative Analysis of Food Industry Framing in WHO Consultations." *Globalization and Health* 16: 76. doi:10.1186/s12992-020-00611-1.

Laverty, A. A., C. Kypridemos, P. Seferidi, E. P. Vamos, J. Pearson-Stuttard, B. Collins, S. Capewell, M. Mwatsama, P. Cairney, K. Fleming, M. O'Flaherty, and C. Millet. 2019. "Quantifying the Impact of the Public Health Responsibility Deal on Salt Intake, Cardiovascular Disease and Gastric Cancer Burdens: Interrupted Time Series and Microsimulation Study." *Journal of Epidemiology and Community Health* 73 (9): 881–87. doi:10.1136/jech-2018-211749.

Lovelle, M. 2015. "Food and Water Security in the Kingdom of Saudi Arabia." Strategic Analysis Paper, Directions International, Dalkeith, UK. https://www.futuredirections.org.au/publication/food-and-water-security-in-the-kingdom-of-saudi-arabia/.

Lutsey, P. L., L. M. Steffen, and J. Stevens. 2008. "Dietary Intake and the Development of the Metabolic Syndrome: The Atherosclerosis Risk in Communities Study." *Circulation* 117 (6): 754–61. doi:10.1161/circulationaha.107.716159.

Massri, C., S. Sutherland, C. Källestål, and S. Peña. 2019. "Impact of the Food-Labeling and Advertising Law Banning Competitive Food and Beverages in Chilean Public Schools, 2014–2016." *American Journal of Public Health* 109 (9): 1249–54. doi:10.2105/AJPH.2019.305159.

*Mexico News Daily*. 2020. "More States Follow Oaxaca's Lead and Move to Ban Junk Food Sales to Kids." August 13. https://mexiconewsdaily.com/news/more-states-follow-oaxacas-lead-and-move-to-ban-junk-food-sales-to-kids/.

Mialon, M., S. Vandevijvere, A. Carriedo-Lutzenkirchen, L. Bero, F. Gomes, and M. Petticrew. 2020. "Mechanisms for Addressing and Managing the Influence of Corporations on Public Health Policy, Research and Practice: A Scoping Review." *BMJ Open* 10 (7): e034082. doi:10.1136/bmjopen-2019-034082.

Michail, N. 2019. "'Overwhelmingly Positive': Chile's Food Regulations Are Changing the Country's Eating Habits." *FoodNavigator-LATAM*, February 20; updated February 21. https://www.foodnavigator-latam.com/Article/2019/02/20/Chile-s-food-regulations-are-changing-the-country-s-eating-habits.

Ng, S. W., J. A. Rivera, B. M. Popkin, and M. Arantxa Colchero. 2018. "Did High Sugar-Sweetened Beverage Purchasers Respond Differently to the Excise Tax on Sugar-Sweetened Beverages in Mexico?" *Public Health Nutrition* 22 (4): 750–56. doi:10.1017/S136898001800321X.

NOM-051-SCFI/SSA1-2010 (NORMA Oficial Mexicana). 2010. NOM-051-SCFI/SSA1-2010, Especificaciones generales de etiquetado para alimentos y bebidas no alcohólicas preenvasados-Información comercial y sanitaria [Mexican Official Standard NOM-051-SCFI/SSA1-2010, [General Labelling Specifications for Prepackaged Non-Alcoholic Foods and Beverages-Commercial and Health Information.] https://www.dof.gob.mx/normasOficiales /4010/seeco11_C/seeco11_C.htm.

Piernas, C., S. W. Ng, and B. Popkin. 2013. "Trends in Purchases and Intake of Foods and Beverages Containing Caloric and Low-Calorie Sweeteners over the Last Decade in the United States." *Pediatric Obesity* 8 (4): 294–306. doi:10.1111/j.2047-6310.2013.00153.x.

Popkin, B. M., and C. Hawkes. 2016. "Sweetening of the Global Diet, Particularly Beverages: Patterns, Trends, and Policy Responses." *Lancet Diabetes and Endocrinology* 4 (2): 174–86. doi:10.1016/S2213-8587(15)00419-2.

Public Health England. 2020a. *Salt Targets 2017: Second Progress Report—A Report on the Food Industry's Progress towards Meeting the 2017 Salt Targets.* London: Public Health England. https://assets.publishing.service.gov.uk/government/uploads/system/uploads /attachment_data/file/915371/Salt_targets_2017_Second_progress_report_031020.pdf.

Public Health England. 2020b. *Sugar Reduction: Report on Progress between 2015 and 2019.* London: Public Health England. https://assets.publishing.service.gov.uk/government /uploads/system/uploads/attachment_data/file/925027/SugarReportY3.pdf.

Ralston, R., S. E. Hil, F. Silva Gomes, and J. Collin. 2021. "Towards Preventing and Managing Conflict of Interest in Nutrition Policy? An Analysis of Submissions to a Consultation on a Draft WHO Tool." *International Journal of Health Policy and Management* 10 (5): 255–65 . doi:10.34172/ijhpm.2020.52.

Rayner, M., P. Scarborough, and T. Lobstein. 2009. "The UK Ofcom Nutrient Profiling Model: Defining 'Healthy' and 'Unhealthy' Foods and Drinks for TV Advertising to Children." Oxford: Oxford Population Health. https://www.ndph.ox.ac.uk/food-ncd/files/about /uk-ofcom-nutrient-profile-model.pdf.

Rayner, M., P. Scarborough, and A. Kaur. 2013. "Nutrient Profiling and the Regulation of Marketing to Children. Possibilities and Pitfalls." *Appetite* 62: 232–35. doi:10.1016/j .appet.2012.06.021.

Reyes, M., L. S. Taillie, B. Popkin, R. Kanter, S. Vandevijvere, and C. Corvalán. 2020. "Changes in the Amount of Nutrient of Packaged Foods and Beverages after the Initial Implementation of the Chilean Law of Food Labelling and Advertising: A Nonexperimental Prospective Study." *PLoS Medicine* 17 (7): e1003220. doi:10.1371/journal.pmed.1003220.

Rivera, J. A., O. Muñoz-Hernández, M. Rosas-Peralta, C. A. Aguilar-Salinas, B. M. Popkin, and W. C. Willett. 2008. "Consumo de Bebidas Para Una Vida Saludable: Recomendaciones Para La Población Mexicana" [Beveratge Consumption for a Healthy Life: Recommendations for the Mexican Population]. *Salud Pública de México* 50 (2). Special article. http://www.scielo .org.mx/scielo.php?script=sci_arttext&pid=S0036-36342008000200011.

Rivera-Dommarco, J. A., A. Velasco-Bernal, M. Hernandez-Avila, C. Aguilar-Salinas, F. Vadillo-Ortega, and C. Murayama-Rendón. 2012. "Obesity in Mexico: Recommendations for a State Policy, Position Paper," in *Obesity in Mexico: Recommendations for a State Policy* 11–41. Cuernavaca: Mexico National Institute of Public Health.

Roberto, C. A., S. W. Ng, D. Hammond, S. Barquera, A. Jauregui, L. Smith Taillie. 2021. "The Influence of Front-of-Package Nutrition Labeling on Consumer Behavior and Product Reformulation." *Annual Review of Nutrition* 41. https://doi.org/10.1146 /annurev-nutr-111120-094932.

Rose, D., M. C. Heller, and C. A. Roberto. 2019. "Position of the Society for Nutrition Education and Behavior: The Importance of Including Environmental Sustainability in Dietary Guidance." *Journal of Nutrition Education and Behavior* 51 (1): 3–15. doi:10.1016 /j.jneb.2018.07.006.

Rose, D., M. Heller, A. Willits-Smith, and R. Meyer. 2017. "Linking Environmental Impacts to Individual Food Choices: The Carbon Footprint of U.S. Diets in the 2005-2010 NHANES." Presentation at the American Public Health Association (APHA) 2017 Annual Meeting and Expo, November 7, Atlanta. https://apha.confex.com/apha/2017/meetingapp.cgi /Paper/391729.

Sacks, G., M. Rayner, L. Stockley, P. Scarborough, W. Snowdon, and B. Swinburn. 2011. "Applications of Nutrient Profiling: Potential Role in Diet-Related Chronic Disease Prevention and the Feasibility of a Core Nutrient-Profiling System." *European Journal of Clinical Nutrition* 65 (3): 298–306. doi:10.1038/ejcn.2010.269.

SAGO (Saudi Grains Organization). 2018. *Baseline of Food Loss and Waste in the Kingdom of Saudi Arabia*. Riyadh: SAGO. https://www.sago.gov.sa/Content/Files/Baseline_180419.pdf.

Sánchez-Romero, L. M., J. Penko, P. G. Coxson, A. Fernández, A. Mason, A. E. Moran, L. Ávila-Burgos, M. Odden, S. Barquera, and K. Bibbins-Domingo. 2016. "Projected Impact of Mexico's Sugar-Sweetened Beverage Tax Policy on Diabetes and Cardiovascular Disease: A Modeling Study." *PLoS Medicine* 13 (11): e1002158. doi:10.1371/journal.pmed.1002158.

Scarborough, P., V. Adhikari, R. A. Harrington, A. Elhussein, A. Briggs, M. Rayner, J. Adams, S. Cummins, T. Penney, and M. White. 2020. "Impact of the Announcement and Implementation of the UK Soft Drinks Industry Levy on Sugar Content, Price, Product Size and Number of Available Soft Drinks in the UK, 2015–19: A Controlled Interrupted Time Series Analysis." *PLoS Medicine* 17 (2): e1003025. doi:10.1371/journal.pmed.1003025.

SFDA (Saudi Food and Drug Authority). 2018. *Policy—SFDA.FD 2483/2018 (Trans Fatty Acids)*. Riyadh: Saudi Food and Drug Authority. https://extranet.who.int/nutrition/gina/fr/node/36039.

SFDA (Saudi Food and Drug Authority). 2020. *Guide to the Use of the Food Classification Model*. Riyadh: Saudi Food and Drug Authority. https://sfda.gov.sa/ar/regulations/79656.

Snowdon, W., and A. M. Thow. 2013. "Trade Policy and Obesity Prevention: Challenges and Innovation in the Pacific Islands." *Obesity Reviews* 2: 150–58. doi:10.1111/obr.12090.

Springmann, M., L. Spajic, M. A, Clark, J. Poore, A. Herforth, P. Webb, M. Rahyner, and P. Scarborough. 2020. "The Healthiness and Sustainability of National and Global Food-Based Dietary Guidelines: Modelling Study." *BMJ* 2020 370: m2322. doi:10.1136/bmj.m2322.

Taillie, L. S., M. Reyes, M. Arantxa Colchero, B. Popkin, and C. Corvalán. 2020. "An Evaluation of Chile's Law of Food Labeling and Advertising on Sugar-Sweetened Beverage Purchases from 2015 to 2017: A Before-and-After Study." *PLoS Medicine* 17 (2): e1003015. doi:10.1371/journal.pmed.1003015.

Thow, A. M., A. Jones, C. Hawkes, I. Ali, and R. Labonté. 2017. "Nutrition Labelling Is a Trade Policy Issue: Lessons from an Analysis of Specific Trade Concerns at the World Trade Organization." *Health Promotion International* 33 (4): 561–71. doi:10.1093/heapro/daw109.

Thow, A. M., and N. Nisbett. 2019. "Trade, Nutrition, and Sustainable Food Systems." *Lancet* 394 (10200): 716–18. doi:10.1016/S0140-6736(19)31292-9.

UN (United Nations). 2020. "Food Systems—Definition, Concept and Application for the UN Food Systems Summit." Paper from the Scientific Group of the UN Food Systems Summit. Draft. New York: United Nations. https://www.un.org/sites/un2.un.org/files/food_systems_concept_paper_scientific_group_-_draft_oct_26.pdf.

Verhagen, H., and H. Berg. 2008. "A Simple Visual Model to Compare Existing Nutrient Profiling Schemes." *Food and Nutrition Research* 52 (February). doi:10.3402/fnr.v52i0.1649.

White, M., and S. Barquera. 2020. "Mexico Adopts Food Warning Labels, Why Now?" *Health Systems and Reform* 6 (1). doi:10.1080/23288604.2020.1752063.

White, M., P. Scarborough, A. Briggs, J. Adams, O. Mytton, R. Harrington, H. Rutter, M. Rayner, R. Smith, and S. Cummins. n.d. "Evaluation of the Health Impacts of the UK Treasury Soft Drinks Industry Levy (SDIL)." Primary Research, started 2017. University of Cambridge. https://www.journalslibrary.nihr.ac.uk/programmes/phr/1613001/#/.

WHO (World Health Organization). 2017. *Decision-Making Process and Tool: Draft Approach for the Prevention and Management of Conflicts of Interest in the Policy Development and Implementation of Nutrition Programmes at Country Level*. Geneva: World Health Organization. https://www.who.int/nutrition/consultation-doi-nutrition-tool.pdf?ua=1.

WHO (World Health Organization). 2019. *Guiding Principles and Framework Manual for Front-of-Pack Labelling for Promoting Healthy Diet*. Geneva: WHO. https://www.who.int/nutrition/publications/policies/guidingprinciples-labelling-promoting-healthydiet/en/.

WHO EMRO (World Health Organization Regional Office for the Eastern Mediterranean). 2017. *Nutrient Profile Model for the Marketing of Food and Non-Alcoholic Beverages to Children in the WHO Eastern Mediterranean Region.* Cairo: WHO Regional Office for the Eastern Mediterranean. https://www.who.int/nutrition/publications/emro-nutrient -profile-food-non-alcoholic-beverages/en/.

Willett, W., J. Rockström, B. Loken, M. Springmann, T. Lang, S. Vermeulin, T. Garnett, et al. 2019. "Food in the Anthropocene: The EAT-Lancet Commission on Healthy Diets from Sustainable Food Systems." *Lancet* 393 (10170): 447–92. doi:10.1016/S0140-6736(18):31788-4.